Love Objects

Love Objects

Emotion, Design and Material Culture

*Edited by Anna Moran and
Sorcha O'Brien*

B L O O M S B U R Y
LONDON · NEW DELHI · NEW YORK · SYDNEY

Bloomsbury Academic

An imprint of Bloomsbury Publishing Plc

50 Bedford Square
London
WC1B 3DP
UK

1385 Broadway
New York
NY 10018
USA

www.bloomsbury.com

Bloomsbury is a registered trade mark of Bloomsbury Publishing Plc

First published 2014

British Library Cataloguing-in-Publication Data
A catalogue record for this book is available from the British Library.

ISBN: HB: 978-0-8578-5846-7
PB: 978-1-4725-1719-7
ePDF: 978-1-4725-7638-5
ePub: 978-1-4725-1718-0

Library of Congress Cataloging-in-Publication Data
Love objects: emotion, design, and material culture / [edited by] Anna Moran and Sorcha O'Brien. — 1 [edition].
pages cm
Includes bibliographical references and index.
ISBN 978-0-85785-846-7 (hardcover) — ISBN 978-1-4725-1719-7 (pbk.)   1. Attachment behavior.
2. Symbolism.   3. Material culture.   4. Love.   I. Moran, Anna, editor of compilation.
BF575.A86L68 2014
152.4'1–dc23
2013045880

Typeset by RefineCatch Limited, Bungay, Suffolk
Printed and bound in India

To our loved ones.

CONTENTS

LIST OF ILLUSTRATIONS

Cover: Pair of women's coral-red silk slip-on shoes, with ribbons and white kid lining, c. 1827. The right shoe bears the label of Melnotte, a French firm of shoemakers and sellers, which boasted warehouses in both Paris and London. Source: 1969.46.6P. The Shoe Collection, Northampton Museums and Art Gallery, Northampton Borough Council. Photograph by John Roan Photography.

NOTES ON CONTRIBUTORS

Fran Carter (School of Art and Design History, Kingston University)

Fran teaches Design Studies at Kingston University and University of the Creative Arts. She has just completed her PhD entitled *Magic Toyshops: Narrative and Meaning in the Women's Sex Shop*. Her research interests centre on the design of sexual retail spaces and notions of female empowerment achieved through the consumption of goods and spaces dedicated to the pursuit of female erotic pleasure. She is currently working on a study of the spatial design of female-orientated sex shop websites.

Professor Jonathan Chapman (School of Art, Design & Media, University of Brighton)

Jonathan is Professor of Sustainable Design, and Course Leader of the MA Sustainable Design, which he co-wrote and launched in 2009. Over the past decade, his teaching, consultancy and research have grown from their early polemical and activist roots, to developing strategic counterpoints to the unsustainable character of contemporary material culture. He has written two books: his monograph, *Emotionally Durable Design: Objects, Experiences & Empathy* (Earthscan, 2005) and his co-edited work, *Designers, Visionaries and Other Stories: A Collection of Sustainable Design Essays* (Earthscan, 2007). He has also contributed chapters to several peer-reviewed books (2008, 2009, 2010) and has published research papers in scholarly journals such as *Design Issues* (2008, 2009).

Dr Adam Drazin (Department of Anthropology, University College London)

Adam is the Coordinator of the MA in Culture.Materials.Design in the Department of Anthropology, University College London. He has published in a range of journals and books on such themes as care as culture in post-socialist urban Romania, photography and personhood and the interaction of anthropology with professional design.

Dr Christina Edwards (School of Education and Lifelong Learning, Aberystwyth University)

Christina completed a PhD in Fine Art Practice at the School of Art, Aberystwyth University. Working in early photographic processes over the last few years she has been researching the wet plate collodion process, and applying this in relation to the family archive. Her research interests are nineteenth-century photographic processes, vernacular photography and the snapshot, and the relationship between the family archive and how we remember.

Professor Catherine Harper (Faculty of Creative and Cultural Industries, University of Portsmouth)

Catherine is Dean of the Faculty of Creative and Cultural Industries at University of Portsmouth. She has specialized in large-scale public art, speculative exhibition work, and performance, and also writes on craft, textiles, the body, gender and subjective narratives. She is UK editor of *Textile: The Journal of Cloth and Culture*, contributor to *Selvedge* magazine, and editorial board member of *The International Journal of Fashion Design, Technology and Education*. She published her first book, *Intersex* (Berg) in 2007, and her edited multi-volume *Textiles: Primary and Critical Sources* (Berg) was published in February 2012. She is writing a 'textile novel' titled *Hyena in Petticoats*, and recently delivered a public lecture at The Shirt Factory Project as part of the City of Culture 2013 celebrations in Derry-Londonderry.

Dr Jane Hattrick (Faculty of Arts, University of Brighton)

Jane is a lecturer in the History of Art & Design at the University of Brighton specializing in fashion and dress history. Her doctoral research investigated the personal identity of the designer Norman Hartnell through a close examination of the material left in his personal collections and business archive. Jane assessed the impact of the private aspects of his life on the designer's creative output through a close analysis of garments and representations of his couture clothing dating between 1921 and 1979.

Dr Elizabeth Howie (Department of Visual Arts, Coastal Carolina University)

Elizabeth received her PhD from the University of North Carolina at Chapel Hill in 2007. She is an Assistant Professor of Art History at Coastal Carolina University in Conway, South Carolina. She specializes in the history and theory of photography.

Professor Victor Margolin (Professor Emeritus, University of Illinois, Chicago)

Victor Margolin is Professor Emeritus of Design History at the University of Illinois, Chicago. He is a co-editor of the academic design journal, *Design Issues*, and is the author, editor or co-editor of a number of books including *Design Discourse*, *Discovering Design*, *The Idea of Design*, *The Designed World* and *The Politics of the Artificial*. Currently he is working on a three-volume *World History of Design* that will be published by Bloomsbury Academic.

Noreen McGuire (Asian Department, Victoria and Albert Museum, London)

Noreen has assisted with research at the Victoria and Albert Museum since 2011 in preparation for an upcoming shoe exhibition opening in 2015. During that time, she also worked on the 'Europe 1600–1800' project, which will see seven new galleries opening at the V&A dedicated to this time period. Noreen graduated with distinction from the National College of Art and Design, Dublin, in 2010 with an MA in Design History and Material Culture, winning best thesis award that year for her thesis titled *Inconspicuous Production: The Genteel Craft of Amateur Shoemaking in the Late Eighteenth and Early Nineteenth Centuries*.

Dr Anna Moran (Faculty of Visual Culture, National College of Art & Design, Dublin)

Anna is Director of the MA in Design History and Material Culture at the NCAD. Her research interests include the interaction between people and objects in the long eighteenth century and she has published several articles in the areas of glass studies, retailing history and material culture. She has served as an editorial board member of *Artefact: Journal of the Irish Association of Art Historians* and is currently on the board of editors of *Irish Architectural and Decorative Studies*.

Dr Sorcha O'Brien (School of Art and Design History, Kingston University)

An industrial designer by training, Sorcha teaches design history and theory to Product and Furniture Design students at Kingston University, and her research interests focus on issues of identity and technology in design and material culture. She is the author of several articles on Irish national identity and technology, and is a sub-editor on the forthcoming Bloomsbury *Encyclopedia of Design*.

Dr Louise Purbrick (Faculty of Arts, University of Brighton)

Louise is Principal Lecturer in the History of Art and Design, School of Humanities, Faculty of Arts at the University of Brighton. Her research is devoted to the understanding of material culture. Her published writing ranges from the nineteenth to the twenty-first century and encompasses the interpretation of industrial artefacts, imperial objects, sites of conflict as well as domestic possessions and everyday things.

Dr Jessica Sewell (Department of Urban Planning and Design, Xi'an Jiaotong-Liverpool University, Suzhou, China)

Jessica is an Associate Professor of Architecture and Head of the Department of Urban Planning and Design at Xi'an Jiaotong-Liverpool University in Suzhou, China. She is currently working on a book on the bachelor pad and masculinity in postwar United States. She has a PhD in architecture from the University of California, Berkeley, and has recently published *Gendering the Everyday City: Women and Public Space in San Francisco, 1890–1915* (University of Minnesota Press, 2011).

Dr Jo Turney (Bath School of Art and Design, Bath Spa University)

Jo is a senior lecturer in the department of Research, Critical and Postgraduate Studies, in the School of Art and Design, Bath Spa University. She co-authored with Rosemary Harden, *Floral Frocks* (Antique Collector's Club, 2007), and is the sole author of the book *The Culture of Knitting* (Berg, 2009). Her research interests focus on everyday textile objects and practices.

Dr Ann Wilson (Department of Media Communications, Cork Institute of Technology)

Ann lectures in Visual Culture and Design History at the Cork Institute of Technology. She has published work on the Irish Gothic and Celtic Revivals, the Arts and Crafts Movement, and on nineteenth-century Irish Catholic material culture, and from 2011 to 2013 was on the editorial committee of *Artefact: Journal of the Irish Association of Art Historians*.

EDITORS' FOREWORD

This anthology of 12 essays interrogates the material embodiments of love, exploring the emotional potency of objects in our lives and the relationships that exist between people and objects. It discusses how objects can become symbols and representations, as well as active participants in and mediators of our relationships with each other, unpacking the ways in which objects engage our emotions subliminally, viscerally and vicariously. It forms a discussion of the ways objects can serve as intentional bearers of significance through embodiment, engagement or control, and has the multifarious issues surrounding love and objects at its core.

In 2008, the editors of this volume, together with their colleague Dr Ciarán Swan, held a conference entitled 'Love Objects: Engaging Material Culture' at the National College of Art and Design in Dublin, Ireland. This collection draws on ideas debated at this conference, together with subsequent scholarly work related to the 'Love Objects' theme. With the premise that objects are endowed with agency and emotional qualities by their owners and users in ways that go beyond the physical characteristics of the object itself, this collection develops the ideas presented at that conference, building on the growing academic interest in the study of the emotions in recent years. Alongside investigating our subjective and emotional relationships with material objects, which is particularly relevant in a world where the digital is increasingly important, this anthology foregrounds the problematic nature of the concept of 'love' in Western culture, as discussed by esteemed design historian Victor Margolin in his introduction. Bearing in mind the increasing scientific interest in emotions and how they can be conceptualized and regulated, this collection adds a new perspective to the discourse on emotions, providing a commentary on an often nebulous topic, yet grounded in the physical reality of material culture and designed objects. In doing so, it utilizes one of the core strengths of research in design history and material culture, expanding the idea of 'history from below' to incorporate not just the voices of the owners of the objects themselves, but also 'reading' the normally mute object and allowing its often fragile materiality to inform the discussion.

The collection brings together international work from a range of perspectives, including Margolin's analysis of the chapters within the collection. Presented within four interlinked themes, each section forms a dialogue about the different ways in which the slippery concept of love can be analysed, expressed, problematized and discussed. The 12 essays are focused around studies of a variety of media and object types, covering a range of geographical locations and time periods. These case studies foreground the idea that emotion is a universal human constant, while at the same time having very specific material manifestations, shaped by specific modes of exchange, performance, agency and objectification. The essays are grouped according to the role that the titular objects play in the negotiation of different types of love, to create biographies, represent identities, embody emotions or negotiate relationships.

The essays within the first thematic, 'The Lives of Objects', address in different ways the biographies of specific objects, the multiple meanings they can hold and the narratives they create for those who may have created, gifted or possessed them. The critical role played by objects in the representation and performance of personal, group and corporate identities is explored in the second section, focusing on the projection and subversion of sexual and gender identities. The third thematic, 'Objects and Embodiment', examines the ways in which objects and bodies interact, necessitating discussion of emotional relationships, whether they be religious, sexual or the affective one between the researcher and the archive. The emotional connections people have with their objects are examined in the final group of essays, together with the ways in which objects can serve as a vehicle for negotiating, materializing and understanding relationships. This section highlights the importance of objects in negotiating absences such as grief, as well as deliberate decisions not to engage, *not* to love objects, in addition positing the question of how designers can use emotion to create affective, sustainable relationships with those objects.

Underlying each essay is a common interest in the personal and subjective nature of the object, and also in the subjective nature of any such inquiry. This consideration of the emotional weight and valence of the object widens our understanding of the material world and is particularly important at a time when ideas about the emotional durability of objects are being promoted as a way of developing a more sustainable lifestyle, whether through the deliberate creation of emotionally resonant products, or by harnessing the reappraisal of traditional handcrafted forms. It also forms an important component of creative practice, as designers and makers interrogate the world of emotions and materiality in a positive and generative manner, incorporating in varied ways the discussion of love in material form within their own practice.

In tackling a range of case studies with these issues at the forefront, this collection deals with core strands of inquiry within design and material culture – such as the relation between object and affect, (im)materiality and the discourse of sustainability, and modes of exchange, performance, agency and objectification. The collection thereby demonstrates an immediate approach to the object, not just as a utilitarian or philosophical presence, but foregrounding the reflexive, ideological and ideational uses of the 'love object'.

ACKNOWLEDGEMENTS

The editors and publisher gratefully acknowledge the permission granted to reproduce the copyright material in this book.

The editors would like to acknowledge their gratitude to the following people, without whom this book would not have been possible. First, we would like to thank our authors for contributing their essays and for being such wonderful colleagues over the duration of this project; their insights, professionalism and good spirits were hugely appreciated. We are very grateful to our colleague and friend Dr Ciarán Swan, with whom we organized the Love Objects conference at the National College of Art and Design (NCAD), Dublin. We also thank the many other people who helped to organize this conference, together with those who attended, contributed to discussions and made it the success that it was. We also extend our gratitude to Niamh O'Sullivan, Professor Emeritus of the Faculty of Visual Culture at NCAD, for her generous support of the conference and this publication. Also at NCAD, we thank Professor Jessica Hemmings, the present Head of Visual Culture, and Neasa Travers. For support and assistance with various funding applications, we are grateful to Dr Siún Hanrahan and Professor Desmond Bell, former and present Heads of Research, and Margaret Phelan of the Research Department at NCAD. Also, we thank the students of NCAD's Masters in Design History and Material Culture, past and present, for their questions, probing research and enthusiasm.

We would like to acknowledge the support of The Modern Interiors Research Centre of the School of Art and Design History at Kingston University, and thank the many libraries, archives and museums that have kindly given permission to reproduce images. We are grateful to Emily Angus for compiling our index, and to Dónal Leahy, Melissa O'Brien and Tom Cosgrave for their help and support throughout the entire process. For our front cover image we thank Rebecca Shawcross of the Northampton Museum, and John Roan of John Roan Photography.

Victor Margolin, Professor Emeritus of the University of Illinois, very kindly accepted our invitation to write an introduction to this collection, and we thank him sincerely. We also extend our gratitude to Dr Tim Putnam and Dr Valerie Swales, to whom we owe a huge debt, together with everyone we have worked with at Bloomsbury Academic, including Simon Cowell, Simon Longman, Rebecca Barden, Abbie Sharman and our anonymous peer reviewers.

The contributors would also like to thank the following individuals and institutions for their help, support and advice:

All of our interviewees; Giles Deacon; Fionn and Leah Garvey Drazin; Françoise Dupré; Tracy Emin Studio; Clare Qualmann; Lisa Obermeyer; France Scully Osterman; Mark Osterman; Garda John Reynolds; Professor Giorgio Riello; June Swann; Emma Whiting; Mrs Claire Williams; Donna Wilson; Jim Wilson; the owners and staff of Coco de Mer and Sh!; Kaywoodie; Rebecca Price of Myla; Deborah Jaeger of Tom Dixon Studio; Ryan Sadamitsu of Visvim/ Cubism; the staff of the British Museum; the Mass Observation Archive; Michelle Ashmore and Valerie Wilson of the National Museums Northern Ireland; The Metropolitan Museum of Art; the National Library of Ireland; Alex Ward and Finbarr Connolly of the National Museum of

Ireland; Rebecca Shawcross of the Northampton Museum; Dilys Blum and Joanna Fulginiti of the Philadelphia Museum of Art; Kylea Little of Tyne and Wear Archives and Museums. Mass Observation material reproduced with permission of Curtis Brown Group Ltd, London on behalf of The Trustees of the Mass Observation Archive. Copyright © The Trustees of the Mass Observation Archive.

Every effort has been made to trace copyright holders and to obtain their permission for the use of copyright material. The publisher apologizes for any errors or omissions in the above list and would be grateful to be notified of any corrections that should be incorporated in future reprints or editions of this book.

Introduction

How Do I Love Thee? Objects of Endearment in Contemporary Culture

Victor Margolin

Love is an emotion to which countless treatises, tracts, and works of art have been dedicated from time immemorial. It is an emotion that human beings care deeply about because it touches the core of our being where the need to be regarded, accepted, or desired resides. It is an emotion that takes many forms and in the end most often eludes comprehension. We have no cultural consensus of what love is and consequently the word is freely appropriated as a floating signifier, available for attachment to a multitude of feelings and the acts that follow from them. At its most extreme, love is a passion that can blind the lover to the need for discretion or the recognition of legal boundaries. Lovers have lost their lives or landed in prison because their amorous intentions have been misguided. They have also been unduly persecuted when their feelings are unjustly deemed inappropriate according to cultural norms.

Even when feelings of love are fulfilled in ways that are socially affirming, the mystery of the emotion remains. In social terms, human feelings are shaped by diverse external sources. First, are the primal feelings that the child develops in response to his or her parents and others who demonstrate the kinds of relational emotions that are possible. Early impressions are the strongest and when parental devotion to the child is lacking or misguided, the child forms an understanding of relationships that is at best slightly skewed and at worst warped. Second, is the understanding of relationships that we adopt through social relations with others outside the primal family, which are shaped by cultural norms that transcend unique individual characteristics. Third, are the ideas of love that are transmitted through cultural forms such as media and the objects of everyday life. Within this complex of influences, we strive to express emotions that are authentic; a process that requires considerable insight and self-awareness – qualities that unfortunately not everyone has the capacity to exercise.

Consequently, there is no consensus as to which cultural norms can best help us understand our emotions. Religious and spiritual texts admonish us to love our fellow human beings, but don't explain the complex nuances of love as an emotion, in part because love can take many forms and its contemporary expression can contradict traditional definitions. The numerous forms of love, in fact, often challenge cultural norms, and one of the principal dynamics of culture is the adjustment of values to accommodate these forms.

The authors in this volume speak directly to the issue of how love intersects with cultural norms, sometimes aligning with them and sometimes creating conditions of critique or opposition. They embed their discussions of love objects – which are based on widely varying premises of what love means – in cultural frameworks that contribute to the ways they make their arguments about what these objects represent. The authors' methodologies constitute a wide range of approaches to the study of material culture, the field that is closest to their enterprise. The point of the essays is not to describe the objects as much as it is to reveal in a multifaceted way different situations in which love becomes central as an emotion. Nonetheless, objects become the foci of the authors' attempts to grapple with the complexities of love as it is played out through the objects' identities both as possessions and as props in the performative enactments of social rituals.

The research strategies of the authors differ considerably. In her discussion of gift giving, for example, Louise Purbrick relies on the Mass Observation Archive – a collection of interviews conducted with British citizens about aspects of their daily lives. From these interviews, Purbrick extracted descriptions of feelings about giving presents and framed her interpretation of these within French anthropologist Marcel Mauss' theory of the gift. Purbrick makes a clear distinction between the gift and the commodity, noting that the commercialization of goods can be overcome by incorporating commodities into a culture of gift giving, which adds a new and significant layer of meaning to them. Purbrick also asserts that commodities can become powerful mnemonic devices that evoke qualities of past relationships and thus accrue added value for their owners. In contrast to object theorists who seek to extract value from the shape or form of an object, Purbrick shows that the memory of a situation in which the object was introduced, regardless of its form, is far more important than its appearance. Her account of how gifts become valuable because of their mnemonic power relates closely to Jonathan Chapman's call in his essay for 'emotionally durable design'. Her account becomes an alternative to the oft-stated belief that designers can make objects more emotionally valuable by creating pleasing forms or useful functions.

Where Purbrick found her stories in a historic archive, Fran Carter relied on interviews with her contemporaries to explore the reasons why women prefer to buy sexual garments and sex toys in stores designed specifically for them, instead of the sleazy sex shops that cater primarily to men. Carter found through her ethnographic interviews that women felt more comfortable when the lingerie and sexual performance objects were presented in a retail atmosphere that empowered them as sexual partners, rather than consigning them to participants in the 'dominant sexual paradigm', in which they play a subordinate role. Through her interviews with female consumers of sexual goods, Carter found, however, that her informants had differing views of the goods and retail spaces. One woman was disappointed with the normality of the retail presentations, wishing for something that would make sex more edgy, while another felt that aestheticizing the objects removed them too much from the actual experience of sexual activity. Such differences are evidence in a microcosm of how complicated the question of love is once it becomes entangled with the cultural processes that make its expression possible.

The complexities of love are addressed differently in Adam Drazin's essay, which explores the way that Romanian immigrants to Ireland negotiate through objects a relationship with their country of immigration as well as their homeland. Like many migrants today, the several informants in Drazin's study have not exchanged their homeland for a new country the way immigrants once did. The possibility of returning to Romania is real and influences the way they choose to live in Ireland. Love, as Drazin notes, is embedded in a plan that includes a stable home, a heterosexual marriage, and children. Migrants who embrace their new country or envision long-term residency, commit to spending money on their domestic environment as well as clothes and entertainment. The others live frugally and save their money in order to return to Romania and buy a residence there. The decision to remain abroad or return home determines the kinds of objects one acquires. The instability of immigrant life can complicate emotional attachments as Drazin demonstrates in his account of one Romanian couple's divorce.

In contrast to Purbrick's reliance on the Mass Observation Archive and Carter's and Drazin's ethnographic engagement with contemporary informants, Christina Edwards, an artist, makes use of a family photographic archive to create an exhibition 'Material Memories', consisting of family snapshots reproduced as ambrotypes, a nineteenth-century form, which consists of photographic images on glass that are viewed against a black background. Edwards' archive is a personal one, thus the images evoke intensely personal memories whose meaning is embellished once they are introduced to the public. For Edwards, auto-ethnography – making use of one's own experience as a basis for producing narrative content – is an essential tool. She writes about the process of making the ambrotypes as one of 'ritual and meditation', which help her to establish a sense of identity in the world.

The issue of identity, prevalent in many of these essays, is either the subject of the essay or else the basis for an interpretation that challenges or subverts existing cultural norms. As an example of both, Jane Hattrick draws on queer identity to foreground the sexuality of Norman Hartnell, a prominent London couturier, whose archive she studied over a period of years to produce both a Master's thesis and a PhD. Hattrick writes that she did not set out to write about Hartnell's sexuality, but its importance emerged after the first two years of archive research. She points out that the term 'queer' has both open-ended and disruptive connotations, thus characterizing an approach to archival research that can identify new strategies of interpretation and yield conclusions about the subject that would not otherwise have been evident. She argues, as well, that a queer theoretical framework gives value to things in Hartnell's archive such as sketches, decorative objects, and personal effects that might not otherwise be considered important.

Sexual orientation is also an issue in Elizabeth Howie's discussion of nineteenth-century male portraits that depict men together in affectionate poses. Howie cautions against assuming too quickly a sexual reading of these photographs. She notes that in the twenty-first century, images of men expressing affection for each other unequivocally signify homosexuality for many, but she cautions against assuming this. She critiques the 'rigidifying classification of sexuality' that resulted in homosexuality as a fixed social category. Instead, she notes that from the 1880s 'sexualities appear to have been more fluid, with a complex continuum of desires, from friendly to erotic to sexual, characterizing intimate relationships'.

Howie's plea for a more open reading of same-sex portrait imagery that reflects some form of emotional attachment, reinforces the claim that cultural norms play a strong role in characterizing and putting value on emotions such as love. Part of the dynamic of contemporary culture is the process of challenging and consequently redefining those norms as experience contradicts them. A similar process is at work in Jo Turney's essay on baby knitting. Turney is critical of the way knitting has been socially constructed to denote a mother's love for her child, especially when the mother knits blankets or booties that become emotionally charged for the child, as psychoanalyst Melanie Klein describes in her theory of object relations. Turney believes that too much love can smother a child and consequently refutes the definition of baby knitting as 'making love with needles'. She sees the equation of knitting with idealized motherhood as a legacy of the nineteenth century that deserves to be deconstructed. I would not go as far as Turney in characterizing knitting as a sign of patriarchal control based on what she calls the 'phallocentric act' of needles penetrating loops or holes formed by yarn, but would certainly agree with her observation that knitting has been historically embedded in a labour economy of women's domestic production without monetary compensation. Turney makes use of semiotic theory to tease out the sign functions of social acts. Knitting, as 'a precarious act that creates strength, but can equally unravel and fall apart', is seen by Turney as a metaphor that 'mirrors the dilemmas of parenthood'. To continue her metaphorical reading of knitting, she adds that the holes in the knitted objects make knitting an inherently vulnerable activity. As a further gesture that deconstructs the equation of knitting and motherhood, she cites artists such as Lisa Obermeyer and Donna Wilson who produce knitted objects that disrupt the conventional connotations of knitting. For her final metaphor, Turney likens knitting to an umbilical cord that must be ruptured and repaired to make the relation between mother and child healthy and dynamic.

The mediation of objects in family relations is also central to Catherine Harper's essay on quilted bed covers. Harper moves from the personal to the speculative as she compares the difference between a quilt made by her grandmother with bed coverings that incorporate smart textile technology. Like the people interviewed for the Mass Observation Archive who equated personal memories with the gifts they received, Harper explains how her grandmother's quilt embodies memories that speak to a consciousness of her own genealogy. The 'unruly sewing and irregular patching of the quilt' signify the hard existence of her grandmother who, she says, occupied both the male space of hard physical labour performed outside the home and the softer interior domestic space traditionally occupied by women. Harper's construction of the quilt's meaning differs from the accounts of objects that were described in the Mass Observation Archive interviews cited by Purbrick. In those accounts, neither the genealogy of the objects nor the conditions of their production was of importance. The objects' value was based solely on the emotional quality of the exchange situations in which they were received. By contrast, Harper sees the quilt as contributing to the construction of her social identity that consists, in part, of the connection through gender and class to her grandmother. Harper's relation to her grandmother's quilt and the needle used to make it, demonstrates how personal relations to objects can enrich the generalized descriptions of object histories that characterize the field of material culture.

However, Harper has another purpose in discussing her grandmother's quilt. She wants to explore, on the one hand, the aesthetic potential of quilts that the art critic Sarat Maharaj characterizes as their 'ability to be simultaneously a "domestic commodity" and "conceptual device" '. As an example, Harper cites the NAMES Project AIDS Memorial Quilt, which consists of more than 48,000 panels and has circulated to over 1,000 venues to signify the extent of the AIDS pandemic. Harper also questions whether new technologies can provide the emotional value of a traditional quilt, raising questions about the potential of new technological objects to evoke feelings of love. She wants to discover 'how and where smart, intelligent technological textiles maintain and celebrate the simpler, slower, emotionally meaningful sensibility'. There are no easy answers to this question, but as technologically driven societies increase our engagement with high-tech industrial objects compared to simpler handcrafted or even manufactured ones, we may wonder whether human beings will still develop emotional attachments to them that transcend their use value alone.

Harper's reading of her grandmother's quilt through gender and class is paralleled by Noreen McGuire's account of amateur female shoemakers in the late eighteenth and early nineteenth centuries. McGuire's explanation of why this activity was transgressive reinforces the strict gender and class definitions of occupations in the period she discusses. Female shoemaking began with embroidering shoe vamps, a traditional women's occupation that often denoted affection, and morphed into shoemaking, which accrued the additional signification of thrifty domestic management, even though, as McGuire points out, '[a] fashionable lady's shoes were therefore more symbolic than functional'. Though not made exclusively for women, most shoes made by the amateur shoemakers were. They tended to be slipper-like and refined in design. What made shoemaking suspect in aristocratic circles was its association with the lower class, and predominantly males, at that. A backlash against women shoemakers accused them of transgressing social boundaries to pursue a hobby. Some critics linked them with sexual misconduct, at least with appearing unseemly as they pursued their craft, and they were accused of intruding into the world of business, which was seen as a male purview. The broader consequence was their exclusion from the history of shoemaking, a gap that McGuire seeks to rectify with her account. Describing the class status of objects is a conventional technique of decorative arts and material culture scholars, but raising issues about craftsmanship that counter the conventions of class introduces a new disruptive element into the categorization of objects and demonstrates, as do other essays in this volume, how objects can pose challenges to established cultural norms.

Besides challenging such norms, objects such as the briar pipe, which is the subject of Jessica Sewell's essay, can also help to create new ones. Sewell describes the pipe as a prop in Hugh Hefner's performance of male sexuality. As the publisher of *Playboy*, an American men's magazine that first appeared in 1953, Hefner embodied a suave, sophisticated, upper middle-class man whose embrace of sensual pleasure eluded the repression and conformity of the prior decade. The *Playboy* man was a connoisseur whose taste in clothes, wines, music, and furniture was impeccable. Sucking on his briar pipe, he exuded a sense of leisure and mastery. Women, by contrast, were portrayed by *Playboy* as bunnies whose principal function was to reproduce, an ironic quality since there was no room for children in the *Playboy* world. The objects in that world were signs of seduction, meant to connote an atmosphere of restrained modernity where everything was under control. The briar pipe too was an object to be controlled. Compared with the cigarette, which had to be smoked quickly before the tobacco burned up, the pipe bowl could house embers that smouldered for hours. A semiotician might read this as a metaphor for sexual pleasure under the man's control, although Sewell interprets the pipe as a signifier of male power rather than a metaphor for sex.

The pipe as a prop in the performance of masculinity is complemented by another type of performance in Ann Wilson's account of the bleeding statues in Templemore, Ireland in 1920. Wilson's essay places the statues at the centre of church politics in that part of Ireland, where the Roman Catholic Church sought to cement its power. More and bigger churches were built and 'papally-sanctioned devotions' were introduced and codified as approved religious practices. The bleeding statues, which Wilson defines as kitsch, generated an emotional response among Catholic believers that was outside the Church's devotional norms. The statues signified, for many people, divine intervention that asserted Irish Catholic identity, protecting Templemore against attacks from British forces. Wilson shows how the statues accrued the power to heal supplicants who made special journeys to see them. Though she does not declare outright that the bleeding was fake, she does recount that a mechanism connected to a fountain pen insert that contained sheep's blood and water was found inside one of the broken statues. In her account, the statues acquired inordinate agency by affecting the feelings of large numbers of people who were distressed by the political turmoil in Templemore. They also satisfied a need for physical and emotional healing due to other causes.

Since Jonathan Chapman's concern is with the future of the planet, this essay aptly concludes the volume. Whereas the voices in these essays range generally from the descriptive to the confessional, Chapman's is exhortatory and prophetic. He foresees the potential of a dire future and he wants readers to act on the basis of what he tells them about the status of objects in the world. His connection to other essayists in this volume is through the issue of evoking meaning. Like them, he agrees that 'an object, material or space cannot hold meaning in and of itself – only our interpretation of these things will produce meaning'. He relates the meanings we give objects to the ways we inhabit the world through building cities, inhabiting buildings, wearing clothes, and using products. In essence, the world consists of what we have put into it and consequently what we take out of it. Chapman is concerned with the skewed relation we have to our environment, which results in a relentless pursuit of novelty and consequently overcrowded landfills and a general 'crisis of unsustainability'. He would like us to consume less and establish more meaningful relations to the things around us that would increase their longevity and reduce our collective waste. Durability, he concludes, is 'as much about emotion, love, value and attachment' as it is about anything else.

As I stated at the beginning of this introduction, readers will not find in these essays a shared assumption of what a love object is. The essayists are American, English, or Irish, and all except two are women. Gender, class, and sexual identity contribute to the divergence of these voices as they do to the nature of the issues the essayists explore. I mention this to confirm that the cultural norms that have shaped them, as well as those that frame the subjects they have chosen to write about, are anything but universal. The forms of love the authors explore range from affection to sexual expression and even to a love of the planet. The voices range from the extremely personal to the more widely reflective. What can carry over to a broader range of cultural situations, however, is the claim that there is an inherent tension between individual emotion and the cultural norms that shape its social expression. What unites these essays, besides the commitment to love objects as subject matter, is the relation of love as an emotion to the cultural framework within which it is expressed. As is evident in the essays, individuals and cultures are sometimes at odds and this conflict is the basis for productive cultural change.

SECTION 1

The Lives of Objects

1

'I Love Giving Presents'

The Emotion of Material Culture

Louise Purbrick

Introduction: a given thing

People become attached to things. 'All my presents hold fond memories for me', wrote a retired Post Office worker of the wedding gifts she received in 1954. Indeed, she held onto her gifts in order to remember. 'I love to take things out of a cupboard and think back to the donor, relative or friend, many long gone' (M1571).[1] The desire to have wedding gifts near at hand is also expressed by a former nurse, married in 1963: 'I am very attached to my remaining wedding presents and if I have to move to a smaller place because of old age I shall do my utmost to take them with me' (L1991). Attachment is not an abstract preference. Things must be kept and kept close to the person. This is often expressed in the same way. 'I would not part', begins a lecturer, 'with the bone china teaset as it holds quite dear memories of the old couple who are now dead' (S1383). She received the china from her in-laws in 1960. A factory worker, who kept all her wedding presents, including Pyrex dishes not yet put to use 30 years after her wedding, repeats the phrase: 'I WOULDN'T PART WITH THEM FOR THE WORLD' (C2579) (see Figure 1.1).

The retired Post Office worker, the former nurse, the lecturer and factory worker are Mass Observation writers. This chapter is based on readings of their writings, collected by the Mass Observation Archive; their writings are but a small portion of this Archive's unique records of everyday life (Sheridan *et al.*, 2000). The retired Post Office worker, the former nurse, the lecturer and factory worker are four of the thousands of people who have joined the Mass Observation panel of writers between 1981 and today; they have all corresponded with the Archive for over 10 years on multifarious matters of everyday life or those effecting it: from body decoration to the bombing of Iraq; shopping to sex. I have read their words to find the meanings of a material culture of domesticity (Purbrick, 2007) and would suggest that their writings can be considered documents of the emotion of material culture. Mass Observation writers do not set out to address the changing agendas of academic inquiry, such as the current concern with affect or emotion, but make an altruistic attempt to respond to the open-ended questions that make up Mass Observation directives, such as those included in a Giving and

FIGURE 1.1 *Pyrex ovenware plate, Corning Glassworks. Photograph by Louise Purbrick.*

Receiving Presents directive sent out in Autumn 1998 on which this chapter is based. They do, however, reflect upon the practices of everyday life.[2] They document their lives, including the emotional, even affectionate relationships with material forms, especially those that have been domesticated, demonstrating the attachment and affinity between persons and things. This chapter considers the relationships with, through and in the material forms in late twentieth-century Britain. It is a study of the domestic exchanges of objects that make up family life: a study of gifts. But first, a few words about the status of Mass Observation as a source for this study and, second, a few more about the implications of finding emotion in material culture.

Mass Observation

Mass Observation writing is the subject of methodological and theoretical inquiries in anthropology, sociology, social and cultural history (Bhatti, 2006; Hurdley, 2006, 2013; Pollen, 2013; Purbrick, 2007; Sheridan *et al.*, 2000; Stanley, 2001). The Mass Observation Archive must be one of the most thoroughly debated collections of documents of the twentieth and early twenty-first centuries. Mass Observation writing, either that generated by its founders Tom Harrison, Charles Madge and Humphrey Jennings through their 1930s documentary collages announced as the 'anthropology of home', or that of the hundreds of participants, 'correspondents' in the Mass Observation Project 'recording everyday life in Britain' (Mass Observation, 2013) initiated in the 1980s, is multivalent: it is meaningful as historical text, sociological data and anthropological material. Few documents tell of everyday life; so many written words, such as these I write here, are shaped by destinations as publications, restrained by the conventions of academic style or by the conventions of individual expression or editorial practices of journalism that eschew the everyday as too obvious to analyse, too routine to ever be newsworthy. Collective recording projects, such as Mass Observation, that generate writing for that purpose only, for the record, are uniquely important; writing is not formulated to achieve institutional targets, to find a market for ideas or to follow fashions in what is supposed to be interesting, worthy of note.

As long ago as 1996, the then Archivist of Mass Observation, Dorothy Sheridan, authored a working paper to address assumptions that Mass Observation was unreliable or unrepresentative and therefore unimportant as a source for academic study (Sheridan, 1996). She countered the criticism that Mass Observation was anecdotal. Drawing on the methodological observations of J. Cylde Mitchell about particular kinds of fieldwork as case studies (Mitchell, 1984), Sheridan developed a theoretical position for Mass Observation as a 'telling' case. Its claim to knowledge is not based on the coverage of demographic types, as required by quantitative survey; it is detail, richness or thickness of description that reveals relationships or structures (Geertz, 1993). Such relationships and structures are inevitably specific – they are specific cases – but it is from specific cases that generalizations, propositions or theories can be made and tested. Thus, the Giving and Receiving directive may not provide evidence of how many gifts of what type are given (a retailing stock-take would do that job far better), however, it might tell much more about the significance of giving as a practice, regardless of the type of gift. Through the Giving and Receiving directive, Mass Observation writers explain why they give gifts, thus a theory of practice of everyday life is produced by those who live that life.

Emotion in material culture

To consider material forms as repositories of affection and not just desire, of longing as opposed to preference, of love of all kinds, demands some rethinking of the status of objects in capitalist and consumer culture. Such feelings show the limits of commodity worlds. If a thing can create affection, then the illusion of human fulfilment falsely promised in the marketplace might actually be real: a fairytale can come true. For Marx, there is no such happy ending. His critique of the commodity, and its subsequent development into a comprehensive and convincing analytical assault upon cultures of consumption, rests upon the fact that the commodity cannot be redeemed from its state of alienation (Marx, 1988, pp. 125–177; Slater, 1997, pp. 63–99). Commodities are empty of all but market values; exchangeable for anything of momentarily equivalent, arbitrary and also empty value, such as money; they are alienated from the moment of being made. A past existence in production is expediently forgotten in the act of exchange, but, even if remembered, there is no redemption in production. Commodities are formed through the calculated productive capacities of a labour force; the labour of those who comprise that force is measured to become as exchangeable and alienated as a commodity. The commodity is a disembodied form, which through repeated exchange, has reproduced a pervasive culture of acquisition and loss. Commodity exchanges determine all other forms of exchange, including those between people beyond their place in production: relationships are commodified, the human condition standardized with only 'the freedom to choose what is always the same' in Theodor Adorno's oft-quoted summary. He also remarked, 'We are forgetting how to give presents' (Adorno, 1997, p. 42).

The dominance of the commodity caused this forgetfulness. Commodities subsume everything; they make all things in their image, including gifts. That something exists outside what Adorno terms the 'exchange principle', the quick transfer of one for another, an article for money, is 'implausible'. Giving appears to be selling. '[E]ven children eye the giver suspiciously', observes Adorno, 'as if the gift were merely a trick to sell them brushes or soap' (Adorno, 1997, p. 42). Thus, the calculating logic of the commodity exchange is imposed upon gift exchange. Calculation is not only the process through which a commodity acquires its price, purchasers also estimate the object as a matter of loss or gain. What will it cost me? Is its value to me worth its price? Will its cost prevent me from getting something better? Adorno sees commodity calculation entering gift relations. Estimation of exchange begins the decline of giving. '[H]ardly anyone' is now able to give:

> At best they give what they would have liked themselves, only a few degrees worse. The decay of giving is mirrored in the distressing invention of gift articles, based on the assumption that one does not know what to give because one does not really want to. This merchandise is unrelated like its buyers. It was a drug in market from the first day. Likewise, the right to exchange the article, which signifies to the recipient: take this it is all yours, do what you like with it; if you don't want it, it is all the same to me, get something else instead.
>
> Adorno, 1997, p. 42

The gift article is the commodity in its pure form (see Figure 1.2). It has an 'unrelated' character. Because it belongs unequivocally to the receiver ('it is all yours') and can be used for exchange and even disposed of. It cannot, therefore, be a gift. The gift article cannot create relationships; it denies the connection between people who ought to be established through their material exchanges. These articles demonstrate the reduced conditions of life in capitalism. Those who do not give, or do not give properly, become dehumanized as individuals. 'In them wither the irreplaceable faculties which cannot flourish in the isolated cell of inwardness, but only in live contact with the warmth of things'. This is a kind of death. 'A chill descends on all they do' and 'recoils on those from whom it emanates'. He who does not give 'makes himself a thing and freezes' (Adorno, 1997, p. 43).

However, the retired Post Office worker does remember how to conduct gift exchanges: 'After all these years it is difficult to remember some of our presents but I'm happy to say we still have many of them and I still associate the giver with the gift when we use them' (M1571). Indeed, she honours the gift in exactly the way its theorist, Marcel Mauss, says she should. His 1925 essay 'The Gift', turns upon the association of giver and gift. Indeed, it is the gift that creates association. It does so because the giver never quite leaves the gift. Gifts 'still possess something of the giver' (Mauss, 1990, p. 12). To receive a gift is to accept the giver along with their offering; it is to allow the giver a part in the receiver's future, at the moment when the gift is inserted into a life. If the gift is a garment, for example, the giver is present when it is worn; if it is food, they are at the table as the meal is eaten. To accept is to acknowledge the presence of the giver in relation to the receiver. This is the effect (and affect) of what Adorno calls 'real giving'. Real giving produces a proper human relationship. He explains: 'Real giving has its joy

FIGURE 1.2 *An example of gift articles in a commercial setting, 2013. Photograph by Louise Purbrick.*

in imagining the joy of the receiver. It means choosing, expending time, going out of one's way, thinking of the other as a subject' (Adorno, 1997, p. 42). A person is recognized in the real gift. In dialectical opposition to an unrelated commodity (and those who exchange it), the gift (and its givers and receivers) is a related thing.

Adorno read Marcel Mauss. The work of gifts in societies where gift exchange is the only form of exchange is the subject of Mauss' essay, but it can be read, indeed it has been read, as a critique of capitalist exchange relations (Carrier, 1995; Gregory, 1982). The commodity transactions of capitalism cannot create human relationships because these transactions have a definite conclusion. A commodity exchange is momentary and is over as soon as an object passes from one hand to another. An exactly equivalent value, most often its price in money, is passed back. A deal is done. Each commodity exchange begins a new brief contract, quickly completed. Thus, commodities create no bonds. Once you have paid the price, you have all rights of possession without regard for another's past relationship to the object: free to use, alone to have. All is alienated. By contrast, gift exchanges are very slowly, if ever, concluded. Giving is always giving back. The gift, according to Mauss, is an obligatory form, an object that must be given, received and reciprocated. The imperative to reciprocate, which generates giving then receiving, receiving then giving, is because a part of the giver remains with the gift. A given thing encloses a debt to the giver or related person; it creates a bond that can only be relieved by giving another gift, and that serves only to extend the debt. Gifts create cycles of exchange, enforcing solidarities of indebtedness, sustaining communities and societies. Gift transactions are irrevocable and sociable. Gifts bind people together.

Real giving

The writings of the former nurse, retired Post Office worker, factory worker and lecturer illustrate the binding together of people through given things. While the gift exists, is present, so to speak, so is the person of the giver, despite apparent physical absence. Having and holding, looking at or touching, a once given thing can overcome the separation of persons over any distance; it can connect the living and the dead. As the Post Office worker explained, to take wedding presents from a cupboard is to recollect their givers, 'many long gone'. Or, as the lecturer stated, 'memories of the old couple who are now dead' are held in the bone china teaset. These accounts of the attachments of people and things relate to the receipt of gifts, but Mass Observation writers also described their practices of giving. Their responses to the Giving and Receiving Presents directive, record and reflect upon their experience of gift exchange. Both descriptive and analytical, their texts raise the matter of concern to Adorno: is 'real giving' still possible? To which I would add the following questions: What is affectionate material culture? Do gifts carry emotion? How can we love objects? Why do we become attached to things? What is the emotion of material culture? But first, what are the patterns of gift exchange?

The Mass Observation correspondent who had worked as a nurse, who also introduces herself as a 'widow', writes:

> As with most people my main present giving is for Christmas and birthdays. I have a small family to give to: on the English side – daughter, son and recently his fiancé, brother, sister in law, niece and nephew. On the Dutch we decided only to exchange presents when we met because of the prohibitive cost of postage. Friends new babies get some things that I have knitted, christenings don't seem to happen these days but I would give a gift. We used to give presents on return from holiday to the children if we had left them behind but stopped because it was such a misery finding something they would enjoy and we could afford . . .
>
> By and large I give to people I receive from. I try to buy without asking for ideas from the intended recipient but if I get stuck I'll ask. I don't see my niece and nephew often enough to know their wants so, after talking to them I now give money. I rarely give tokens.
>
> Ideally I give presents by hand, my brother and I meet for lunch each December to exchange gifts, the children live locally or I'll use the post. I use a mail order flower service for people to whom I would like to say hallo but don't really want to get into the habit of regular present giving, this has been very successful, people seem to like it.
>
> L1991

The former nurse practises 'real giving' or, at least, she attempts it: she buys presents for a person, searching for her own ideas about what is appropriate for that person until settling upon one or getting 'stuck'. She is, as Adorno put it, 'thinking of the other as a subject' (1997, p. 42). Giving began, as it should, with 'choosing, expending time' but falls apart when ideas for, or of, the person fade. The niece and nephew are a case in point. She knows them in their relation to her, but cannot gather enough thoughts about them to envisage a material form that might match their lives. For her they lack a specific subjectivity; they are simply her brother's children. The intergenerational familial relation is sustained by a devalued form of giving wherein the space of the gift is taken up by its exchange value: money. Giving money does not conform to Adorno's idea of 'real giving'; it requires neither 'choosing' nor 'expending time'. Money, furthermore, is a lesser material form; it lacks substance. They are acknowledged as part of the family, but less recognized as persons in a gift without content. The former nurse does recognize that something is amiss in the gift transactions with her niece and nephew. The acceptable practice of the past is brought to an end with negotiation ('after talking to them'). The need for negotiation is often a sign that a common understanding is failing or a customary practice faltering. Giving money needs to be agreed rather than just given because it is not a proper gift in a material form; money is the exception that proves the rule.

Notwithstanding this exception, the gifting of the former nurse does, in a Maussian manner, create societies; it constitutes the contemporary family as an affective community with nieces and nephews included at its outer limits. The extent of giving reaches, although it only just reaches in its reduced form, the children of a brother and defines the family as a related affair, a group of people connected through the courtship patterns of siblings as well as children. As the writing of the former nurse implies, now that her son's fiancée has started to receive presents on 'Christmas and birthdays', she has become part of their family. Attachment is the work of the gift, its effect and affect; it pulls upon emotions. Through the gift, the family is cast more widely than the members of an individual household; moreover, its inner and outer limits, what is often referred to as a close and an extended family, is repeatedly reaffirmed. All gifts are reciprocated. 'I give to people I receive from', writes the former nurse. Reciprocal exchanges take place twice a year, every year: at Christmas and on birthdays, which function as recurring moments of recognition of the extent of the family, keeping it together. Members of the family are distinguished by being more or less successfully imagined and materialized; the giver's thoughts settle upon a physical present for those who are close, whereas ideas are inconclusive for those on its extended edge; these are offered the means to get their gifts. But all such exchanges are personal, given by hand in the meeting between a sister and a brother at 'lunch each December'. In contrast, gifts to friends, the mail ordered flowers, are deliberately distanced from the person of the giver, an arranged gesture rather than handed over. Cut plants are not intended to last; their curtailed life does not carry the continuing obligations of the gift to form permanent relationships.

One Mass Observation writer gives in a remarkably similar way to another. The retired Post Office worker gives 'to my family, husband, son and daughter, their families, especially grandchildren, to my sister and her family. 'I knitted a "Sooty and Sweep" sweater for my grand-daughter aged 6 for Christmas' (M1571). At the time of writing, the former nurse was not a grandmother, but since she knitted for new babies, it is safe to assume that she, too, would give to grandchildren. Indeed, both Mass Observation writers demarcate the life cycle of the related family, the affective community defined by courtship, with gifts. As the retired Post Office worker explains: 'On marriage of course the family presents increase but then sadly with the passing of years we lose our elderly relatives but "little people" arrive at the other end of the scale so the present giving list remains fairly constant' (M1571). The extent of her family also lay with nieces and nephews. The familial relationship between siblings and siblings' children is reaffirmed in a recurring pattern of perpetual gift exchanges but the retired Post Office worker, like the former nurse, reluctantly gives in its emptied form: 'I do give money to my nieces and nephews for birthdays, Christmas, Congratulations etc. for the simple reason that they live far away and its seems the only sensible option – when they were children I sent presents but now as teenagers I really can't keep up with computers etc.' (M1571).

Geographical distance ensures that 'real giving' as a practice of 'thinking of the other as a subject' is more difficult. Losing sight of the potential recipient affects the accuracy of their representation; there are no recent images to produce a clear picture. Yet, the position in the family does not alter and an outline identity is projected, a familial subjectivity conceived, from the position of the parent's generation. The material presence of niece and nephew is a child. Their ageing unsettles the order of familial present giving; they have grown up into consumers more knowledgeable than their aunts and uncles in the market of technological commodities. Yet, the retired Post Office worker still continues to celebrate the ageing of family members with a gift; she marks the rites of passage of birth and growth with material forms; she gives presents 'for birthdays, special anniversaries, for a new baby'.

Family life cycles are at the centre of the retired Post Office worker's giving practices, but her gifting increased to include friends once she began her working life. 'As a child I gave small presents to my sister and parents', she recalls. 'When I became a wage earner I set aside a little fund for presents, my present giving then increased to include friends' (M1571). Her expanded gift relations are premised on a measure of independence, especially financial independence, from the family. However, it is the emotion of the object to be given: 'I just love to give presents, I find the greatest pleasure is in choosing the present or in the case of children's presents seeing the joy in the face of the child when the present is unwrapped' (M1571). The joy of giving at the moment of its receipt is well known, but the retired Post Office worker's love of 'choosing' is closer to Adorno's joy of 'real giving'. Choosing a gift is a process of questioning what object is most appropriate for this person; the chooser of the gift keeps on imagining the person with the different objects until the material object fits the person; it is representation as materialization. Certainly, choosing is 'expending time' upon a person, but it is also constantly choosing what constitutes the person.[3] 'I like to choose a present for a particular person', she adds.

The factory worker also declares: 'I LOVE GIVING PRESENTS'. The extent of her gift community is similar to that of the retired postal worker: the related family defined by courtship plus friends:

MOST OF THE PRESENTS I BUY ARE FOR RELATIONS, BUT A FEW ARE FOR FRIENDS CHILDREN. I ALWAYS BUY CHRISTMAS AND BIRTHDAY PRESENTS FOR MY HUSBAND, MY MOTHER-IN-LAW, BROTHER, SISTER-IN-LAW, NIECE, AUNTIE, HALF SISTER AND MY HUSBANDS SISTER AND HER HUSBAND, ALSO MY COUSINS SON. TWO OF MY CLOSEST FRIENDS HAVE CHILDREN AND I ALWAYS BUY THEM PRESENTS. I ALSO BUY EVERYONE SOMETHING WHEN I GO ABROAD ON HOLIDAY. PLUS I BUY HOLIDAY GIFTS FOR MY FRIENDS AT WORK.

THE OTHER TIME I BUY PRESENTS IS WHEN SOME ONE AT WORK RETIRES. IF IT IS SOMEBODY I HAVE WORKED WITH FOR A LONG TIME, I LIKE TO BUY THEM SOMETHING SPECIAL FROM ME, AND NOT JUST SOMETHING WHICH WE HAVE ALL CONTRIBUTED TO. I ALSO BUY PRESENTS FOR FAMILY AND WORKMATES WHEN THEY HAVE A SPECIAL WEDDING ANNIVERSARY.

C2579

The affective community created by the factory worker's gifts is wide; her family, for example, includes a cousin's son. What distinguishes her gift practice is the generous application of intergenerational giving. While some friendships are affirmed with gifts directly to the friend, for themselves, 'CLOSEST FRIENDS' receive presents for their children, an intergenerational and familial practice of giving.

The love of the factory worker for giving gifts is not matched through their receipt. Her gift exchanges do follow the reciprocal principles of Mauss and patterns of other Mass Observers. 'MOST OF MY FAMILY WHO I BUY FOR', she states, 'DO GIVE ME A PRESENT IN RETURN'. There are some exceptions. Some cannot reciprocate because, she explains, 'TIMES ARE A BIT HARD FOR THEM, ITS THE SAME FOR MY FRIENDS'. The factory worker indicates that she is relieved not to receive in return; clearly she prefers unequal or 'asymmetrical' (Komter, 1996) gift exchanges:

I HAVE TO SAY THAT I HATE RECEIVING PRESENTS. I FIND IT HARD AND I USUALLY BREAK DOWN IN TEARS. I NEVER HAD MUCH BECAUSE WE WERE POOR, BUT NOW, AFTER WORKING HARD AND BUYING A HOME AND BEING ABLE TO SAVE, I WANT TO GIVE IT TO MY FAMILY AND FRIENDS WHO ARE NOT SO FORTUNATE AS ME ... MY FAMILY GIVES ME PRESENTS, AND THIS YEAR (1998) WHEN I WAS ILL, I RECEIVED ABOUT 20 BOUQUETS OF FLOWERS FROM WORKMATES AND FROM WORKMATES WHO HAD RETIRED AND WHO HAD LEARNT THAT I WAS ILL. I DO FIND IT HARD TO RECEIVE PRESENTS. WHEN I DO I USUALLY BREAK DOWN AND CRY.

C2579

Her hatred of gifts is qualified later in her Mass Observation account when she states she has received 'SO MANY OVER THE YEARS WHICH HAVE GIVEN ME SO MUCH PLEASURE'. It is possible to suggest, then, that it is not the gift she hates but the discomfort of the moment of its receipt. Tears are a sign of excessive emotion, a surfeit of feeling that cannot be contained inside the body and brims over onto its skin. The rising tide of emotions experienced by the factory worker includes the shock of present achievements contrasting with past hardships, as well as the amount of affection in a given material form: 'PRESENT GIVING TO ME IS MOST IMPORTANT, BECAUSE SOMETIMES YOU CANNOT SHOW PEOPLE HOW MUCH THEY MEAN TO YOU. BUT BY GIVING THEM A PRESENT I FEEL THAT IN SOME WAY SHOWS HOW YOU FEEL ABOUT THEM' (C2579). The gift expresses real feelings, to borrow Adorno's use of the word 'real'. Herein lies its bodily effects; its ability to disrupt the surface of a person's appearance, causing her (or maybe even him) to cry. In front of a present, a body may fragment, if only temporarily, before pulling itself together to receive the present with a smile. The clarity of expression of the gift, the way in which it can communicate emotion so effectively, is because it is material. Its substantial nature demonstrates the scale of significance of a relationship ('SHOW PEOPLE HOW MUCH THEY MEAN TO YOU'). Its power and affection derives from its materiality.

The far-reaching affect of the gift, the emotion of material, can be revealed in reverse, when the principles of giving and receiving are not upheld. The former nurse, whose gift exchanges were similar in most respects to other Mass Observers, recalls the disaffection of failed gift exchange: 'Presents for my mother were very difficult, if she did not like what she was given she would simply give it back and furthermore decline anything else, it was very painful and a real rejection' (L1991). The pain of rejection is often manifested in a flinch: the person reels back from the thing that caused the pain. Despite, or because, she experienced the incisiveness of pain upon of the refusal of a gift, an act that is 'tantamount to a declaration of war', according to Mauss (1990, p. 13), her Mass Observation account concludes with the importance of giving to human life: 'I think present giving has an important role, human interaction is the basis of living and reciprocity underpins this. Thinking of others, and being thought of, oils the wheels and does much to both value and be valued as human beings' (L1991).

She offers a theory of gifting, a little differently expressed to that of Adorno, but not unlike his in its configuration of the proper relation between materiality and humanity. It is about time to return to his injunction: 'We are forgetting how to give presents'. It seems we have not yet forgotten. Indeed, Adorno never argued that we had forgotten, but that we are always just about to forget. Our present condition lies somewhere between remembered and forgotten. Giving appears in his 1951 essays as a past practice that we struggle to complete in the present; the gift is a memory of how things should be.

Forgetting

The lecturer is the last Mass Observation writer to be discussed here. The lecturer's account of giving is an expression of the struggle to practise the proper giving of the past. The lecturer gives to the same people on the same occasions and, like the former nurse, retired Post Office and factory workers, to the related family and a small number of friends: 'relatives plus one or two close friends. e.g. my children, brother, sister, niece, husband, old friend, parents in law, grandchildren' on 'birthdays, Christmas and occasionally leaving presents when people leave work' (S1383). The same people return gifts to her. The consistency of Mass Observation accounts suggests that reciprocal giving that maintains affective communities of around 20 people is a common and a stable social practice. However, the lecturer reflects: 'How things have changed over my lifetime'. She continues:

> When I was a child we only got presents from our mum and dad and sometimes our brother and sister although not always. Usually presents for me were practical e.g. a new coat for Christmas, or new shoes for birthday. We would also get sweets and a little toy as well. Relatives did not give presents then and Christmas was not the nightmare it is now as we did not buy for relatives either. I do believe we were more delighted with modest gifts then than children are now as they are bombarded with expensive, often electronic toys which break down on Christmas Day.
>
> S1383

Her Mass Observation account contains a familiar refrain on the commercialization of Christmas, especially in relation to the price and quantity of technological objects given to children:

> Now I find Christmas particularly worrying as I have three children, three brothers and sisters, a close friend, a niece and nephew, husband to buy presents for as well as five grandchildren plus two stepgrandchildren. It is costly and difficult to choose. I would prefer modest fun presents for the adults with toys for the children but it never seems to work out like that so I end up buying clothes usually for my children and relatives, and toys for the grandchildren.
>
> Working out what people like is the worst nightmare. My husband and I do not go Christmas shopping together any more as he has different views on how much to spend and what kind of presents people might like. So I do it alone and don't enjoy it. Sometimes I give tokens or money but rarely as I feel this is a boring kind of thing to open on Christmas day and shows no imagination or thought at all. Even if you get a present you dislike someone has at least thought about it and got it wrong!
>
> S1383

While she does not love giving presents as the retired Post Office worker or factory worker do, she attempts the 'real giving' of 'thinking of the other' through time spent deciding upon an appropriate material form for a person. The choosing causes conflict, disagreements between her and her husband; it has a high price, but she still does it. This is a kind of love: a fulfilment of an arduous obligation. She understands the material forms of the gift as fully expressive of receiver as recognized by the giver (a person in the relationship with another) and thus the lecturer, as other Mass Observation writers, tries to avoid settling upon 'tokens or money' and fails. They attempt to give against a commodified world.

Keeping giving

Real giving persists, then. For some, such as the lecturer, 'thinking of the other as a subject' and properly fulfilling the obligation to give is a hardship. The large numbers of lonely shoppers who crowd the streets every December share that burden: searching for ideas of a person, an intended recipient of an as yet unformed gift; they try to match an image of that person with the objects in the shops and then work out whether that appropriate object is affordable. They must give something. Whatever it is and however long it takes to find it, the search for an offering is preferable to succumbing to the dehumanized condition that Adorno attributed to not giving. To give is to fend off social isolation, to try to survive as a person.

Gifts are powerful things. As described by Mass Observation writers, gifts are acts of love; they can express the significance of a person that cannot be contained in words; their exchange creates attachments, acknowledges and affirms the extent of a family; they are the cause of tears of sadness and joy. They can recall the dead. The opening citation from the retired Post Office worker bears repeating: 'I love to take things out of a cupboard and think back to the donor, relative or friend, many long gone' (M1571). The circulation of gifts constitutes a domain of material culture that could certainly be characterized as emotional: the things given have bodily effects and affects, they produce feelings; they sustain relationships between people across families that do not see each other, negotiate the distance from nephews and nieces, keep attachments between the living and the dead. Both personhood and sociability, the social life that makes a person, are realized in this emotional domain of material culture. Here, the encroachments of the market are held at bay.

For Mauss, for Adorno, for others, the gift is the antithesis of the commodity. It is also this in practice as well as theory: gift exchanges continually dissent from commodity culture; giving is an everyday practice of opposition. The exchange of gifts has a more lasting affect than the commodity exchanges that provide the dominant paradigm of culture. They are the things to which we can become attached. For that we are grateful, both for the things and the way it makes us feel. Thus, the gift could be considered a hidden history of the commodity. The sheer quantity, never mind the significance, of things sold and bought in order to be given might alert anyone who wanted to take up a dialectics of commodity culture that it is dependent upon the very thing that it has relegated to a secondary position. Paradoxically (or not), these things exert their power materially and intimately but less discursively and decisively than commodities. One way of thinking about the antithesis of commodity and gift is an object lesson in maintaining the hierarchy of market over home, capitalist culture over family life. Overcoming the difficulties of shopping for an extended family every Christmas, as the lecturer does, in an effort to reaffirm affectionate relationships and recognize, as far as possible, the particularities of persons, is fuel for commodity culture. We make many of our gifts from commodities. At its best, when the gift is just the right present for that person, the gift is an anti-capitalist form, a human thing. That people give and receive the very things they need every day, could be held up as routine victories over capitalism; the struggle to be a person is won through gift relationships with others. The ties that bind people together are strong. Attachment is the power of the gift. The gift is coercive; it forces inclusion across asymmetries and hierarchies of social life. Thus far, the domain of the gift, an emotional material culture, has been offered as a criticism of capitalism, but in conclusion I should say a few words of warning about the given objects of love.

Conclusion

While there may be brief moments of equality within gift relationships, most gifting occurs in families where this is not often the case. Some family members, usually siblings, might be treated equally by being given goods that carry the same personal worth, but families are characterized by asymmetrical gift relationships. Aafke Komter has analysed the asymmetry of giving: females in families, particularly those in the role of the mother, participate in giving and receiving to a far greater extent than males, including fathers (1996, pp. 119–131). Women carry out the work of gifts and are rewarded for it: they give more and receive more, but not in equal amounts. The Mass Observation testimony bears this out. All female writers assumed responsibility for family gifting, giving on behalf of male family members for the family as a whole. Furthermore, whilst Mass Observation writers might attest to the love of gifts, an aspect of familial love is that it occurs in (or is even an affect of) the hierarchy of an older over a younger generation; parents over children. Imagine children showering parents with presents at Christmas. Children are not initially expected to reciprocate their gifts and when they do, the gift is not an equivalent. Indeed, failure to give in return or to return a less than equivalent gift is expected since acceptance of the position as a child, less than equal and dependent upon a parent, may be the gift's desired effect (Godlier, 1999). Thus, gifts can arise from inequality and continually enforce it. An emotional material culture of the gift might dispel the market, but it does not banish hierarchy; it softens the effect of inequality, enables it to be tolerated, even embraced.

Notes

1 Mass Observation writers are anonymized in the Mass Observation Archive and then identified by letters and numbers. Excerpts from their correspondence with the Archive have been reproduced here in the written form closest to their own. In cases where the correspondent wrote in capital letters, those excerpts have also been reproduced in upper case. Mass Observation material reproduced with permission of Curtis Brown Group Ltd, London on behalf of The Trustees of the Mass Observation Archive. Copyright © The Trustees of the Mass Observation Archive.

2 See entries for the University of Sussex Special Collections held at The Keep: http://www.thekeep.info/collections/mass-observation-archive/ and http://www.thekeep.info/collections/getrecord/GB181_SxMOA2_1_55 (accessed 17.3.14).

3 For another account of 'expending time' see Pierre Bourdieu's 'Work of Time' (Komter, 1996, pp. 135–147), an extract from *The Logic of Practice* (1990).

2

(S)mother's Love, or, Baby Knitting

Jo Turney

Boys are so jolly lucky when mummy likes knitting.
ADVERT FOR SCOTCH WOOL HOSIERY STORES IN *HOUSEWIFE*, SEPTEMBER 1956, P. 6

The significance of knitting to the contemporary world is multifarious, but emanates predominantly from the symbolic potential of both activity and object as myth (Barthes, 1973). Within Western popular culture, merely the word 'knitting' conjures ideas and ideals surrounding the cosy, homely, familial, traditional, thrifty, feminine and hand-made. Such linguistic association positions knitting within an ahistorical and sentimental framework, which is simultaneously past and present, and therefore symptomatic of a permanent state of nostalgic longing. Such assumptions create a mythology that presupposes linearity and longevity that consequently sites knitting as a constant; an example of stability in a fashion-led culture dominated by obsolescence. Such an analogy is problematic on two counts: first, the discipline of hand-knitting is stifled by its self-referentiality, and, second, the prerequisite of memory in perpetuating the 'meaning' of knitting offers subjective and selective mythologies that naturalize the dominant ideology, particularly the patriarchal constructs of the 'good woman' and the 'good mother', which are inherent in these sociocultural constructs (Goodwin and Huppatz, 2010, pp. 1–3). Connotations of 'make-do-and-mend' – a do-it-yourself ethic, so central to the contemporary knit revival, recalling working through hardship, a narrative stemming from wartime – situate knitting within wider social issues that include domestic ideologies, neo-liberalism, and financial and household management (Reynolds, 1999, p. 327). Such concerns are heightened through perceptions of knitting as a thrifty activity, a skill that is both money saving and money making; one can make clothing for one's family more cheaply than buying (although this is largely a myth) and one can knit to sell, i.e. *pin money* to add to the household budget (Nelson and Smith, 1999, p. 123; Strawn, 2007, p. 114). The recent re-popularization of knitting pays testament to the 'new domesticity' (Hollows, 2006, pp. 97–118) because such iconology plays and offers resistance to the current economic instability experienced by Western nations and a return to traditional gender roles (Samuel, 1996, p. 280). Consequently, knitting acts as an ideal vehicle for communicating stability in unstable times and communicating Victorian ideals of femininity that promote selflessness and prudence (Davidoff and Hall, 2002, pp. 28, 114), implying that national stability is dependent upon traditional women's roles and the creation and maintenance of a stable family (Bamberger, 1974, p. 265; Davidoff, 1973, p. 51; Hirschon, 1993, p. 66). Knitting is therefore not merely part of the iconography and iconology of patriarchy, but an element of moral economy that polices and binds women to their family through loosely defined notions of love (Goodwin and Huppatz, 2010, pp. 1–2).

Much like knitting, this analogy is full of holes, a myth that needs busting or at least revisiting. This essay[1] questions the seemingly 'natural' link between women's domestic work (knitting) and social roles (motherhood), considering the paradoxical construction of ideals that include both. Love, here, is a double-edged sword; one must love, but not too much; one must nurture but not stifle; or one must 'mother', but not 'smother'. It is, of course, impossible and undesirable to measure love, to ascertain when enough tips into too much, and thus the successful attainment or sustainability of such ideals is precarious to say the least, frequently leaving mothers paralysed by the fear of impending failure. Ultimately, the mother (much like a knitter) must sacrifice personal time, energy, thoughts, for the betterment of her loved ones (Miller, 1998, p. 100). Here I will argue that although knitting for one's children may be considered 'making love with needles', it is a repetitive and painful exercise that is fruitless, thankless and endless; one that must be unpicked and reworked in order to achieve a sense of success. Knitting, in this essay, will be investigated as a cultural paradox; indicative of a mother's love but simultaneously of too much love, or smothering. Knitting is therefore presented as a fluid, rather than static entity; the expression of polarity and difference, rather than unchanging familiarity. These dichotomies are the focus of this discussion which draws from psychoanalytic and feminist theories that consider the re-instigation of the patriarchy within contemporary culture; one that considers feminism a threat and, somewhat paradoxically, as a sign of reparation of the status quo. Examples are drawn from textile art practice and are supported with oral testimonies solicited in 2011 from British mothers who discussed their relationship with wool.[2] These disparate perspectives have been selected in order to demonstrate the ubiquity and cultural depth pertaining to the relationship between knitting and nurture and the ways in which the hidden, emotional and sentimental anxieties of motherhood find form. The 'naturalness' of knitting is perpetuated by its ordinariness, its ease and ubiquity, and, much like motherhood, the naturalness extends to the sacrifice of time and the self for the well-being of another. The breadth of exemplar within this essay bears witness to the extent that 'good' mothering is not natural, but a source of constant anxiety and a patriarchal construct that wears knitted booties. The wolf is wearing the sheep's clothes.

The iconography and iconology of knitting are intrinsically linked with the mythologies of idealized femininity developed in the nineteenth century. From, and as a consequence of, the Industrial Revolution, hand knitting has been largely, in the West, a domestic pursuit. Knitting can be seen, therefore, to inhabit a decidedly female domain, existing as part of a moral economy; an alternative to fashion, 'work' and the masculine world of modern capitalist business. Indeed, knitting is a phallocentric act; needles penetrate loops or holes formed by yarn, and by association can be assessed as a sign of patriarchal control.

Knitting is both familiar and familial, the stuff of everyday life, epitomized by the enduring image of a granny knitting in her rocking chair. Although 'granny' may not be the ideal poster girl for contemporary knit, she remains a potent signifier of knitting as a female and family-centric occupation. Historically, children, particularly girls, were taught to knit by their mothers or grandmothers, and until relatively recently this form of intergenerational sharing of knowledge was commonplace. Initially seen as a means of useful occupation, knitting was imbued with the concept of 'work' rather than leisure, as with embroidery, and had a dual purpose of providing an outlet for idle hands and a means of future employment, most frequently within the home (Boris, 1994, pp. 1–2). In the late twentieth century, this was less the case and knitting, however potentially useful, was a means of creating bonds and relationships between female relatives (Turney, 2009, p. 12). This remains a concern for young mothers now:

> [the children] wore a number of knitted garments made by their grandmother. Very often I would ask her to make a particular style that I liked, or she would show me patterns that she had had from her mother and things that she'd made for her children and she'd recreate them. And one of the things that I particularly loved that she made for [the children] were little blankets for their cots which were really old-fashioned patterns. And I particularly cherish those because they were so unusual. I got lots and lots of pleasure from people stopping me in the street and asking me where I had got the blankets from because they were so unusual. They would then regale me with their own memories of things that their parents would make. [She] is in her late 70s now so obviously a lot of the patterns she had were very, very, very old. And some of them are written with tiny, tiny writing, in pencil and you can just about read them because they have been so pawed over for years, but they were written either by herself by remembering what her mother had told her or by her mother. . . . I wanted it to have lots of memories, so it wasn't just the knitting itself, it was the creation of that artifact that I thought was really important. It held lots of importance for [the grandma] and the family in general, because of course all the family were aware of it, and lots of memories would come out of it even in discussing the pattern and the colour; she'd tell me lots of stories about her mother and all her memories of her mother creating things and there'd be memories of her making things for her own children, and that's now been passed on to my children. So I really, really cherish all the little knitted garments she made.
>
> Sharon

Knitting, as this testimony outlines, is a means of connecting; of forging and maintaining links with female family members through the production of what may become an 'heirloom' item (Gauntlett, 2011, p. 2). This is both sharing and bonding; respectful and repetitive. Here, one mother appreciates the efforts and skills of her elder, whilst by association, acknowledging her success as a mother. Love, nurturing and time spent on knitting for the family have become badges of honour, souvenirs of sacrifice, that are articulated through patterns, garments, skills and knowledge. On the one hand, the knitting is projective, a nurturing map for the younger woman's journey through motherhood, on the other, it is retrojective, connecting the present with the past and a history of mothers.

In a similar manner, as a craft practice, knitting is a tacit skill passed from one person to another, i.e. it is much easier to learn through watching and doing than from a written or illustrated text. From this perspective, knitting is a relatively simple activity to teach to young children, as it requires concentration, but can also produce an outcome quite quickly and thus prevent boredom. It instils discipline, whilst fulfilling a utilitarian function and can thus be seen as demonstrative of intergenerational instruction, of behaving 'like a girl'. So, by learning to knit, girls are indoctrinated in patriarchal roles; they are learning to be 'good' wives and mothers.

Indeed, the connotations that link knitting to the role of the 'good mother' are so entwined that frequently women learn or take up knitting whilst pregnant, an act that seemingly bonds mother with unborn child, fulfilling maternal urges for nesting and nurturing. Such an analogy is evidenced in *Blood-line* (2006), a knitted sculpture by Lindsay Obermeyer, in which the umbilical link between mother and child is both flexible and unbroken; a link that extends beyond the body and is seemingly endless (see Figure 2.1). What is witnessed in this work is a bond fraught with concern – a lifeline – that rescues and bonds. Obermeyer knits the connection between mother and child, emphasizing the inherent, continuous sacrifice of the self for the sake of another, as in

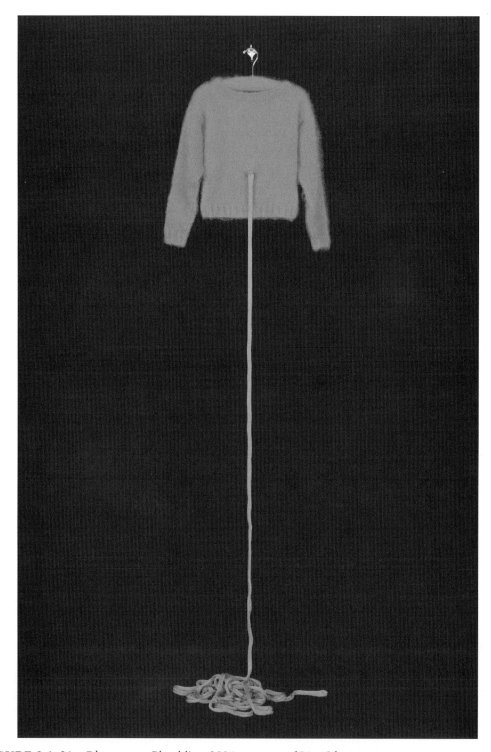

FIGURE 2.1 *Lisa Obermeyer – Blood-line, 2006, courtesy of Lisa Obermeyer.*

Kristeva's analysis of the abject. Here, the knitted umbilicus is both *of* the mother and *not* the mother, thus representing disruption and meaning (Keltner, 2010, p. 45). In Obermeyer's sculpture, we can see the lifeblood sucked from the mother, endlessly nurturing and sustaining, and extending or developing the meaning or purpose of the woman as mother. Here, the mother is a conduit; the umbilicus hinders her movement whilst the child must free itself from its constraint.

The dichotomous position the mother finds herself in is twofold: to focus on the self or the child and/or to nurture too much and limit the development of her offspring. These concerns are exemplified in Clare Qualmann's sculptural cosy *Knitted Cover for 3 Kids* (2003), in which the concept of knitting as a protection from the world outside is particularly evident (see Figure 2.2). Qualmann stated: 'This piece was inspired by a spate of news about child-safety debates over whether children should be allowed to walk to school alone or to play outside. I thought that if you put them in one of these they'd be safely protected from the world, and very warm' (Qualmann in Mowery Kieffer, 2004, p. 179).

The notion of binding babies is not a new one; from traditional forms of swaddling, to wrapping children 'up tight' as protection from the elements, textiles as security blankets is manifest. For Qualmann, the rather humorous visual reference to the 'cosy' or knitted cover is both poignant and ambiguous. The 'cosy' is a symbol of home, of stability and refuge, and by completely covering her children she is enveloping them in the mythology of home and its comforts; making *them* 'cosy' (both in terms of the noun and adjective).

Knitting is the creation of a surface through the looping and entwining of a single thread; a precarious act that creates strength, but can equally unravel and fall apart. Such an act mirrors the

FIGURE 2.2 *Clare Qualmann – Knitted Cover for 3 Kids, 2003, courtesy of Clare Qualmann.*

dilemmas of parenthood, the frailty of an innocent in a corrupt world. Qualmann's work indicates the impossibility and futility of such an endeavour. Movement and growth is restricted by the cosy, vision is impaired and the world outside completely hidden. The message is simple: one can try to wrap one's children and protect them, but to do this would stifle their development and experience of the world. One may love, keep warm and protect, but this love is impairing, even harmful.

The dilemma of child protection and nurturing is evidenced in Françoise Dupré's *Brooder* (1999), which was inspired by manipulating babies and children's socks (see Figure 2.3).

FIGURE 2.3 *Françoise Dupré –* Brooder, *1999, courtesy of Françoise Dupré.*

Through manipulating the heel of the sock it became reminiscent of a nest, and of the mythical imagery of the stork carrying newborn babies in a papoose. Dupré noted:

> The egg is a very obvious choice, but one that I at first rejected, but chose at the end because it is a simple and clear metaphor for life, food and motherhood. The fresh heavy egg, often too big for a nest, stretches the fabric around the hook. There is an element of fragility and danger in the installation. The room filled with eggs is a brooder (a heated house for chicks), a factory farm. A brooder is also a person who broods, and the installation aims to raise questions about fertility.
>
> Dupré in Scott, 2003 p. 117

For Dupré and Qualmann, knitting provides a protective surface, a barrier between the inside and outside, or in Dupré's case, life and death – if the knitted papoose gives way, unravels or loosens from its hook, the egg will fall and break. Both examples draw attention to the precariousness of parenthood and the impossibility of achieving and maintaining the complete safety of one's charges (and indeed, the self) in a precarious and unstable world (Ruddick, 2004, p. 161). It is possible to extend this metaphor to the knitting itself; it looks like it can protect, but because it is made not merely from loops of yarn, but also from holes, it is inherently vulnerable. Motherhood, as expressed through these examples, appears as a series of paradoxes that need to be negotiated, each one offering potential disaster. The protection of one's young is central to the continuation of the species, so regardless of how many children are born, it is their survival to reproduce in later life that is the focus of social discourse (Blaffer Hrdy in Banyard, 2010, pp. 182–183).

Maternal instincts and ideals, along with the symbolic properties of knit, inform the work of Donna Wilson, whose knitted toys express a familiarity through their genre, materials and techniques, but become horrifying examples of hidden fears and desires through the subject matter. For example, in Wilson's *Cannibdoll*, a monstrously angry doll 'eats' its baby, questioning the notion of motherhood as nurturing and addressing the ultimate parental nightmare – could I kill the life I have given? Can I really sacrifice myself, my needs and wants, for those of another? By highlighting this common social taboo, strangely absent from parenting manuals, Wilson pays homage to the Medea syndrome, in which infanticide, incest and other horrific behaviours are enacted through a conscious choice. This choice is understood as indicative of the calculating 'evil' inherent in women, as opposed to the 'accidental' or unassuming behaviours of the male counterpart, as in the Oedipal complex (Salecl, 2004, pp. 101–102). For Freud, motherhood was a means through which women could attempt wholeness or as a release from the self as in orgasm; a means of temporarily bridging the sexual gap or 'lack';[3] an act of repairing, of closing the gaps, as so ably and humorously demonstrated by Wilson's *Cannibdoll*.

Such work questions notions of femininity, for both woman and child, suggesting that women's presumed social role can be subverted, inverted, questioned and represent inner turmoil. In relation to the mythology of Medea, we might also see Wilson demonstrating the mother's sacrifice, to surrender or destroy the thing she loves most in order to be accepted as a 'whole' woman (Salecl, 2004, p. 102). Freud calls this the death drive (Alford, 2006, p. 4), whilst for psychologist Melanie Klein (1988) this intensive desire for annihilation is merely a phase that facilitates future reparation as the basis for child/parent relationships, resulting in a combination of guilt and love that fuels a need to restore harmony.

Whilst the mother may be fraught with guilt over surrounding impulses to over-nurture or kill, child development follows similar and equally complex juxtapositions of love and hate. For both Freud and Lacan, the baby starts its life as an entity driven by need; it has no separate identity as its survival is reliant on its mother, i.e. food, warmth, comfort, etc. These needs are satisfied by an object such as a breast, blanket or clothing, and so on, but the baby has no concept of the object as separate from itself or as part of another being (mother), so therefore everything it needs is essentially an extension or part of itself. For Lacan, in this stage, the baby exists in the 'realm of the real'. This is not a physical place or space, but a world that exists in the mind; a perfect world, which is devoid of loss and lack; the pre-linguistic, primal, pre-social state that is inhabited before speech, self-awareness, difference and recognition are developed. The child develops through a process of identity formation that involves a distancing, or breaking away, from the mother. This act instigates a fragmentation, rupture, a move from the world of dependence towards one of independence and into the world of culture and signification. This rupture establishes a sense of loss and the realization that its world will never be the same again. This loss is understood as a break from unity, where the baby and everything it needs is satisfied in an arena that predates (for the baby at least) language and signification. From this point onwards, the child is constantly seeking to restore this loss. This loss may be fulfilled, temporarily at least, through objects and their possession (a form of sublimation) so comfort might be gained from sucking a blanket, stroking a pet, or from buying a product that offers something seemingly lacking, such as love, friendship, style, status and so on.

As Melanie Klein noted in 1933:

> To begin with, the breast of the mother is the object of his (the infant's) constant desire, and therefore this is the first thing to be introjected. In phantasy the child sucks the breast into himself, chews it up and swallows it; thus he feels that he has actually got it there, that he possesses the mother's breast within himself, in both its good and bad aspects.
>
> Klein in Dufrense, 2000: 72

By metaphorically ingesting the mother, the child is destroying the object that he/she loves most in an attempt to both acknowledge and fill the lack. This paradox becomes a continual quest for reparation, of making up for the harm executed in a state of fantasy. This continues throughout the child's life, and reparation becomes a balancing act in which the desires of the self and the needs of others are constantly in conflict.

Likewise, the mother compensates for her destructive feelings through guilt and over-protection. Mothering becomes smothering. In relation to knitting, this is demonstrated literally and metaphorically. First, by knitting for one's children, the mother makes amends; she demonstrates her love (and nurturing and protective instinct) by sacrificing time and making garments that will protect her child's body. Additionally, through wearing said garment, the child takes a piece of the mother wherever they go. The mark of the mother (maker) is on them. Whilst physically absent, the child is wrapped in his/her mother, a reminder that wherever they go and whatever they do, they are loved and watched over, encased in a three-ply cover.

Such an act of love and caring is precarious as the child attempts to formulate his/her own identity and establish a distance from his/her parents, and is evidenced by the number of children who refuse to wear handmade sweaters. Regardless of the time and effort invested in a sweater's construction, these items are rejected as they signify parental control and a loss of the child's personal identity. One might see this as a motherly need to 'make' the child in her own image; to inflict her taste, values and beliefs onto an offspring determined to ultimately reject her.

The burden of the hand-knitted garment overshadowed Giles Deacon's over-sized knits (2007), in which models were shrouded by and dwarfed in mummifying swathes of sweaters and scarves. The protective qualities of knit enveloped the form, constricting the body like a woollen straitjacket. Wool appeared less comforting and cosy and morphed into its converse, as heavily weighted chains, restricting movement; itchy and cumbersome. Here, mothering smothered; over-protection stifled progress, dominating and obliterating the individual. In Deacon's collection, the clothing overpowered the models to Lilliputian proportions, critiquing the loss of the individual amidst existing social mythologies and problems. By communicating our inability to protect others or ourselves by hiding beneath a seemingly cosy veneer, we are merely avoiding greater social concerns. As Jessica Benjamin argues: 'The public world is conceived as a place in which direct recognition and care for others' needs is impossible – and this is tolerable as long as the private world "co-operates" ' (Benjamin in Bauer and McKinstry, 1992, p. 1). This cooperation becomes apparent when one considers post-feminist responses to knitting, which primarily respond to concepts of the 'real' world and knit as a 'mute' object/ practice that needs to find its own language. Essentially, this standpoint considers the potential for knit and its manipulation, but also the articulation of fluidity and spatiality, the distortion of perception and of the expected. In this respect, the stable and familiar is questioned, as if it were a trick of the eye, and the expected is transformed into not merely the unexpected, but presented as a series of discourses in which no one perception is dominant. Critically, this position draws from Mikhail Bakhtin's reading of the carnivalesque, a world turned upside-down, which is pertinent to conditions of post-modernity and feminist discourse (1984). By referring to Bakhtin, feminists have started to assess the ways in which the public, the masculine, rational world, can merge with the emotional, irrational feminine private sphere and act as a means of reclaiming power (Bauer and McKinstry, 1992). This position establishes a dialogic based on irreverence, particularly in respect of size and scale, and disproportionate forms of representation.

Within the carnivalesque, the body is a metaphor for heaven and earth, of high and low, of life and death, with the torso upwards indicative of the heavenly, and below, the earthiness or baseness of death, bodily functions and, consequently, giving birth. From this standpoint, all that is deemed devalued becomes valuable, and from a patriarchal position, women's work, such as knitting, is celebrated. Yet the carnivalesque is merely a temporary measure, a means of drawing attention to social inequalities rather than making any real change to them. And whilst knitting can be seen as a feminist paradox, conforming to patriarchy or denying female creativity simultaneously (Pagett, 2007; Rigdon and Stewart, 2007; Stafford 2007), in a post-feminist climate, women's domestic practice appears to be celebrated, albeit on capitalist terms (Sparke, 1995). This in itself is a form of reparation, a form of seemingly subverting from within, whilst simultaneously accepting the status quo; i.e. knitting is seen as women's work, but is also an expression of women's creativity and pleasure. It is dichotomous – two opposing concepts co-existing. Likewise, motherhood can be interpreted in the same way; the need to care, love, protect and to meet impossible standards is simultaneously juxtaposed with the acceptance of imperfection, as played out televisually via 'reality' shows such as *The World's Strictest Parents*, *Supernanny* and *Wife Swap*.

Knitting is the creation of a surface through the looping and entwining of a single thread. With each knitted loop, the fabric is formed and a deliberate hole made, an imperfection which contributes to the creation of a potentially 'perfect' whole; a paradox that perhaps exemplifies the role of woman as mother. So, knitting, like parenting, is an act that drives the prospect of completion (a job 'well done'), of puncturing and repairing simultaneously, that can be seen as 'making better' or 'making up' for imperfections inherent in the maker/mother, and ultimately, the actualization of reparation, a repetitive and continuous task, in which love is both made and expected.

One can never truly 'make' love, and one can never make it last. Yet these are expectations that pervade our popular culture. Love, like knitted items, has a start and an end, one that must continuously be made and remade. It must aim for the perfect fit – not too tight, too itchy or uncomfortable, and as the child grows and develops a distinct identity, so must the size and style of garment. Although knitting is like an umbilical cord, a continuous thread linking mother to child, it must be ruptured and repaired or bonded to maintain the appearance of a love line.

Notes

1 A portion of this text previously appeared in an earlier version in Turney, J. (2009), *The Culture of Knitting*, Oxford: Berg.

2 The testimonies used within this paper emanate from a wider project, which investigated perceptions of wool and its use within clothing in British homes. This was ultimately a wardrobe study, which was a contrasting element to the same study undertaken in Norway. The purpose of these studies was to ascertain the level of understanding of fibres, both in reality and as an aspect of popular memory to construct narratives of locally sourced wool and its potential uses.

3 Each surface (textile or body), has margins, boundaries at which fragmentation is more apparent, and this is marked for Jacques Lacan by gaps, or the rim or cut. The cut has erotic potential, it is literal inasmuch as it connotes sexualized areas of the body such as the vulva, tip of the penis, anus, eyes, ears, mouth, pores in the skin, etc. Yet it is more than a physical entity, as the cut is representative of discontinuity, and therefore exerts no sense of continuity or meaning. To be whole would mean that all of these gaps, rims, cuts would need to be filled, which in real terms would lead ultimately to the death of the individual, i.e. one could not breathe, eat, excrete, etc. Yet, individuals realize as a response to their earlier confrontation with 'lack' that they must attempt to do so, to join, conceal or cover the fragments, or to make meaning where there is none. For Lacan, it is this process that is most significant; for this is desire, the bridge between fraction and potential completion. See Warwick and Cavallaro (1988).

3

Sex, Birth and Nurture Unto Death

Patching Together Quilted Bed Covers

Catherine Harper

Introduction

When Bart Simpson's dog shredded up the Bouvier family quilt, Bart's mother Marge (née Bouvier) was more than upset: 'My quilt! Six generations, ruined!', she wept. The highly charged, intensely emotional relationship between Marge, her family's history and her quilt typifies much of the discussion in this essay. Love objects, indeed love subjects, have all the cultural potency of fetish, symbol, totem, devotional, index and ideology, for those on whom that power impacts. Those outwith that, by contrast, focus on their own significant objects: Homer, her husband, responded thus: 'Now Marge, honey honey, honey. Come on, come on, don't get upset. It's not the end of the world. We all love that quilt, but we can't get too attached to . . . OHH!!! MY COOKIE!!!' The Simpsons are arguably us at our all-consuming best, so why Marge's particular trauma at the loss of an old bit of fabric?

It is creation, not consumption (I contend), that creates object attachment, and the Bouvier quilt represents the making and the perpetuation of Marge's history and heritage, captured through six generations and held in trust for the seventh. Homer missed the point – Marge was already 'too attached'. Her quilt's linkage of past, present and future was its essential value, and Marge's upset indicates just how potent the attachment and the object were.

This essay uses a methodology that insists on the readability of cloth through memory, familiar signification, narrative and a kind of low history. Writing through my practice, I explore historical contexts of making and using objects that are emotionally rich and affective, in this case inherited quilts made by known ancestors. Smart textiles can – and do – complement and extend these objects. Previously established forms of object-attachment and signification, and the contexts of their use – particularly the complex activities and emotions relating to bed – may be argued, then, as pertaining equally to quilts industrially produced from innovative technological fabrics *and* their humbler handmade counterparts. This is especially potent when textile and/or familial chronologies reference the extended linear nature of technological and intergenerational evolution.

Reflection on personal encounters with objects that became attached to memories of class, location, skill and family enabled my reference to other objects of attachment in various cultural and historical contexts. I discovered through writing this narration, that the object I thought was my emotional link with a textile past and a technological future – the quilt – was not. It was a needle, rather, translated into an electric wire and back into a needle, shape-shifting for context, that was my attachment to my history and my anchor to the now. My needle is my textile talisman, a love object and my trade's tool, an apotropaic and emotional attachment that protects me still.

Maternal memory

When my childhood dog gave birth to seven pups on my bed on my father's mother's quilt, my own mother was less disturbed than Marge. She burnt it, and bought me a duvet with a poly-cotton cover. In 1975, that was my mother's desired object, a textile technology that would machine-wash at 40 degrees. My paternal grandmother's quilt was neither skilfully made nor especially beautiful. Compared to the fine white-on-white embroidery and drawn linen threadwork of my *mother's* mother, this was a poor 'country' thing, a thin textile sandwich of striped ticking, two grey woollen blankets, and a top covering of irregularly pieced patchings of patterned cotton. Because my grandmother wasn't given to idle chat, my father – after her death – named each fabric scrap as the Sunday 'bests', working shirts, and dance dresses of his sisters: 'there's Alice, there's Lily, there's Eileen'. As a child, I couldn't match the flowers, checks and stripes of the attributed fabric scraps with the youthful histories of my staid and serious aunts, but I was mesmerized by the stories.

In academic terms, my grandmother's was an Ulster utility quilt (Wilson, 2002), evidence of a make-do-and-mend salvage mentality necessary in working-class Ulster homes in the early part of the twentieth century (see Figure 3.1).[1] It links cross-historically with the so-called 'britches quilts' of the impoverished and slave communities of nineteenth-century United States, and similar frontier-spirit, home-spun utility textiles created by working-class immigrants forming the diasporas of Australia, the United States, and so on (Harper, 2001; Suit, 2004). Unlike many women of that class and time in the north-west of Ireland, my grandmother was not involved in the massive shirt-making concerns, which had begun particularly in Derry City in the middle of the nineteenth century and which lingered (to some extent and in travail) in a city of great unemployment and political strife until nearly today (Gavin, 2002).

While many women worked either in the factories or as outworkers, augmenting their shirt-making income, with its supply of surplus fabric scraps, by making and selling patchwork quilts to friends and neighbours, my grandmother was a small farmer in an isolated and barren valley in rural County Derry. Maggie Harper (née McCully) rode a horse, gathered 'purdies' (potatoes) from their drills, snared hares, reared five children to adulthood, claimed a usable field from a bog, walked and worked 'like a man'. She went miles to worship her god, and boiled pins to ward off the evil eye. A stoical and undemonstrative woman, her sewing, like her farming, lacked finesse or superfluity. It was done with as much care as was necessary to create a functional bed covering, no more and no less.

When I consider my grandmother, my image is of a woman with earth-roughed, clumsy big hands stabbing a needle back and forth, making stitches that shifted and changed direction with and against the grain of the fabrics of her quilt. I'd like to say my grandmother gave me my love

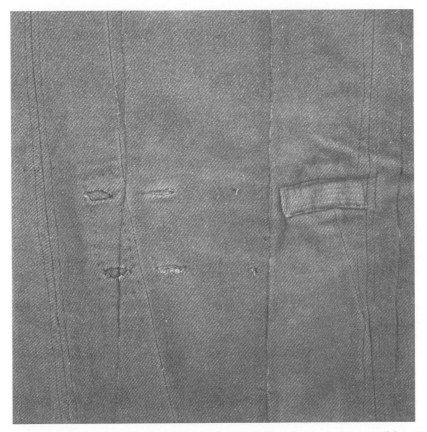

FIGURE 3.1 *Unknown maker, detail of Ulster utility quilt, wool coat and cotton fabric, Ballyrobert, near Bangor, Northern Ireland, c. 1900–1910, 94 × 165 cm, HOYFM 577-1976 (TR247/7). © National Museums Northern Ireland. Collection Ulster Folk & Transport Museum.*

of textiles and my desire for stitch. She didn't per se, but the memory of the undecorated, not-so-great quilt she made is strangely affective. It speaks to me of more than six generations of Scots-Irish puritan stock, a genealogy of work ethic, plain fare, simple ways, hard graft, muddled with the coarse and fearful superstition of country folk. This emotive heady mix is *my* genealogy, and the memory of that quilt is its signifier.

Coarse craft

My paternal grandmother's quilt was the 'bad craft' yet functional equivalent of my other grandmother's careful and highly decorative embroidery. The latter epitomized the combination of great technical skill, particular care, and detailed design unique to specific and arguably privileged understandings of craft (Watney, 1997). The former typified an alternative (historical) crafting concerned simply with producing objects necessary for life (Smith, 1986) or indeed doing well enough what is required for life (Johnson, 2000). The quilt introduced above was fundamentally the result of a hand process creating an essentially utilitarian craft object (Lucie-Smith, 1981). To leave its definition at that, however, would be to negate the key emotional content which it carried forward in its material and subsequent memory form.

The 'bad craft' unruly sewing and irregular patching of the quilt is a signifier, for me, of my grandmother's ambiguous status as a woman. Where her rural counterparts were finding finesse in the flourishing shirt factories, she salvaged and held her tiny farm on a rocky hillside. Holstein, writing of eighteenth- and nineteenth-century American quilts, locates them in a pre-industrial historical frame, aligned to an actual or mythic homestead, in which ancestral hand skills represented an alternative domestic industry of the home (Holstein, 1973). Holstein's words are densely packed, and I begin my unravelling of their meaning with his allusion to the homestead. Long before the exquisitely beautiful handcrafted quilts of settled US white communities were made from the mid-nineteenth century onwards, women and men – immigrants from Ireland and the rest of Europe – shifted their families painstakingly across an unforgiving and unfamiliar new land of opportunity. The women made utility quilts 'as fast as [they] could so [their] famil[ies] wouldn't freeze . . . and as beautiful as [they] could so [their] heart[s] wouldn't break' (Chase, 1976, p. 9).

Before the notion of home as an interior domestic space for household industry was established in the log cabins of 'new' Americans, homesteads were literally carved out (salvaged) (colonized) as patches of land stitched together by force of pioneering will. The mythic or actual pioneers/colonists of Holstein's study activate a sense for me of my grandmother's hard existence, and the uncompromising functionality of her roughly sewn quilt is strongly flavoured by that. My grandmother inhabited an ambiguous set of spaces incorporating the historically masculine external property of her field as well as the interior domestic space that Holstein (1973) ascribes to a notional 'traditional feminine'. The household industry symbolized above by hand making was only *part* of my grandmother's remit and not her primary drive. I choose to read her 'half-handed' stitches as indicative of her partial habitation only of the territory and emotional space of 'women's work'.

In the Hollywood film *How to Make an American Quilt* (1995), women of three generations work collectively both to create a traditional marriage quilt and confirm the central youngest character in the traditions of her 'feminine role'. The protagonist's ambiguity around her 'feminine destiny' is gradually dispelled as the quilt and its metaphors take shape throughout the film's narrative. The quilt in the film is a formidable contemporary example of a particular kind of mid-nineteenth-century Pennsylvanian traditional album quilt, and it is highly symbolic of the 'good craft' associated with a form of 'successful womanliness' (see Figure 3.2). That is, the balance, intricacy and care manifest in such a quilt becomes what Holstein urges is a visibly manifesting and highly expressive representation of a set of culturally valued 'feminine attributes' including frugality, diligence and domesticity.

References to the practices of collecting, salvaging and hoarding of fabric scraps and the associated textile craft techniques of cutting, piecing and stitching are in the domain of women (Constantine and Reuter, 1997). Indeed, Lippard asserts the quilt as the 'prime visual metaphor for women's lives, women's culture' (1993, p. 18). Such references are frequently and variously problematized, utilized and complexified in respect of essentialisms and definitions of femininity, domesticity and textiles. Just as Parker (1984) asserts the duality of, for example, embroidery in terms of both its inculcation of femininity in women and its enabling of a negotiation of its constraints, I will argue for my grandmother's use of so-called 'badly crafted' stitching to both indicate her double-gendered employment in the home and on the farm, and express her misgivings (if not her exhaustion and her fury) at its demands on her.

FIGURE 3.2 *A patchwork bedcover (quilt), hand pieced 'template' style of Turkey red, and plain white cotton, HOYFM.2013.76.2. © National Museums Northern Ireland, Collection Ulster Folk & Transport Museum.*

Further, I might argue that fabric salvage to hand-sew bed coverings was of little excitement compared to the salvage of a strip of field from a barren bog, the salvage of a sick calf from its early death, or the salvage of a potato crop from the ever-present threat of blight. Rather than being of 'traditional feminine' stock, my grandmother's quilt is both a signifier of her feminine ambiguity, and, nevertheless, a symbol by its very presence of her commitment to 'six generations, saved!'

That is not to ignore other contemporary readings and significations of historical and traditional quilts. There is some intrinsic value in the time and labour investment in the meticulous piecing of fabric scraps, perhaps at least as an articulation of a more static skills economy, a descriptor of an emotional currency signified by simplicity and stability. The emotional content of such economy provides a critical foil to the speed of a perceived impersonal industrial production. Where, then, sits this pre- and post-industrial context in relation to developments in smart, intelligent, technical textiles and a retained investment in emotionally meaningful sensibility?

Beds and blankets

Functional, utilitarian and decorative – traditional quilts mark the commonplace rituals and universal emotions of bed (sex, death, birth, sleep, comfort, warmth, nurture, and so on), and the momentous and miniscule events and significations of life. Recurrent motifs in traditional American quilts include, for example, wedding rings, drunken walks, 'women's work', regional symbols and architectural signs. Such quilts therefore are embedded – in their composition, design, image content, and in their bodily usage – with human emotions, operating as textile interfaces where human subjects performatively meet and merge with designed objects. If cloth itself is in some fundamental way a container of human experience (Barnett, 1999), and thread a 'malleable transmitter of ideas' (Johnson, 2000, p. 19), they are co-joined in a quilt to extremely powerful effect.

Contemporary examples of quilts of great emotional significance are numerous and varied. British artist Tracey Emin memorably gave us her bed (*My Bed*, 1998–1999), and told us who she'd slept with (*Everyone I Have Ever Slept With (1963–1995)*, 1995). No shy seamstress, however, it is her appliquéd blankets that tell us the stories of that bed (*Automatic Orgasm*, 2001), and the love, sex and death that gets sited there (see Figure 3.3). The NAMES Project AIDS Memorial Quilt (ongoing since 1987) showed by its massive scale, its tiny personal detail, and its use of the quilt-sign of comfort, how monumentally devastating the AIDS pandemic was and continues to be. Faith Ringgold's quilted and sewn pictures of her family and neighbours in Harlem (*Echoes of Harlem*, 1980) resonate with the lived experiences expressed in quilts made by North American former slaves like Harriet Powers (1837–1911).

Maharaj reminds us that the quilt's emotional affectivity lies in its duality, its ability to be simultaneously a 'domestic commodity' and a 'conceptual device'. With all other meanings intact, the quilt remains for him – and in the examples above – inextricably bound, even obliquely, to 'the notion of wrapping up, keeping warm, sleep and comfort, some feeling of hearth and home' (Maharaj, 2001, p. 5). I have proposed the quilt as variously a symbol of genealogical history, a container of memories, a covering to keep us warm, a troubled signifier of gender, an example of hard handwork and time investment, a well or poorly crafted object, a token of domesticity, and ultimately an emotionally affective textile. In contemporary textiles, then, what correspondence might we see between the fabric scraps of Sunday 'bests', the working shirts and skirts and the dance dresses of my aunts preserved in my grandmother's quilt?

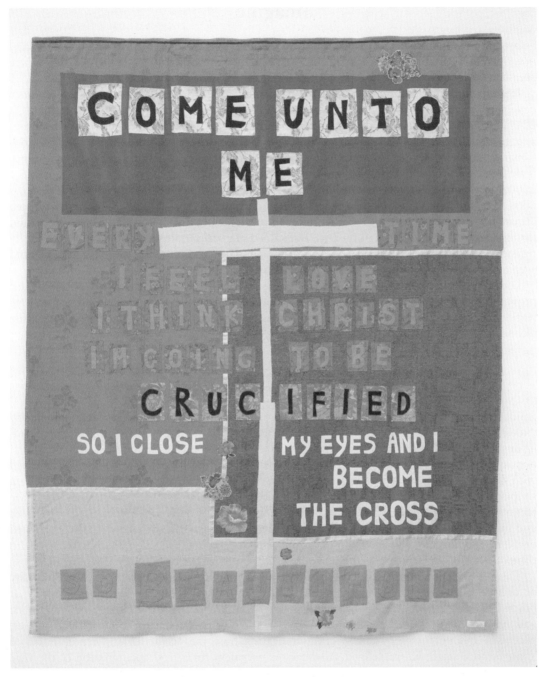

FIGURE 3.3 *Tracey Emin,* Automatic Orgasm, *appliquéd blanket, 2001, 263 × 214 cm. Tracey Emin, courtesy of White Cube. Photograph: Stephen White.*

Imagine

Smart and intelligent fabrics are now almost ubiquitous as massive shifts forward in textile (and other) technologies provide us with fabric and fibre scenarios our grandmothers would not have dreamt of, even greater indeed than a poly-cotton duvet, machine washable at 40 degrees.

Imagine the new technology bed scenarios made potentially possible by contemporary developments in smart textiles science, its programmable sensors, phase changing potential (Qi, 2012) and responsive materiality. Automatic and magical design possibilities open up future-science dream scenarios where duvets cuddle up, sheets talk across continents, and pseudo-somatic comfort may be drawn from 'intelligent' blankets (NASA, 2012). Electroluminescence is already employed by Rachel Wingfield in her 'Digital Dawn' bedding and blinds designs (since 2000), wakening the sleeper 'naturally' with a 'digital sunrise'. 'E-broidery', conductive printing inks and electronically activated thermochromic woven fibres all provide communication, transmission, emission (Dong, 2012) and digital connectivity (Chu *et al.*, 2008) from and through the textile substrates of the bed. Embedded medical monitoring technology potentially registers vital signs and well-being as the sleeper slumbers, and bio-mimicry technologies could even allow fabrication of bedding that operates as an extended skin.

Locating and exploring the narrative and cultural implications of my grandmother's quilt provokes negotiation of the relationship between a historical, traditional and nostalgic textile crafting, an embodied heritage and memorializing reliquary, and the magic of textile technology.

Material magic

Smith (2004) articulated the problematics of these textile scenarios, especially to textile designer-makers interested in textile craft. She noted the tendency to think oppositionally, pitting 'hand' against 'digital', sensory versus rational, the tactile facing the technological, the flawed in opposition to the perfect, even the human in contrast to the machine. My project was concerned with finding how and where smart, intelligent technological textiles maintain and celebrate a simpler, slower, emotionally meaningful sensibility. Human culture, cloth and craft are inextricably linked to myth, artefact, magic, and ritual. The potential for new textile processes and materials to surprise and delight must not be overlooked in the race to solve perceived problems of efficiency, power, communication, reliability, connectivity, intelligence, security and control. Our future challenge is to harmonize *and* humanize the technological world.

There is evidence of a search for something more 'felt' than merely cool, efficient technology or chemical 'magic tricks'. Designers such as Hella Jongerius, through the methodology of practice (both textile and textual), effectively question how digital technologies, new materials and innovative methods of production impact on the very particular traditions, characteristics, processes and outcomes of textile craft, indicating how the aesthetics and materialities of 'craft futures' might be (re)defined. Advocacy is prevalent for a fresh examination of the very particular traditions, characteristics, processes and outcomes of hand-crafted, fabric-salvaged, highly functional, labour-intensive, emotionally invested, collectively stitched, pre-industrial, domestic, nineteenth-century Ulster/American/Australian (it has to be said, colonialist, impoverished, enslaved) quilts, working towards a vision of how technological textile innovations and advances might allow emotionally rich, quality-measurable, poetically valuable designed future living.

Blush

In 2000, I was commissioned to create a permanent artwork for the new Women's Centre, Derry. My work – *Heart* – is a rose-pink, Canadian smocked, velvet cotton ceiling in the counselling space of the new building. The work was exactly tailored to the room's dimensions and was laboriously hand-stitched in conscious and performative reference to women's historical and time-consuming labour, to Derry's historical textile industries and to my grandmother's quilt. Essentially, it reflected attachment to the emotive and emotional subject of female genealogy and endeavour, personally and politically forefronting 'labour of love' as a method.

In 2004, I returned to smocking, piecing and patching, snipping and snatching, in my 'craft futures' project – an interactive extension of the dual (communication and comfort) nature of traditional quilting. I embarked on the creation of a series of 'hybrid quilts' using a cross-disciplinary approach to traditional hand-stitching, patterning, and the processes and products of technological textile advances. In the quilt pieces, I variously worked with innovative electronic engineering, fabric electro-conductivity, digital and thermochromic fabric printing, and laser-cutting, feeling my way – needle and electric wire in hand – towards a concept of 'engineered emotion'. I pieced a textile quilt called *Blush* (2004) that emoted gently, pinker or paler in turn (see Figure 3.4).

FIGURE 3.4 *Catherine Harper,* Blush, *velvet fabric and thermochromic inks, 2004, 280 × 220 cm, courtesy of Catherine Harper.*

My grandmother's thin and irregular quilt covered my narrow childhood bed: a functional 'utility quilt', it evidenced frugality, salvage, isolation, Puritanism, stoicism, and lacked finesse, decoration or pleasure (Wilson, 2002). It was highly invested with her tough and hard emotions. But, as I have alluded, the bed is a site of sexual passion, procreative delight, coy amusement and sleepy pleasures. My grandmother married twice, produced five children, and a blushing cheek is symptomatic of them all. *Blush* was time-invested and meticulous, representative of my emotional engagement through the seductive pleasure of skilled making, focused crafting and traditional technical expertise. The creation of emotional meaning then allowed space for the intervention of a technical textile product: the velvet fabric used was over-dyed with thermochromic ink, and the changing temperature was provided by a thermostat-operated heat pad on the reverse of the quilt (in place of heated bodies). The work appeared uniformly cream and white, but at random intervals it was suffused with a pink glow integral to its very fibre. That is, the quilt itself – its actual fibres – blushed.

Blush alluded to the functional, but its function was shifted from that of the bed-covering providing protection, warmth and privacy, to a 'conceptual function' concerned with both expressing and eliciting an emotional and technologically exciting affect. It was therefore created and offered as a performative interface between an emotional human subject and an emotionally designed, emotionally signifying object. *Blush* exactly activated Maharaj's 'quilt duality', wherein the quilt operates as both domestic commodity and conceptual device (Maharaj, 2001). My grandmother would have both recognized it and never have dreamt of it. Certainly, I proposed that the surprise and delight the blushing quilt activated went some way to the harmony and humanity of technology in a tender work that was richly emotional, of measurable quality and of poetic value.

Nonetheless, the relationship between my work in 2004 and the quilt of my childhood, on which my dog had her pups and where my aunts' dresses found a final resting place, seemed uneasy and even strained. I could not settle it. I had reached backwards into my personal history to make contact – through tactility and technology – with Maggie Harper, but her quilt was burned and the link was imprecise.

And then I remembered: my grandmother had given me my first sewing box, and in it – the lowest of textile technologies – the needle. There, in that love object, had been a reaching across, a gesture, from an old woman with few words to a little girl with a love of fabric scraps, to a grown woman as seduced by the digital world as its material counterpart. My grandmother boiled pins to ward off the evil eye, I created a blushing quilt to comprehend textile technology and make it emotionally resonant for myself. Contexts differ, and object attachment changes with contextual specifics. Technologies are a continuum, highest to most lowly. The pertinence of textile tradition to craft futures is absolute. And for me, it is the needle, *not the quilt*, that is my object-connection to that undemonstrative woman of the bog. *Making*, with the needle as its emblem, turned out to be the soundest link between us.

Note

1 Ulster refers to the northern quarter of Ireland, comprising today's Northern Ireland plus three additional counties that remained part of the independently governed Irish Free State (Éire) following partition of Ireland in 1921. Since my paternal grandparents were Protestant, the term 'Ulster' was frequently used interchangeably, if incorrectly, with 'Northern Ireland' to indicate allegiance to the British crown. I use it here in a kind of nostalgia for the simplicity of their formulaic political thinking.

SECTION 2

Projecting and Subverting Identities

4

Bringing Out the Past

Courtly Cruising and Nineteenth-Century American Men's Romantic Friendship Portraits

Elizabeth Howie

Introduction: a rediscovered genre of photographic portaiture

In 2001, art historian David Deitcher curated 'Dear Friends: American Photographs of Men Together, 1840–1918' at New York's International Center for Photography, exhibiting photographs commemorating men's romantic friendships. The show revealed the importance of a genre of portraiture popular from around 1840 to 1920 which lost favour in the face of the late-nineteenth-century pathologization of homosexuality and the concurrent rise of homophobia. The portraits appear to represent an ideal lost world in which long-stigmatized desires could be openly expressed and satisfied: male couples gaze adoringly at each other, link arms at the elbow, interweave fingers or wrap arms around each other's shoulders. Rediscovered by captivated contemporary viewers, their recuperation represents much more than a quirk of collecting; it both affirms the transhistorical evidence of homosexuality and is a radical, socially destabilizing political act. To borrow the words of historian Thomas Waugh, the photographs provide 'a visual manifesto of the right to love' (1996, p. 102).

Scenes of fully reciprocated, ideal romantic love visualize the longed-for outcome of desire celebrated by the medieval poetic genre of courtly love. Perhaps courtly love, with its ostensibly heterosexual construction of the unattainable courtly lady eternally desired by the male troubadour, seems an unlikely theoretical approach with which to assess homoeroticism in photographs. Yet interpretations of courtly love by Lacan, Barthes and Žižek disrupt that heteronormative reading and provide a queer courtly methodology with which to analyse these enigmatic photographs: the desires they inspire, what they withhold, and their embrace by contemporary gay collectors seeking traces of pre-twentieth-century gay subjectivity. In particular, Lacan's concept of sublimation, the psychological enhancement of an ordinary or even disparaged object with powers which imaginarily promise satisfaction, suits the way these images and objects function in relation to desire.

Picturing men's romantic friendships

The earliest romantic friendship portraits were professionally made daguerreotypes. Many thousands must once have existed; an estimated total of 30 million daguerreotypes were produced during the 1840s and 1850s (Ibson, 2002, p. 38). Most of the published images are anonymous photographic orphans, separated from historical information. How images from this once-abandoned genre were used is unclear, but each was once a prized possession, an object to be held and touched. Having survived an interim during which what they pictured was unacceptable, they have resurfaced to become treasures for contemporary viewers, an entire orphaned genre rediscovered by collectors browsing flea markets and antique stores. What a lovely surprise it must have been to flip through vintage wedding portraits, photographs of children wearing long dresses and knee breeches, or solitary suited men, to discover a photograph of two men with their arms around each other, lifting a veil to reveal a lost male world of love. The recuperation of these images demonstrates, as Deitcher says, 'the potential for personal desires to lead to the disclosure of public truths' (1998, p. 34).

It is not clear how widely such portraits were made, but they were not exclusively American. Photographs of African-American and Asian friends are uncommon, interracial photographs even rarer (Ibson, 2002, p. 45). Despite written evidence of women's passionate friendships (Smith-Rosenberg, 1975), scant photographic evidence of them has emerged, although affectionate images of women cross-dressed as men exist (Smith and Greig, 2003, pp. 107–108, 116–117). During the time that romantic friendship portraits were popular, men photographed together demonstrated physical affection and intimacy more often than women together, or men and women together (Ibson, 2002, p. x). Men and women were rarely photographed together, except for wedding pictures and family portraits. Romantic friendship photographs present an alternative past in which, instead of being closeted, male-male affection is visually predominant, and intimate physical affection between men was widely condoned. Their freedom to express themselves that way looks remarkable, even from the more liberal vantage point of the twenty-first century. The photographs offer heterosexist culture an alternative vision of a non-heterosexist past, embedded in photography's insistent indexicality.

A gold-framed daguerreotype from 1850 of two unidentified young men provides a striking example (see Figure 4.1); they look like affectionate, virile lovers, comfortable with each other's bodies, secure in their mutual attraction. Tight framing emphasizes the men's remarkable physical intimacy. Both wear frock coats, identical beards and short, knotted cravats. The man on the right has handsome, expressive features, an elegant moustache, collar-length wavy hair and slightly wistful eyes that nevertheless look boldly at the camera. The man on the left, a bit stern, plants his right hand firmly on his friend's thigh where it crosses his own, his long fingers lightly gripping his friend's leg. His left arm wraps around his companion's shoulder, fingertips almost caressing the velvety lapel of his friend's coat, index finger intriguingly raised ever so slightly.

FIGURE 4.1 *Anonymous, nineteenth century* (Two Young Men), *c. 1850. Daguerreotype, 10.8 × 8.3 cm (4¼ × 3¼ in.), gift of Herbert Mitchell, 2001, 2001.714, courtesy of The Metropolitan Museum of Art, New York, USA. Image source: Art Resource, NY.*

The man on the right leans back into his companion with legs spread apart, and where his right leg crosses his companion's left, the contrast between his dark trousers and his companion's light-coloured ones emphasizes their interlocked limbs. But where are his hands? The left is buried in his trouser pocket, not even a sliver of wrist discernible, although the hand's form shows beneath the fabric of his pants, pointing toward – touching? – his groin. His right hand disappears behind his knee in the vicinity of the friend's upper thigh. There can't be much room for that hand, between the darkly clad thigh and the lightly clad hips; it could almost be in his friend's pocket. Or, perhaps, his pants. Their contact declares their right to touch each other, and their confidence in visualizing affection through touch.

A twenty-first-century collector's comment demonstrates the tension around the enigma of these portraits: he asserted that 'the same-sex affection such photographs record was, of course, "legitimate" '. For Deitcher, this remark indicated that the collector 'wanted neither to aid nor abet what he suspected might be my gay historical agenda' (2001, p. 35). In twenty-first-century American culture, such touches signify sexuality. In the nineteenth century, they signified less clearly; conventions of articulating affection between devoted friends, male or female, make expressions of intimate romantic friendship difficult to distinguish from declarations of erotic desire. Their sheer numbers and varieties mitigate the ambiguity of the love displayed in individual images. The most accurate thing to be said is that some of these men loved men exclusively, some had sexual experiences with other men, all felt a freedom to express love for other men that has largely been lost to homophobia, and perhaps most transgressively, men who sexually desired other men could not and cannot be visually distinguished from men who desired women. The men who sat for these warm photographic testaments commemorating their relationships were, Deitcher comments, 'innocent of the suspicion that such behavior would later arouse' (2002, p. 50).

Men's romantic friendships in context

This photographic genre dates from a time when sex between men was a crime. In 1786, Pennsylvania removed sodomy (a term which denoted male-male anal intercourse, as well as bestiality and other 'unnatural' sexual acts) from the list of capital offences. South Carolina was the last former colony to repeal the death penalty for sodomy in 1873 (Crompton, 1976, pp. 286–288). While no longer a capital offence, punishments for sodomy convictions ranged from one year to life in prison, at times including forfeiture of property. The lessening of punishment actually resulted in a greater number of prosecutions and convictions (Katz, 2001, p. 63). The acts were punishable; individuals were not necessarily stigmatized for their desires or identifications alone.

The existence of gay subjectivity before the late nineteenth century has been debated, and finding historical traces of male-male sexuality demonstrates the previously largely unacknowledged deep roots of this culture. Close romantic friendships of the type represented in the photographs are a casualty of the rigidifying classification of sexuality that resulted in the category of homosexuality. Ironically, naming and stigmatization led to the consolidation of homosexuality as an identity (Foucault, 1980, p. 43). As literary scholar Graham Robb notes, 'a society of strangers ... was informed of its own existence by its persecutors' (2003, p. 34). Before Hungarian writer Káaroly Mária Kertbeny's coining of the term 'homosexuality' in 1869 (Ellenzweig, 1992, p. 15) and its pathologization beginning in the 1880s, sexualities appear to have been more fluid, with a complex continuum of desires, from friendly to erotic to sexual, characterizing intimate relationships. Deitcher explains: 'Unable to be certain of which among these photographs actually constitutes the discarded traces of historic queer love, they all become symbolic of the mutability of same-sex affection, of masculinity, male sexuality, and the limits of same-sex intimacy as homosocial relations between men transmuted into homophobic ones' (1998, p. 34). The acceptability of fervent passion between friends, expressed physically, could veil sexual passion. Michel Foucault reasons, 'as long as friendship was something important, was socially accepted, nobody realized men had sex together' (1997, p. 171). The ever-present possibility of legal punishment tragically clouded the potential freedom afforded by romantic friendships.

Finding and flirting

Contemporary collectors seeking out images of historical male-male affection continue a tradition of adopting mainstream, socially sanctioned imagery to acknowledge desires that dominant culture condemns, an important part of the development of gay subjectivity. Nineteenth-century academic male nude photography, originally marketed to artists, became part of what film historian Thomas Waugh calls gay men's 'history of appropriated eroticisms' (1996, p. 62). The fact that male-male pornography co-existed with romantic friendship portraits evidences a growing homosexual sensibility of which at least some of the sitters would have been aware (Waugh, 1996, p. 295).

The ambiguity of the romantic friendship portraits enhances their allure, as Deitcher acknowledges when he describes his relationship to them as: 'akin to flirtation. It parallels the sense of limitless possibility that depends on not knowing very much more about a man than is suggested by his presence . . . As in flirtation, the collector's desire to sustain a relationship with these photographs and to the men they record embraces uncertainty' (2001, p. 16). Deitcher suggests possibilities occasioned by anonymity that perhaps parallel the practice of cruising. Barthes (1975) advocates a cruising approach to reading, in which the reader awaits a flirtatious wink from the text (Kritzman, 1989, p. 101). Barthes' fondness for Parisian hustlers, beautiful Moroccan boys and the gay corners of Tokyo attests to his blissful partiality to cruising (1992). He describes cruising as 'the voyage of desire . . . The body is in a state of alert, on the lookout for its own desire' (1985, p. 231). The ambiguity and anonymity of the romantic friendship portraits fosters this unpredictable dialectic of desire.

Cruising photographs opens the viewer to the experience of the Barthesian *punctum*, an innocuous detail that the viewer experiences free from any obvious intent of the photographer. It reaches out to a particular viewer, even 'rises from the scene, shoots out of it like an *arrow*, and pierces me' (Barthes, 1981, p. 26). Art historian Kris Cohen suggests that the 'prick' of the *punctum* may be read in relation to gay sexuality. It enters the body as if, Cohen writes, it startled Barthes from behind (1996, p. 10). This sexualized, homoeroticized *punctum* adds another queer layer to the practice of cruising photographs.

The Barthesian cruiser may attain momentary but inadequate satisfaction; desire keeps him on the move, each fulfilment displaced by more desire, compelling the cruiser to try to satiate it anew. He shares some qualities with the courtly Barthesian lover of *A Lover's Discourse: Fragments* (1978), who, like a medieval troubadour, revels in the sweet anguish of unrequited, perpetual desire. Both lover and cruiser seek for and decipher signs of desire from the other(s); desire flourishes.

Courting the past: idealization and desire

Barthes and Lacan share an interest in courtly love's relationship to desire; while Barthes is known for his distrust of psychoanalysis, Lacan's influence on him has been demonstrated (Iverson, 2007, p. 57). Lacan models his theory of desire and the impossibility of the sexual relationship on courtly love, describing it as the erotics of uncertainty, withholding, absence, distance and unsatisfiable desire, centred on the courtly lady, a formulaically idealized and necessarily unavailable beloved (1991, p. 145). For Lacan, this structure of desire makes all love, not only heterosexual, courtly, permanently asymmetrical (Ragland, 1995). This slippage between homo- and hetero- is part of the ambiguity of nineteenth-century sexualities. Courtly love has homosocial aspects because of how the exchange of women structured relations between men. To further queer courtly love, the lady, often of higher social status than the troubadour, was at times masculinized; if the troubadour bent to her will, he could be feminized (Burns, 1985, 2001).

For Lacan, courtly love fosters the lover's belief that culture creates desire's obstacles – for example, courtly codes and regulations, and impediments like marriage, class and prohibited same-sex love – rather than being inherent in relations between lovers. This was certainly true of nineteenth-century same-sex love. But courtly love hides the object's essential unavailability, bolstering the lover's belief that without those obstacles, he could achieve satisfaction with the object (Žižek, 1993, p. 100). Lacanian sublimation is the process by which the lover elects a beloved object as that which can imaginarily fulfil desire. Nevertheless, for Lacan, fulfilment is impossible. But the lover persists against all odds; courtly obstacles cause desire to take what Lacan calls a detour, promoting desire by denying its fulfilment (1991, p. 152). Courtly love interests Lacan because he interprets it as raising the value of medieval women, who were, in many ways, chattels (1991, p. 147). For Lacan, the courtly lady is a woman who has been sublimated. Because Lacanian sublimation raises or idealizes the object, increasing its value, sublimation is an ethical issue. The romantic friendship photographs, items whose subject matter was at one time not only neglected but pathologized and demonized, are sublimated: idealized and valued, they promise satisfaction, but keep their secrets, keeping desire aroused.

Photography has an inherent courtliness: the photograph's referent appears to be present but is always absent, a paradox which keeps the viewer's desire inflamed. The unavailability of the referent, the asymmetry of the relationship between viewer and referent, and the desires photography arouses resonate with the desires aroused by the unavailable courtly lady. What photography gives, what it denies and the desires it inspires are often courtly. The romantic friendship portraits present a dream in which even though homosexual acts were criminalized, the convention of romantic friendship could conveniently veil the fulfilment of same-sex desires, making cultural obstacles appear easily surmountable. Time becomes the obstacle in the contemporary viewer's relationship to the vintage photograph. Today's viewer seeking and possibly finding evidence of idyllic gay love in the past, when obstacles were greater than they may be today, is a courtly lover, desire inflamed by this glimpse of fulfilment.

For Lacan, ancient Greek homosexual love is 'not the same thing' as courtly love, 'but it occupies an analogous function . . . it is quite obviously of the order and of the function of sublimation' (n.d., II 12). The Greek love relationship interests Lacan because a kind of balance exists between the two lovers; the adult man, the *erastes*, does not know what he is lacking, while the boy, the *eremenos*, does not know 'the hidden thing he has, what gives him his attraction' (Lacan n.d., III 4). Nevertheless, what the lover lacks is not what the beloved has hidden in himself – love is always asymmetrical.

The courtly Barthesian and Lacanian lovers voraciously seek signs showing that the beloved reciprocates their desire. Random events illusorily foretell desire's satisfaction. Very occasionally, what Lacan calls the 'answer of the real' rewards the courtly lover when, at least briefly, the beloved returns the lover's desire. Žižek (1992, p. 31) explains:

> a totally contingent coincidence is sufficient . . . we become convinced that 'there is something to it'. The contingent real triggers the endless work of interpretation that desperately tries to connect the symbolic network of the prediction with the events of our 'real life'. Suddenly, 'all things mean something', and if the meaning is not clear, this is only because some of it remains hidden, waiting to be deciphered. The real functions here not as something that resists symbolization . . . but, on the contrary, as its last support.

In courtly love, the answer of the real has surprising and destabilizing effects: 'the long-awaited moment of the highest fulfillment . . . is neither the Lady's surrender, her consent to the sexual act, nor some mysterious rite of initiation, but simply a sign of love from the side of the Lady, the "miracle" of the fact that the Object answered, stretched its hand back to the supplicant' (Žižek, 1993, p. 106). Such an act reverses the position of lover and beloved. This shift permits the appearance of the gift of love: 'We witness the sublime moment when *eremenos* (the loved one) changes into *erastes* (the loving one) by stretching his hand back and "returning love". This moment designates the "miracle" of love, the moment when . . . the real waves back' (Žižek, 1993, p. 106). Nevertheless, the Lacanian sexual relationship remains impossible, as both subjects recognize the other's lack. But that momentary glimpse of fulfilment drives the lover on.

These photographs relate to courtly love and Greek love similarly. If a contemporary viewer is a troubadour, he is also the *erastes*, the desirous lover. Like the disempowered medieval woman or Greek boy, the photographs have been marginalized; their redemption sublimates them. The finding of the photographs, discovering a longed-for validation, is the gift of love, the real waving back. It destabilizes the separation between present and past. Like Lacan's *eremenos*, the photographs in a way do not know what they have: they don't have a concrete answer or proofs; they have love.

An 1890 tintype beautifully displays such love (see Figure 4.2). A bespectacled man with a small neat moustache sits on his friend's lap, right leg crossed over left, right foot intriguingly clad in a striped sock. Holding a cigar, his hand rests on an ashtray balanced on his thigh; he is not going anywhere anytime soon. He looks somberly off-frame over his friend's head, his somberness belied by the warm way his left arm wraps around his friend's shoulder, pulling him close so that his fingers wrinkle the fabric of his friend's jacket. The pipe-smoking companion, hair thinning, inclines his head slightly upward, fondly and even tenderly angling his eyes towards the face of the man on his lap. His left hand disappears between his thigh and his friend's. Such comfort and affection hails us from the past, demanding a close look.

Hidden in plain sight

Late-nineteenth-century insistence on the dichotomy of straight and gay fabricated the closet and closed the door. In the past world of fluid sexualities, perhaps there was not a closet but a curtain or veil, allowing for a continuum with the conventional world. For Lacan, the veil

FIGURE 4.2 *Unknown, American (Two Men Smoking, One Seated in the Other Man's Lap), 1880s–1890s, tintype. Image: 8.6 × 5.9 cm (3 3/8 × 2 5/16 in), irregular. Plate: 9 × 6.2 cm (3 9/16 × 2 7/16 in). Private Collection, Courtesy of The Metropolitan Museum of Art, New York, USA.*

arouses desire by implying that it hides something, allowing the subject to persist in believing that an object exists which can satisfy the subject's desire, when there is actually nothing there (Kay, 2001, p. 201; Lacan, 1994, p. 106). Lacan demonstrates this with a story from Pliny the Elder: in a competition to paint realistically, Zeuxis painted grapes so effectively that a bird tried to eat them (1998, pp. 103, 111–112). But Parrhasius painted a veil so convincingly that Zeuxis asked him to pull it aside so he could see the painting behind it. The fruit arouses the appetite of the bird; the veil arouses the desire of the subject (Iverson, 1994, p. 462). We desire what we cannot prove is there, awaiting the answer of the real. The story demonstrates, literary theorist Charles Shepherdson argues, that:

> The function of art is to incite its viewer to ask what is *beyond*. Art ... leads us not 'to see', as Lacan would put it, but 'to look'. For the human animal is blind in this respect, that it *cannot simply see*, but is *compelled to look* behind the veil, *driven*, Freud would say, beyond the pleasure of seeing. (1995)

The pleasure of seeing images like the romantic friendship portraits arouses the desire of the viewer – of some viewers – to know what is beyond them. Nevertheless, like Parrhasius's painting, their veil, the photographic representation, cannot be opened. Yet in this case, perhaps, the veil is a fantasy. Instead, what could satisfy the viewer's desire is there on the surface. Like Parrhasius's painting, these photographs are not veils themselves but images of veils, picturing the veil that protected men's desires for other men, which could exist in plain sight. This veil has nothing to hide.

Conclusion: courting ambiguity

To assert that the romantic friendship portraits depict no evidence of male-male desire, as some have, is to insist that there is something behind the veil (Deitcher, 2001, p. 95). To assert that they show incontrovertible proof of male-male desire is to do the same. But leaving their meaning open simultaneously validates the individuality of the sitters, and keeps in play all possible relationships between the men, and between the photograph and its viewers. What cannot be denied is the love and affection expressed through touch and physical intimacy.

The risk of ascribing sexual intent to expressions of male physical affection must be balanced with the greater risk of continuing to suppress a history that has been neglected and deliberately hidden, by the persecutors and also, tragically, by those who feared persecution. Queer theorist Michael Warner states forcefully: 'The dawning realization that themes of homophobia and heterosexism may be read in almost any document of our culture means that we are only beginning to have an idea of how widespread those institutions and accounts are' (Warner in Restuccia, 2006, p. 145). The indefinite sexuality of the romantic friendship portraits, taken at a time when sexuality retained to some degree its own indefiniteness, must be neither occluded nor overinterpreted. Instead, we may accept what we see: men's love for each other existed in a broad continuum whose photographic visualization was not only more permissible but more desirable than it often is today.

Such ambiguity fosters a courtly cruising of the images, keeping desire perpetually inflamed. To dream of a time without homophobia, when all men could show physical affection with pleasure and without fear is not to imagine a world without gay identity, but instead, to dream of a future when politics no longer necessitate a community needing to defend itself. It is to persist in one's desire, undaunted by obstacles. The portraits are a sort of Barthesian 'prophesy in reverse' (Barthes, 1981, p. 87).

The Barthesian *punctum* can operate in terms of sublimation by bestowing a unique relevance on a photograph to a particular viewer. The embrace of the genre of men's romantic friendship portraits is a sublimation that welcomes difference even as it is a form of identification. Their courtliness keeps desire in play, motivating a search for a hidden past. The gay community's recuperation of these photographs, and their subsequent visibility and popularity in the wider art world, is the beginning of a process that disregards heterosexist assumptions, that desires gay people and idealizes freedom of sexual preference. It is a courtly, ethical sublimation.

5

The Genteel Craft of Subversion

Amateur Female Shoemaking in the Late Eighteenth and Early Nineteenth Centuries

Noreen McGuire

Introduction

Female amateur shoemaking in the late eighteenth and early nineteenth centuries was a leisure activity of the upper and middle ranks of society that is almost completely absent from both the history of shoemaking and the history of women's craft.[1] Yet it was an activity that was far from insignificant. To a qualitatively greater degree than every other acceptable female pursuit of the day, female amateur shoemaking managed to simultaneously project and subvert gender and class identities. On the one hand, numerous threads from pre-approved, dutiful female activity converged in the new hobby, yielding handcrafted, domestically produced tokens of affection and material evidence of feminine industriousness and love of one's family. The emotional connection between maker and recipient was made manifest in the home-made shoe, and helped to position the activity within the realm of sanctioned female interests. However, on the other hand, this pastime skirted the forbidden realm of male trade, and low-ranking male trade at that. At a time when class and gender boundaries were rigidly policed, privileged female transgressions of same would require careful negotiation. This essay will explore how it was possible for such privileged women to emulate low-ranking members of the labouring classes. It will also examine how the historically interesting narrative that both subverted and projected gender and class identities could have been the very anomaly that condemned it to obscurity for many years.

Evidence of the shoemaking hobby survives in Britain and Ireland in the form of amateur shoemaking toolkits, illustrations of women engaged in the activity (see Figure 5.1) and contemporary literature referring to the new craze, which apparently infiltrated all classes.[2] It is

FIGURE 5.1 *S. W. Fores, 'Coblers of Fashion or Modish Pastime for 1813', satirical etching from a folio of caricatures, London, 1813, 25.1 × 42.5 cm. 1935,0522.7.24. © The Trustees of the British Museum.*

difficult to say when the activity began, but it appears to have reached its height in the first and second decades of the nineteenth century. Demand for shoemakers to give lessons in the craft came from 'all sides and at all costs' according to Stirling (1913, p. 177). The flat, slipper-like shoes popular from the last decade of the eighteenth century into the early decades of the nineteenth century, were of simple construction compared to their high-heeled predecessors (see Figure 5.2 and cover image). They were also made of lighter materials such as fabric or kid, which made it easier for amateur shoemakers to make their own. The shoes shown in Figure 5.2 illustrate the type of shoe fashionable at the time of the shoemaking hobby, which were probably similar to the shoes produced by the hobbyists. To date, there is a lack of clearly provenanced examples of amateur-made shoes in existence.

Tokens of affection

The making of shoes might not be a particularly 'cultivated' activity like the typical accomplishments of music, drawing and embroidery, but embroidery may actually have been a strong contributing factor to the uptake of shoemaking by refined women. Women had been embroidering shoe vamps for years before shoemaking became popular.[3] Although embroidery had carried negative connotations of vanity and aristocratic decadence, these problems could be solved if the embroidery was carried out for others (Parker, 1984, p. 142). The hours spent producing highly decorative stitching to embellish the home were physical proof of the woman's

FIGURE 5.2 *Women's blue kid leather slip-on shoes, c. 1810. BS340 1976.60P, courtesy of The Shoe Collection, Northampton Museums and Art Gallery, Northampton Borough Council.*

devotion to, and love for, her family. In a similar way, amateur shoemaking could produce tokens of friendship or love, strengthening the emotional bonds that women were expected to maintain. The provision of these wearable items would also no doubt bolster bonds with extended family members separated by distance. Jane Austen wrote to her niece Anna in September 1814 that 'your Grandmama desires me to say that she will have finished your shoes tomorrow & thinks they will look very well' (Austen in Byrde, 2008, p. 38). A letter dated 10 January 1783, in the form of a poem to Penelope Geast, describes the fabrics and embellishments used in the decoration of a pair of shoes for the recipient, as well as indicating where she might wear them:

> The Shoes I now send ye – are paultry enough,
> The one is of Sattin – the other of Stuff.
> But to make them appear more bright at a Ball
> I have work'd 'em with Silks, Worsteds, Spangles, and all.
> Now fear not to wear them, but dance it away,
> And be ever blythe, merry, good humour'd and gay.

For when these are worn out, I will work ye some more
As I've both Silk and Sattin, and Worsted good store.

Letter to Penelope Geast 1783

The shoes mentioned in the poem are explicitly fashioned with someone else's happiness in mind, and may even have provided an opportunity for the wearer to advertise the affection that existed between her and the maker. Amanda Vickery states that '[g]ifts were valued in themselves and as material proof of the kind thoughts of others ... Home-made presents were usually offered by women and were seen as time, labour and affection made concrete' (Vickery, 1998, p. 188). The slipper table held at Tyne and Wear Archives and Museums in Newcastle includes wooden shoe lasts in both adult and child sizes, with the names 'Lady Frances' and 'George' written on them respectively, possibly suggesting that Lady Frances was making shoes for both of them. Figure 5.3 illustrates the shoe last used to make George's footwear. The craft could also be perceived as an exercise in thrift, as scraps of fabric could be transformed into footwear. Elizabeth Shackleton was unimpressed by her son's failure to keep scraps, complaining that 'he sho'd keep bits. If they had not done so at Newton, how co'd the old Lady have made my own dear, nice little [grandson] a pair of shoes' (Shackleton in Vickery, 1998, p. 151). Thriftiness was expected, regardless of personal wealth. Shoemaking was an inoffensive way to engage in domestic crafting activity – producing useful, inconspicuous items for oneself, friends and

FIGURE 5.3 *Shoe last marked 'George', early nineteenth century, courtesy of Tyne and Wear Archives and Museums.*

family, which were mostly hidden under long skirts. It also reinforced idealized visions of industrious middle-rank femininity – balancing domesticity with refinement – without appearing to be menial drudgery or aristocratic decadence. The home-made shoe could be seen as a symbol of both affection and shrewd domestic management – both admirable qualities in a woman.

Performance, props and privilege

While the practice of shoemaking can be perceived as an important performance of class and gender distinction in itself, the shoes produced and their careful public display also worked to signify status. In an 1878 publication, Lord William Pitt Lennox describes how women's home-made evening shoes were not suitable for heavy wear.[4] He states that '[s]o long as the wearers remained in-doors, or drove out in a carriage, all went well, but when these articles . . . were put to the test in the promenade or ball room, the chances were ten to one they would not stand the wear, and that a heel or ball of the foot would obtrude' (1878, p. 45).

The very delicacy of these creations spoke of the wearer's own delicacy. The author of the *Manuel du bottier et du cordonnier* (1831), Jean Morin, claimed that shoes worn by working women had to be similar to men's shoes, conveying masculine strength and labour, and clearly showing the social position of those women: 'their round shape and their overall external appearance must always establish the difference that will be used to distinguish and make everyone know the kind of woman they are made for' (cited in Riello, 2006, p. 33). By contrast, the flat slipper-like shoes of privileged women were generally made of more refined materials like fabric and kid, and were white or lightly coloured (see Figure 5.2). They were not supposed to be hardwearing because she was not expected to walk anywhere or to labour. According to Giorgio Riello, the only purpose of walking in town 'was to see and be seen and therefore it was appropriate only as an urban leisure activity . . . If walking did not have a clear social function, it was considered as activity for the lower sorts or those who could not afford a coach' (2006, pp. 61–62).

Delicate shoes went hand in hand with a mode of transport which elevated the owner both physically and metaphorically from those lower down the social scale. A fashionable lady's shoes were therefore more symbolic than functional. If they disintegrated at a social occasion, it merely advertised that she had made her own shoes, and regardless of their durability, 'the lady who, at balls, could boast that her feet had been shod by her own fair hands was an object of envy to all the less talented' (Stirling, 1913, p. 177). The time it would have taken to make the shoes, combined with their unsuitability for heavy wear, expressed important information about the wearer's character and means. According to Linda Young, '[t]he genteel habitus required the right kind of environment in which to live, shaped by a battery of material goods to enable management of the self-controlled body and presentation of the self-conscious social person' (2003, p. 153). Material goods provided both the stage and the props in the performance of gentility (2003, p. 153).

While the shoes and coach were props in the performance of genteel behaviour outside of the home, the shoemaking toolbox served as a prop in the private performance of the craft itself. The fine materials and decorative techniques used in the manufacture of such tools were also important signifiers of the user's status. Surviving amateur toolboxes held in Dublin (see Figure 5.4) and Aylesbury are almost identical except for the use of turned ivory in the handles of the Dublin tools and the use of dark wood, possibly ebony, in the Aylesbury tool handles. Ivory turning was also an aristocratic hobby during the seventeenth and eighteenth centuries, on a par with embroidery (St Aubyn, 1987, p. 115). The noble associations of ornamental turning no doubt

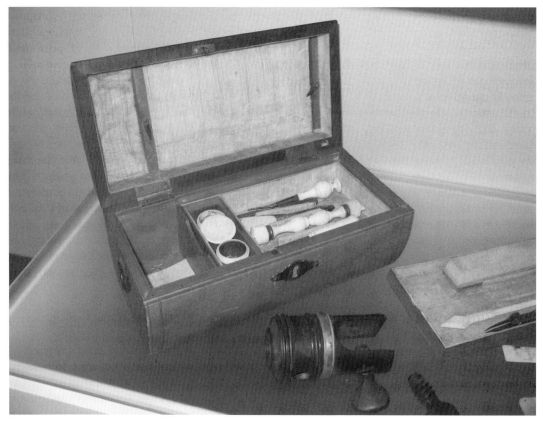

FIGURE 5.4 *Amateur shoemaking toolbox, early nineteenth century, courtesy of National Museum of Ireland.*

prompted interest in the activity by the increasingly wealthy, aspirational middle classes. Young explains that in order to understand middle-class construction it is necessary to 'disentangle its relations with aristocratic culture, at once yearned for and yet moralized as decadent and unproductive' (2003, pp. 14–15). By incorporating a luxury material like turned ivory into a set of tools normally associated with the lower classes, the appearance of aristocratic leisure could be tempered, while the craft could be elevated. The beautifully crafted tools – beyond the practical requirements of a tradesman – helped set the user apart from a professional shoemaker.

This marriage of refinement and useful work may suggest that amateur shoemaking originated within the middle classes, and thus far their ideology seems to align with the practice. Its occurrence among members of the upper strata may then be a result of the spread of the genteel ideology of dutiful feminine behaviour up the social hierarchy. This runs counter to Thorstein Veblen's *The Theory of the Leisure Class* (1899), which argues that the members of the wealthy, high-status leisure classes display their superiority through wasting time and money on extensive leisure activities – conspicuous consumption and conspicuous leisure (1899, p. 85). Those lower down the social hierarchy then try to emulate this behaviour in an attempt to bolster their own status (1899, pp. 103–104). However, by using the lower classes as the inspiration for their new pursuit and by engaging in the production of their own footwear, the upper classes would appear to debunk Veblen's theory. Rather than a top-down filtering of leisured behaviour there would have been a bottom-up appropriation of productive work. In *Distinction*, Pierre Bourdieu provides an explanation for this sort of behaviour, which still affords the upper classes higher status. The upper classes' appropriation of lower-class work could outflank the ambitious middle classes and foil their attempts to emulate those above them in the social hierarchy (Bourdieu, 1984, p. 62). By taking up an activity associated with the lower orders of society, the upper classes could cause the middle strata to appear lower down the social hierarchy should they attempt to emulate them.

Whether shoemaking was a bottom-up appropriation of middle-class values or an outflanking manoeuvre by the upper classes, either explanation gives a more complex picture of inter-class relations than Veblen's one-directional downward flow of tastes. Regardless of who started the hobby, the popularity of amateur shoemaking most likely lay in its balance of domesticity and accomplishment, which was central to the middle-class vision of womanhood, but increasingly relevant to women of the upper strata also. A woman of high rank was not exempt from the office of housekeeper, although it was more of a discretionary activity (Vickery, 2009, p. 159). The sophisticated interplay of props, end product and setting used, not only in the performance of the craft, but the public display of the finished shoes, helped establish the hobby as a strategy of maintaining social position.

Reinventing the shoemaker

Despite utilizing the amateur craft, the shoes produced and the crafting paraphernalia to project refinement and femininity, the shoemaking amateur was still appropriating an activity from the lower orders, and one associated predominantly with male trade. The low cost of a shoemaking apprenticeship, in comparison to other more profitable trades, meant that it attracted the sons of the poor (Hobsbawm and Wallach Scott, 1980, p. 99). A description of the pre-factory craft written in the late nineteenth century stated that: '[a]s a class . . . the common shoemakers were neither clean nor tidy in their habits and persons, and the calling was looked down upon as one of low social grade; a fitting employment to which to apprentice the boy inmates of workhouses' (Arlidge in Hobsbawm and Wallach Scott, 1980, p. 99).

In addition to its performance in the aforementioned domestic setting, shoemaking as a low status trade would have required reinvention as a suitable activity for middle- and upper-class women. A refined woman's foray into what was essentially a trade of the lower strata might appear to challenge the promoted ideal of masculine endeavour outside of the home and female management of the domestic environment away from the world of paid work. However, the skills she would learn were most likely a watered-down version of the professional craft, as it took years of apprenticeship to qualify as a master shoemaker. According to eighteenth-century determinist philosophies, women and men had inherent differences, which rendered women incapable of anything but simple thought and imitation, while men were creative and able to exercise judgement (Edwards, 2006, p. 12). Edwards states that '[i]n the fields of "art and crafts", this led to the distinction between amateur women and professional men' (2006, p. 12). Assumptions about female abilities, or lack thereof, effectively neutralized any professional associations shoemaking might have.

While separating the high-ranking female amateur from the low-ranking male professional might appear to be a logical step in the preservation of class and gender boundaries, there is a

possibility that certain commonalities were emphasized in order to elevate the status of the trade
and its practitioners. This would probably have been necessary to some degree as shoemakers
were entering the homes of their social betters as tutors of a kind. Although professional
shoemaking was dominated by men, Hobsbawm and Wallach Scott explain that 'small, weak or
physically handicapped boys were habitually put to this trade' (1980, p. 89). The strength required
by a female amateur could surely at least match that of a small, weak boy. While shoemaking may
have been less physically challenging than other masculine trades, 'the gentle craft' of shoemaking
also had a more positive reputation for being populated by intellectual workers due to the 'quiet
and semi-routinized nature of much of their work, which could be readily combined with
thinking, watching and conversation' (Hobsbawm and Wallach Scott, 1980, p. 97). In addition:

> his frequent isolation during working hours threw him on his own intellectual resources . . .
> the training of apprentices and the tramping of journeymen exposed him to the culture of the
> trade and to the culture and politics of a wider world . . . the lightness of his tool-kit actually
> made it easier than in some other trades to carry books with him.
>
> Hobsbawm and Wallach Scott, 1980, p. 89

This combination of gentle work with either reflective isolation or cultured discussion could
conceivably parallel the experiences of countless well-read crafting ladies in their drawing rooms.
The alignment of certain aspects of the tradesman's daily routine with those of his privileged pupil
could possibly have feminized the tradesman to a degree, rendering his presence in the drawing
room less provocative to the established social hierarchy. Ironically, this blurring of gender and
class boundaries – elevating and feminizing the lowly tradesman – could have made this subversive
act appear to be non-threatening. The elevation of the male professional would also have appealed
to one of the core values of the middle classes – self-improvement. Young describes the 'essential
drive' of the middle classes as 'the urge of aspiration, of self-improvement, of upward mobility':

> In practice it contained a hollow element of promise that good or at least correct behaviour
> would achieve the reward of higher status. In this lies the source of the dynamic structure of
> minutely differentiated levels of genteel practice, offering infinite possibilities to move up and
> up.
>
> Young, 2003, p. 15

Regardless of his inauspicious beginnings, a humble shoemaker could most likely educate
and better himself through the 'thinking, watching and conversation' Hobsbawm and Wallach
Scott attributed to him earlier. This is not to say that the crafting students would have welcomed
the tradesman into their social circle outside of his role as instructor. With more and more
people gaining access to greater income and education, 'a constant struggle ensued to establish
a position, to protect it from others, and perhaps to advance it without opposition: truly a
conundrum of contradictory purposes' (Young, 2003, p. 14). But the chasm between the low-
ranking male and high-status female could have been bridged to an excusable degree to allow
interaction at a teacher/pupil level.

While drawing parallels between low-ranking men and women of rank might be a risky
undertaking if attempting to justify one's engagement in the hobby, drawing on the history of
shoemaking for vindication may have been a safer bet. Shoemakers had a long and distinguished
history, which was reprinted innumerable times, however fanciful it may have been. Privileged
women interested in reading and making shoes would certainly have been familiar with *The*

History of the Shoemaking Craft (Anonymous, 1810a), printed at a time that coincides with the craze for shoemaking. The book details the royal lineage of Sir Hugh, which was no impediment to him learning the trade. In his travels to forget his unrequited love for Winnifred, he met a merry band of shoemakers who lifted his spirits with their songs and stories, and in time taught him their skills. Add to this the story of the young royal princes Crispin and Crispanus fleeing persecution from Maximinius, and the noble history of shoemaking appears to be indisputable (1810a, n.p.). Both found refuge with a merciful shoemaker, who happened to be in the employment of the emperor, and he taught them the trade. Crispin and the Princess Ursula ultimately fell in love through their shoe-related encounters at court and married in secret. She fled the palace to give birth to their clandestine child – an event which gave rise to the phrase 'A Shoemaker's Son is a Prince born' (1810a, n.p.). Another royal association with the shoe trade was recorded in *The History of the King and the Cobler* (Anonymous, 1810b), in which a disguised King Henry VIII befriended a humble cobbler, and enjoyed his hospitality and good humour only to return his kindness at court.

These stories of Sir Hugh, St Crispin and the king and the cobbler painted those in the shoe trade as merciful, romantic, brave and noble, as well as cheerful enough company to earn a place at court. The gulf between the worker of low status and members of the elite could conceivably be overlooked when the former revealed such admirable character traits, or better yet, a secret royal lineage. Amateur shoemaking ladies, whether of upper or middling rank, could invoke these stories should anyone question their participation in the craft and give it greater cultural and moral weight. The upper classes could relate to the noble lineage of Sir Hugh and the two princes, while the middle classes could aspire to social recognition by those above them. These stories would also further separate the shoemaking craft from the world of trade and infuse it with an air of virtue.

Backlash

Interaction with low-status men, regardless of how cultured their reinvented image might be, challenged strict class and gender boundaries, which did not go unnoticed. A significant backlash against amateur shoemaking betrayed a clear sense that women were transgressing social boundaries in their pursuit of the hobby. Accusations of economic destruction were laid at the feet of the female amateurs. *Crispin Anecdotes* explain that 'the lighter half of the cordwainer's trade, was not only placed for a while in considerable jeopardy, but actually much affected by a species of rivalry which sprang up in a quarter where it was least to have been expected – among the fair sex' (Anonymous, 1827, p. 174). The absence of amateur female shoemaking from the history of women's craft may be due to the complicated class and gender transgressions, which it went on to embody.

While other female crafts were passed on from mother to daughter or via literature aimed at crafting ladies, shoemaking required the initial tuition of someone outside the normal circle of women of rank – the lowly male shoemaker. This transgression was seized upon and met with a sense of moral panic by satirists and others, who levelled accusations of lewd behaviour at the amateurs. In *The Repository of Arts*, the fictitious Mr Cordovan criticized the ladies of fashion 'who, neglecting their own affairs, would be for making shoes, instead of mending their husbands' stockings and drawers' (Ackerman, 1810, p. 17). He lays the charge of 'indecency' against the privileged female shoemakers – his description of their participation in the activity laden with sexual innuendo:

I think I see one of your dashing women of fashion, a baroness or a marchioness, dressed out in all her finery, down upon a low stool, with her tools before her, bending her elegant neck and bosom over her last, a huge 'lap-stone' between her thighs, working away with the 'rubbing-stick'; her beautiful little hand, still fragrant from almond-paste or palm-soap, bedawbed all over with cobler's [*sic*] wax.

Ackermann, 1810, pp. 17–18

Any noble lineage that the shoemaking trade may have had was readily forgotten by detractors, who linked female shoemaking with sexual misconduct and intrusion into the male world of business. The home-made shoe morphed from a lovingly crafted symbol of affection to physical evidence of time spent in the company of a low-status man.

Conclusion

The production of lovingly crafted shoes by privileged amateur women in a domestic setting might initially seem to be rather uncontroversial. Utilizing skills gleaned from embroidery and combining them with a talent for household economy to create modest tokens of affection would appear to meet with pre-approved, middle-class ideals of dutiful feminine industry. The home-made shoe became a signifier of that identity as well as the material embodiment of love. Performance of the craft was also carefully choreographed – using beautiful tools appropriate to one's rank, creating shoes that reflected one's social standing, and executing the production and the public display of the shoes in appropriate settings. All of this worked to separate the high-status craft from the low-status trade, which may provide a partial explanation for its omission from the history of the professional craft. But the omission of the hobby from the history of women's craft might be indicative of a selective historiography, including only that which fits neatly with more clear-cut portrayals of eighteenth- and nineteenth-century women's behaviour. Low-status, male-gendered work was taken up by high-status women, who despite, and also because of, their efforts to elevate the craft and redefine class and gender barriers, fell foul of contemporary critics. This complicated negotiation of work and leisure, as well as gender and class, may help to explain the historiographic oversight, which largely ignores the phenomenon.

Notes

1 June Swann's 1982 book *Shoes* gives a comprehensive overview of footwear styles and includes a paragraph on the female amateur craft of shoemaking, identifying primary sources that have recorded the activity, namely *Mrs. Calvert's Souvenirs* and *Crispin Anecdotes*. *Shoes* also records the existence of shoemaking toolboxes held in The Museum of Leathercraft, Northampton and Aylesbury Museum, Buckinghamshire. Swann is the exception, among both shoe historians and historians of women's craft, in offering more than a passing reference to female amateur shoemaking.

2 See Blake (1911, p. 98); Stirling (1913, p. 177); and Anonymous (1827, p. 174).

3 The vamp is the front part of the shoe upper, covering the top of the foot.

4 I am grateful to June Swann for bringing this source to my attention.

6

Performing Masculinity Through Objects in Postwar America

The Playboy's Pipe

Jessica Sewell

Introduction

In 1959, a newly divorced Hugh Hefner, the founder of *Playboy* magazine, reinvented himself as 'Mr Playboy', living the life promoted in the pages of his own magazine. For this, Hefner writes, he needed several 'props': 'the pipe, the red velvet smoking jacket, the white Mercedes Benz 300SL and the magnificent mansion' (Hefner, 1998, p. 11). Of these props, the pipe was the most visible: from this point until 1984 (when he had a stroke and gave up smoking), Hefner was virtually never photographed without a briar pipe. Each of these four props symbolized an important aspect of the playboy and the pleasure he took in life. The smoking jacket showed the world that he lived a life of leisure (although he in fact continued to work very hard). The mansion clearly showed his riches, while also serving as a setting for legendary parties. The smoking jacket and the mansion together referenced a life of sybaritic pleasure constructed against the repression and conformity of the 1950s (Hefner, 1998, p. 12). The sports car served both as a signal of his money and of masculinity, its horsepower a metaphor for his power. But what about the pipe? Why was a briar pipe a central attribute of heterosexual playboy masculinity and a totem object for Hefner? This essay explores the pipe as a material object that embodied and performed heteronormative masculinity in 1950s and 1960s America, unpacking the meanings that the pipe carried for Hefner and other would-be playboys.

The pipe is not only associated with Hugh Hefner. It appeared regularly as one of the attributes of the playboy within *Playboy* magazine, even before Hefner began smoking one himself. Pipes were advertised more heavily in *Playboy* than cigars or cigarettes, even though cigarette smokers greatly outnumbered pipe smokers among *Playboy*'s readers.[1] Pipes were also used as props in articles, pictorials and ads for other products. The briar pipe sometimes served as a stand-in for the playboy, in advertisements and centrefolds. At times, it referenced Hugh Hefner, as it was well known as his totem object. But more importantly, it suggested the presence of the reader, a fellow playboy. It became a way for a reader to imagine himself in the sophisticated world that *Playboy* presented, with access to the very willing girls next door. But in order to enter into this fantasy, the reader needed to be a pipe smoker, or at least think of himself as one.

The playboy bachelor and the postwar crisis of masculinity

Both the playboy and his pipe are best understood in the historical context of what postwar sociologists and others argued was a 'crisis of masculinity'.[2] In this crisis, the traditional domains in which American heterosexual middle-class men's identity were based – work and family – were seen as no longer sufficient. Contemporary writers blamed the crisis of masculinity partly on the conformity of corporate America (Ehrenreich, 1983, pp. 30–40; Riesman, 1950; Whyte, 1956) and partly on women (Moskin, 1959; Wylie, 1958). Men's individuality was seen to be crushed through their experience at work, where critics claimed there was 'no place for individuality' and 'teamwork and personnel relations reigned over all' (Leonard, 1958, p. 97). Men had become corporate drones, with no space for individuality or creativity. Life was no better for the man at home. Women were understood as controlling men's sexuality, through control over sexual limits before marriage, and control of conception and demands for orgasm after (Moskin, 1959). In addition, the wife was seen as controlling her husband's working life, through her desire to consume to keep up with the neighbours and concomitant pressure on her husband to make money (Moskin, 1959; Wylie, 1958).

In a 1958 essay on 'The Crisis of American Masculinity', Arthur Schlesinger Jr. argued that for men to become men again, they needed to 'recover a sense of individual spontaneity. And to do this, a man must visualize himself as an individual apart from the group, whatever it is, which defines his values and commands his loyalty' (1958, p. 65). Visualizing himself as a bachelor, living a life of leisure, provided just such an opportunity for a man to recover his individuality. The image of the bachelor playboy, promoted most heavily by *Playboy* magazine, but also articulated in films and other realms of popular culture, served as an alternative model of heterosexual masculinity. The playboy as imagined in American popular culture, was a professional, and thus had more autonomy than a typical office (or factory) worker. As he was unmarried, his home was purely his own. Most importantly, his identity was not based on work or family, but on consumption and leisure. His identity as a playboy came from his individual, masculine consumption, quite distinct from the family-based consumption paid for by the office drone.

The playboy's masculinity is defined through leisure and consumption, through his acquisition of stylish things and the pleasure he takes from them. The playboy is a connoisseur, an expert on jazz, clothes, food, design and culture, and he surrounds himself with things that proclaim his confident masculinity as well as his impeccable taste. Even a married man with a humdrum job could participate in the playboy's sophisticated masculine consumption and thus bolster his sense of self. He could use the same objects the playboy used – the stereo set playing jazz, the sports car, the wet bar, the briar pipe – to construct his identity as a man. Of these objects, the briar pipe was comparatively inexpensive and highly portable, which made it significantly more accessible, and of particular interest to college students, playboys in training.

This essay looks more closely at the pipe in this context. Why was the pipe, as an object of material culture, important to constructing this alternative model of heterosexual masculinity in the face of a masculinity crisis? The pipe, I argue, had three important and interrelated attributes. It was understood as a particularly masculine object, expressing the masculinity of the man who smoked it. It also served as a marker of middle- and upper-middle-class status, letting others know that its user was a man on the rise. It was associated with connoisseurship and collecting, and thus expressed the expertise and cultural capital of its owner. In addition, as with the playboy's other props, the pipe served as an opportunity for male individual consumption and was above all a source of pleasure. The pipe was important to would-be playboys because of the particular form of masculinity – cultured, leisured and worldly, based not on physical activity but on knowledge, collecting and pleasure – that it embodied.

Smoking and masculinity

Tobacco and pipes have long been associated with men in American culture. In the context of the highly structured gender roles of the Victorian era, men were not even to smoke in the presence of women, as smoke was seen as an affront to women's delicate natures. Men were advised not to smoke in any room that women were in the habit of frequenting, whether or not women were present; nor while walking in the company of a woman; nor on crowded promenades or fashionable streets; nor ideally while walking on any street during the daytime (Anonymous, 1865, p. 290; Green, 1904, pp. 229, 243; Humphry, 1897, p. 32; Louis, 1881, p. 225; A Woman of Fashion, 1898, pp. 177–178; Young, 1881, pp. 148, 260). Smoking functioned as a ritual of male bonding, and took place in special male-only smoking rooms at the theatre, operas, balls and parties, as well as in the dining room after dinner, once women had withdrawn to the parlour (Green, 1904, pp. 110, 229; Roberts, 1913, pp. 200, 207).

This social smoking focused on the consumption of cigars, often provided by the host. In contrast, pipes signalled a more private, contemplative sort of smoking. The pipe functioned, according to the author of *Habits of Good Society*, as 'the bachelor's wife', 'the worst rival a woman can have', because it was never nagging or needy and offered calm pleasures that improved with age (Anonymous, 1865, pp. 288–289). The intimate relationship between a man and his pipe is marked by descriptions of the pipe as 'beloved' and a 'comfort and companion' (Roberts, 1913, pp. 207, 393). In contrast, cigars were seen as a source of pleasure, but were not described in language that suggests an intimate and long-lasting bond. Iain Gately even suggests that the pipe was, at times, confused with sex itself (2003, p. 192). The private, even sexualized associations of the pipe were such that smoking a pipe on the street was seen by some etiquette experts as beyond the pale, even when a cigar was acceptable (Anonymous, 1865, p. 290; Louis, 1881, p. 129). This shifted significantly by the 1950s, when pipe smoking, while still associated to a great extent with contemplative smoking in masculine spaces in the home, was also seen as appropriate in public, particularly during outdoor leisure activities, such as fishing, as well as 'tooling his sports car along in a rallye, skiing, golfing, yachting' (Anonymous, 1959a, p. 80).

In the twentieth century, with changes in gender ideology, women increasingly took up smoking. By the 1910s, etiquette books acknowledged women as smokers, and allowed that they might smoke in private, or in the company of women (Roberts, 1913, pp. 207–208, 268–269, 273, 343). But when women smoked, they smoked cigarettes. Cigarettes from their origins were associated with women, as they were first made out of tobacco scraps by Spanish women cigar rollers for their own use (Gately, 2003, pp. 179–180). In addition, of all the modes of tobacco consumption, cigarettes are both the mildest and require the least skill to smoke, and thus were seen as more appropriate for women than pipes and cigars. In the context of women's adoption of the cigarette, the gendered meanings of smoking changed, but the pipe and the cigar remained as distinctly masculine modes of tobacco use, while the cigarette became relatively gender-neutral.

Gender, class and the pipe

In the context of the American postwar crisis of masculinity, the masculinity of the pipe became one of its major selling points. Advertisements for pipes emphasized their masculinity. A 1960 Kaywoodie advertisement promoted the pipe as not merely a manly prop, but a weapon for men to fight for their embattled masculinity (see Figure 6.1):

> Help fight creeping matriarchy! . . . Smoke your Kaywoodie often *especially among women*. Flaunt its manly grain. Tantalize them with the lush tobacco-and-briar aroma. But never let them savor a puff! Kaywoodie flavor, mildness, and relaxation . . . are strictly male. Will this return women to bondage? Maybe not. But it will be a brave exercise of your male prerogative . . . and pleasurable to boot.

In this advertisement, the idea that the pipe is not accessible to women is central. It promotes the pipe as a refuge from a world in which women are increasingly powerful and demanding more rights.

But the masculinity of the pipe is only one element of its appeal as a playboy's prop. Another important attribute is its gendered class associations. The playboy interpolated by *Playboy* magazine was firmly marked as an upper-middle-class professional, and in fact the readership of the magazine reflected this ideal as their median income was 30 per cent above the national average (Anonymous, 1958, p. 76). *Playboy* magazine can be seen as, among other things, a manual for the upwardly mobile man. *Playboy*'s readers were young – over 75 per cent of them were between 18 and 34 in 1958 – still working their way up the ladder of success, and *Playboy* was a tool to help take them there (Anonymous, 1958, p. 76). Articles on fashion, goods and furnishings taught men how to furnish their apartments and themselves to mark their desired class status. Recipes and bartending instructions taught readers how to entertain. Articles on jazz told readers what music to play for their guests, as well as how to speak intelligently about their taste in music, shaped by *Playboy*'s reviews and annual jazz poll. Interviews and articles on culture and politics gave readers fodder for sophisticated conversation. This conversation was also modelled for them by *Playboy*'s 1959–1960 television show, *Playboy's Penthouse*, which combined musical performances with conversations with writers, musicians and other culture-makers on a wide range of topics. On this show, Hugh Hefner served as the host of the party, pipe always firmly in his hand. We can see the playboy lifestyle as a hip version of upper-middlebrow class culture, charted in a 1949 article in *Time* magazine by Russell Lynes (1949, pp. 99–101). In this context, *Playboy* was instructing its readers in the taste culture associated with the class position they either held or aspired to hold. Modern art and furniture, fashionable but tasteful clothing, the best contemporary literature, the newest technology, and the newest jazz were all attributes of the hip highbrow taste promoted by *Playboy*. Knowing how to behave and what to own (or aspire to own) was particularly useful for the college students who made up 23 per cent of *Playboy*'s readership (Anonymous, 1958, p. 76). Through college, these young men hoped to get ahead. *Playboy* helped them learn how to dress and act like the successful professionals they hoped to become. In this context, the pipe helped to mark the certifiably adult status of its playboy users. Pipe makers such as Kaywoodie took advantage of this, marketing less expensive 'starter' pipes directly to college students in their 'campus collection', advertised in *Playboy*. Pipe smoking was, as Gately argues, a particularly adult activity (2003, pp. 193–194). While teens might try cigarettes or chewing tobacco, a briar pipe was more expensive, more difficult to use, and

FIGURE 6.1 *Advertisement for Kaywoodie Pipes,* Playboy, 1960, *reproduced with permission of Kaywoodie.*

took a longer time to smoke. More importantly, the pipe marked its young smokers as middle or upper class.

The briar pipe

The pipe had not always been a marker of middle-class status, but the briar pipe, the pipe smoked by the playboy, was a middle-class item from its invention in the mid-nineteenth century. Earlier pipes, made of clay, were easily broken. The briar pipe, made from the rootstock of the Mediterranean bruyere tree, is made of a rarer material, takes more skill in its making, is much longer lasting, and is much more expensive. For example the pipes in the 1960 Kaywoodie advertisement quoted above sold for $5–$15, equivalent to $35–$100 today; 'starter' pipes in the campus collection cost roughly the equivalent of $25–$30 today. In addition, as briar smokes cooler than clay, it can be made in a wider range of shapes, allowing its users to express individuality in their pipe choice. Gately argues that for these reasons, 'The middle class found its totem in the pipe. It was the perfect device for expressing both individuality and respectability' (2003, p. 188).

In the nineteenth century, briar pipes came to have middle-class associations in part because of their contrast with other modes of tobacco use. They were distinguished from the clay pipes used by some of the working class, the cigars preferred by the elites, and cigarettes, which were smoked rarely (Gately, 2003, pp. 186–187). Briar pipes contrasted even more strongly with the chewing tobacco used by the vast majority of nineteenth-century American tobacco users (Gately, 2003, p. 173), which, with its spitting, fit poorly with the genteel bodily control of the ideal middle-class man (Anonymous, 1865, p. 291; Louis, 1881, pp. 223–224; A Woman of Fashion, 1898, pp. 178–179). Because of the ubiquity of chewing tobacco in the nineteenth century, spitting was seen as the 'curse of the American people', and was so impolite that 'A Woman of Fashion' wrote that 'a man who can not live without spitting should take to the woods and reside there alone, forever. And then he is not good enough for the beasts that roam there' (1898, pp. 178–179).

Similarly, meerschaum pipes, made from hydrated silicate of magnesia from Anatolia and typically elaborately carved, were also associated with the middle class (Gately, 2003, p. 189). In comparison to briar pipes, meerschaums are both more expensive and more fragile, meaning that they tend to be reserved for smoking at home. In addition, their elaborate carvings mark them as objects of leisure. In contrast, the briar pipe is much less fragile, thus can be easily used in a wide range of situations, including outdoors and in the office. It is also less expensive. While Carl Weber argues that 'no man who does not have at least one genuine meerschaum in his possession can be called a true lover of pipes', meerschaums are greatly outnumbered by briars for most pipe smokers (1962, p. 27). For example, the 1959 Kaywoodie Presentation collection of pipes included 28 briar pipes, but only one meerschaum (Anonymous, 1959b). Thus, while the meerschaum retained a masculine and middle-class identity, it was the briar pipe, with its clean, modern lines and sturdy practicality, that became a symbol of middle-class masculinity, used and carried by the architect, the bowler-hatted businessman and the professor alike.[3]

Buying a briar pipe required not just money, but also a certain level of connoisseurship. Would-be pipe smokers needed to be able to recognize imperfections in the grain of the briarwood and understand what flaws were merely cosmetic and which affected the function of the pipe. They also needed to choose a pipe shape and make sure that it had an appropriate stem. Most importantly, according to the 1962 *Weber's Guide to Pipes and Pipe Smoking* (still a revered text among pipe smokers), a man needed to find a style or shape in keeping with his particular character. Weber suggests that a pipe shopper 'Try on the pipe as you would a hat or an overcoat. If the pipe looks out of place in your mouth, put it back on the shelf and try another one' (1962, p. 55). Smokers would also choose different pipes depending on their intended smoking site, choosing a bulldog or apple for active sports, a long-shanked pipe with a lid for driving, a medium pipe with a flat bottom for office use, and a large 'half-hour' pipe with a curved stem and bit for relaxing at home (Anonymous, 1959a, pp. 80, 97). Once a pipe was chosen, similar care must be taken in selecting the tobacco to smoke in it, whether a commercial blend or, ideally, a custom blend made for the smoker by a tobacconist or blended himself. Actually smoking a pipe similarly required specialist knowledge. The smoker must know how to break in a pipe, how to maintain it so that it has just enough of a protective cake to smoke well, and how to fill, light and clean it. All of these elements of skill and knowledge added to the pipe's mystique. More than other forms of smoking, the pipe both requires sophistication and provides an opportunity for individuation, especially in the creation of a personal tobacco blend, but also in the choice and maintenance of pipes. Its cost, the knowledge it entails, and its relationship to self-development all help to mark it as a middle-class item.

Pipe collecting

Smoking a pipe also became an opportunity for collecting. As Weber argues, 'Most interested pipe smokers become collectors sooner or later . . . every smoker eventually learns that he should have at least four or five pipes and smoke them alternately' (1962, p. 115). *Playboy* went further, arguing in the 1959 article 'Playing the Piper' that 'anything less than a dozen pipes, selected in accord with your tastes and activities, is frowned upon as the mark of a tyro' (p. 97). Collections could include pipes of all sorts from all over the world, but even a smaller selection of new and non-exotic pipes could be understood as a collection, in part because of the careful selection process involved in the choice of each pipe. Pipe manufacturers also encouraged pipe collecting through expensive matched sets of briar pipes. These ranged from Kaywoodie's seven-day set, including more elaborate and rounded shapes for Saturday and Sunday, to their elaborate presentation collection, which included 28 matched briars, plus carved head, meerschaum and calabash pipes in a walnut cabinet, for the astronomical sum of $2,500 in 1959 (roughly $20,000 today, and more than the Renault convertible sports car recommended in the same article) (Anonymous, 1959b).

Collecting can function as a masculine mode of consumption (Auslander, 1996; Gelber, 1999, pp. 100–106). While women's consumption was historically focused on the household, working to keep up with the Joneses, men's collecting has historically focused on the self. When women did consume for themselves, it was generally understood as producing only pleasure, while men collected to express and cultivate their taste, helping to distinguish themselves as individuals (Auslander, 1996, pp. 85, 87). Collecting was a way to demonstrate and create knowledge about the authenticity of objects, as well as to create order in the world, and thus to collect was to demonstrate and cultivate power and expertise (Auslander, 1996, p. 86). The idea that collecting helped construct men's individuality and authority was particularly important in the context of the postwar crisis of masculinity, as men's conformity was a central trope of this crisis. In addition, men's collecting has typically been focused on things that are valuable, are explicit tokens of maleness, or are both (Gelber, 1999, p. 102). These sorts of object reflect well on their collectors, sharing their qualities of value and masculinity with them. Collecting, then, was one way for men to be individuals, participating in a valuable activity removed from the rat race of work and household consumption.

Pipes and contemplation

Collecting pipes, as well as smoking them, required knowledge and research. In keeping with this, by the 1950s the pipe was associated with studiousness and contemplation. It was a regular prop for academics and intellectuals whose most important work was thought. It was thus a fitting object for the playboy, who was improving his mind, and thus his class position, whether through the formal education of college or the informal education of the pages of *Playboy*. The importance of studious contemplation to the playboy is notable in the designs for ideal bachelor pads that ran in the magazine from 1956 until 1970, each of which included a study as one of the most important rooms (see Anonymous, 1956, pp. 79–80). The study in the bachelor pad is the space most expressive of the bachelor himself, the only room where he is not performing for others. While potentially a place of work, expressive of the playboy bachelor's class position as an independent professional, it is primarily a place where the bachelor works on himself, reading and thinking, cultivating his mind, proving both his independence in a world of conformity and his distance from working-class culture. The pipe is the perfect companion to this activity.

The pipe marks its user as both contemplative and leisured. As Weber writes, 'the pipe smoker belongs to a breed apart from other men. His pleasures are contemplation and relaxation, he does not rush, he is not nervous. His joys are the casual and meditative ones' (1962, p. 7). The pipe is also what one smokes when one has the time to relax and enjoy it, while the quick cigarette is the more likely choice during a hectic workday. As the playboy is defined precisely by his access to leisure, as well as his pursuit of pleasure, the pipe is an appropriate choice. As Hugh Hefner wrote in an essay introducing the first issue of *Playboy*: 'We don't mind telling you in advance – we plan spending most of our time inside. We like our apartment. We enjoy mixing up cocktails and an hors d'oeuvre or two, putting a little mood music on the phonograph and inviting a female acquaintance for a quiet discussion on Picasso, Nietzsche, jazz, sex' (1953, p. 3). The *Playboy* bachelor, although a professional, is defined not by his work, but by his life at home, as well as his lively and enquiring mental life. His profession serves primarily to give him sufficient leisure to pursue the *Playboy* lifestyle, including the leisurely, pleasurable and cultured pipe.

Conclusion

The pipe proved the perfect object for the playboy bachelor, whether real or aspiring, whom we can understand as a creature of the 1950s American crisis of masculinity. Both the playboy and the pipe were intimately tied to this historical moment, and both became obsolete during the youth revolution of the 1960s, which challenged the gender norms in relation to which both the playboy and the crisis of masculinity were conceived. Through the playboy's connoisseurship and urbanity, through his collecting and his sophisticated use of highly gendered objects, including the pipe, he marks consumption as not only safe for men, but as a mode for constructing heterosexual masculinity. In smoking a pipe, he demonstrates both masculinity and skill. In choosing, buying and collecting pipes, he expresses his carefully cultivated personal taste, knowledge, purchasing power and class position. The pipe supports his project of self-improvement through leisure as well as the centrality of pleasure to his self-definition. The very presence of the pipe telegraphs to the world the sort of man he is. As *Playboy* argued about the pipe in 1959, just as Hefner had taken it up as his personal totem, 'there has not come into the world ... a more enjoyable way to take tobacco, nor a more prestigious, masculine symbol' (Anonymous, 1959b).

Notes

1 27.8 per cent smoked pipes vs 69.9 per cent cigarettes (and 29.9 per cent cigars) in 1961. *Playboy* had the highest percentage of male smokers among its readers (77.1 per cent) of any leading American magazine (Anonymous, 1962, p. 43).

2 While the 'crisis of masculinity' has since been used as a trope to understand gender transformations both in earlier periods and more recently, it is in the 1950s that the idea of masculinity in crisis was invented. As Cuordileone has argued, while the turn-of-the-century preoccupation with masculinity shared many themes with the postwar masculinity crisis, it is not until the 1950s that the issue was framed in psychological terms as a 'wholesale loss of self' (2000, pp. 525–526).

3 For example, the briar pipe served, along with his round glasses, as a totem for the architect Le Corbusier, who would often take photographs of his interiors that included his pipe. It is also one of the attributes of Magritte's surrealist everyman and Jacques Tati's befuddled M. Hulot.

SECTION 3

Objects and Embodiment

7

Seduced by the Archive

A Personal and Working Relationship with the Archive and Collection of the London Couturier, Norman Hartnell

Jane Hattrick

Introduction

Driving down the hill towards the house on the water one rainy day in October 2007, adrenalin flooded through my body, my heart suddenly began to lurch and then race very fast. I felt as though I was driving to meet a lover after a long absence. It was not a lover's touch that I was eagerly anticipating, however, but time alone with the archive, to handle the paper, to engage with the objects. I am one of 'those sad creatures . . . solemnly hunched over a list of names' that Carolyn Steedman has written about. Breathing in the 'dust' and the unique smell of it, I am a willing victim of Derrida's 'archive fever', or Steedman's 'feverlet' (Derrida, 1998; Steedman, 2001, pp. 18–19). As Steedman has written, those whose form of writing originates in the archive believe that their output can reflect what is not present amongst the documents as much as what has been found: a form of writing that celebrates the constraints on it, constraints that – so it is said – are made by the documents themselves: 'what they forbid you to write, the permissions they offer' (2001, p. xi).

The archive in question is that of the London couturier, Sir Norman Hartnell (1901–1979). Hartnell's career as a fashion designer began as a young man aged 22 in 1923, dressing the debutante sisters of his university friends and their mothers, and continued until his death in 1979. His fashion collections were immediately followed with interest by the international press. Described as a 'dress artist' during the 1920s, Hartnell produced pencil and watercolour sketches of each ensemble from which his workroom staff created a toile, then a paper pattern. Rather than copying French models, he produced fresh designs more suited to English taste and Society life. Each collection included formal evening gowns, cocktail dresses, dresses for court presentations and balls, tailored suits and coats, as well as wedding dresses. By the mid-1930s, Hartnell had become Britain's most celebrated couture fashion designer working in London's high-end clothing district of Mayfair. By this time, the House of Hartnell had become extremely profitable, and by the 1950s it was the largest, most established and internationally famous fashion house in London. The couturier designed two fashion collections a year, from March 1924 until his death in June 1979 (see Figure 7.1). He is best remembered, however, for dressing British royal clients for major events such as Princess Elizabeth's wedding in 1947 and her coronation as Queen Elizabeth II in 1953.

In 2005, I discovered Hartnell's lost company and personal archive and collection, containing elements of every aspect of his private and working life in an empty house once lived in by the

FIGURE 7.1 *Norman Hartnell, original pencil and watercolour sketched design for an evening gown with swatches of fabric pinned to the corner, c. 1938, courtesy of the Hartnell-Mitchison Archive.*

man who shared Hartnell's private, social and working life, George Mitchison, and George's wife Doris, now both deceased. It was their daughter Claire who kindly agreed to show me what she could find in the house relating to her godfather 'Uncle' Norman's life and work. I was unprepared for the vast quantity of bags and boxes spilling over with original fashion sketches, business paperwork and garments that awaited me in a large bedroom in the house. My doctoral research took place in the house where Hartnell had slept, surrounded by hundreds of his possessions. These included not only the vast paper archive generated by the fashion business over a 60-year period, but also his personal effects such as his hair brush set, and items of clothing once worn by him, as well as examples of his furniture and decorative objects.

This essay unpacks my personal and working relationship with the archive and collection between 2005 and 2009, from the paper archive generated by this couturier's life and work, to the objects collected and displayed by him. It also probes the biography of these things and analyses their current meanings and place in the world. My aim is also to reflect upon my research processes and methodology, and to that end I take an autobiographical approach to my account of being in the archive. My research journey began as dress historian who approached this archive hoping to research Hartnell's design work through sketches, photographs and extant garments. Hartnell's homosexuality became evident throughout his archive, and over a period of two years with the material, it became clear to me that the sexual identity of the man was central to his life and work and that it should not be 'glossed over'. Framing an analysis of the life and work of Britain's most celebrated royal dressmaker within queer theoretical approaches, however, went against the existing public narrative. I argue here that my own personal queer identity caused me to choose this way into Hartnell's archive and personal possessions, and that the personal identity of the author impacts on their approach to their subject of research. Casting my queer eye over the designer's personal possessions alongside his design work generated across a lifetime, provided the opportunity to examine just how a designer's private, personal identity might be reflected in his creative output.

It is not often that academics position themselves within their research so clearly on the page, or reflect about research processes and methodology in the first person. As in the case of Judith Halberstam's approach to writing as 'low theory', which goes against the accepted ways of writing, it is not considered legitimate within masculinist art-historical practice to write in a self-referential way (Halberstam in Williams, 2012). One dress historian who has done so is Professor Carol Tulloch, who has explained that as a black-British-Jamaican woman 'unquestionably, race is in the foreground of my work ... with an eye on the black British experience' (1998, pp. 366–377). Tulloch uses empirical research in the Jamaica Archives in Spanish Town to 'uncover the self-presentation practiced under the shadow of imperialism and colonialism by African-Jamaican ... women' and states that 'had I neglected to investigate this source, I would have continued the legacy of disallowing these other "truths" to be heard' (1998, p. 369). It is Tulloch's black-British-Jamaican identity that led her to identify the overlooked histories and to uncover these other 'truths'.

A life in the archive

Rather than being remembered for his contribution to British fashion design, it is the embroidered State gowns designed for Britain's Queen Elizabeth from 1937 and for her daughter, the country's current monarch Elizabeth II, that are considered Hartnell's legacy. Neither Hartnell's design and production of two couture collections per year between 1924 and 1979, nor his signature house style had been analysed in-depth before I embarked on my doctoral research.[1] My research posits that Hartnell's house style has its roots in his personal, sexual identity and cross-dressing, and that his overtly feminine taste in colour, material and embellishment is present in all his fashion and royal designs and in his collections of decorative objects. Within the dominant heteronormative cultural bias, a designer's work is not usually discussed in terms of his/her sexuality. In her essay on the textile designers and same-sex couple Phyllis Barron and Dorothy Larcher, Bridgett Elliott notes design historian Peter McNeil's remark that 'issues of the designer's sexuality have been supressed in most of the design literature' (Elliott, 2006, p. 6). I argue, however, that Hartnell's sexuality is central to his identity and therefore his creative output. In 2012, I published an essay that explored the ways in which Hartnell staged the interiors of his private homes for photographic representation and what the collection and display of decorative objects reveals about his queer identity and his intimate personal relationships (Hattrick, 2012, pp. 136–152). My research therefore goes beyond a focus on royal dressing and an analysis of Hartnell's design practice to consider the spaces and places in which he worked, his collecting and display of objects and furniture, interior decorative schemes, and his relationships with his everyday possessions, revealing his sexual selfhood. The ways in which he constructed his personal and public identity through material culture, and the biography of these things now extant in the archive and house, reveals a complex, layered history.

The biography of the Hartnell archive

The paper archive and couture clothes from the Hartnell Salon were removed by George Mitchison, then executive director at Hartnell's, after the company was sold in 1989. This enormous collection of unidentified material was discovered still in the Hartnell carrier bags in which it had been transported 20 years earlier. It includes over 200 garments, hundreds of sketched designs, embroidery samples, fashion photographs, bound volumes of press cuttings, and paperwork relating to the business between the early 1920s and the 1980s. There are also many personal letters from British royal clients. Hartnell's personal life (and death) is reflected in everything from his birth certificate to his death certificate, private letters and family photographs.

Hartnell met Mitchison in 1938 when Mitchison was a young Guardee stationed at a London barracks. Mitchison took up residence at Hartnell's London home in Regent's Park and is described as Hartnell's secretary in an inventory of the house taken in 1939 (Maple & Co. Ltd., 1939, p. 40). Mitchison married Doris in 1939 and their first baby, Norman, was born during the war. After the war, Hartnell elevated Mitchison to the position of business manager and he remained at the fashion house from 1946 until it was sold in 1989, at which point he was executive director. Hartnell left Mitchison his entire estate on his death in 1979, and Mitchison and his wife moved to Cornwall in later life, taking what was left of Hartnell's possessions and archive. Hartnell's and Mitchison's riding boots and spats were found displayed together in Mitchison's bedroom in 2005 along with photographs of Hartnell, his hairbrush set and other personal effects, furniture, paintings and prints on the wall representing 40 years of the two men's strong personal attachment.

Close analysis of photographs of Hartnell's and Mitchison's homes, their interiors and the objects displayed within, revealed that Hartnell's objects, seen in images taken between 1936 and 2008, travelled through time, their meanings shifting according to the stage in what Igor Kopytoff would describe as their biographies or social lives; according to whether they were owned by Hartnell or subsequently by Mitchison (and now Hartnell's goddaughter) (Kopytoff, 1986).

After Hartnell's death in 1979, his objects and furniture were used to furnish Mitchison's own large house in Kent. As further photographs of the interior of this property taken in the mid-1980s illustrate, the same colour schemes were used for both the drawing room and the dining room as had been used at Hartnell's homes Lovel Dene and Rose Place. The objects simply moved from one house to another house of similar proportions. Photographs of the archive house taken in 2008 illustrate the eerily similar fashion in which the interiors are decorated, the objects arranged and displayed much as Hartnell had displayed them in his lifetime (see Figure 7.2). Revealing either a conscious or unconscious system of memory cues, the similarity between the hall of the archive house in 2008 and the hall at Lovel Dene, reproduced on the cover of *Ideal Home* magazine in 1947, was remarkable (*Ideal Home*, 1947). The same Venetian glass mirrors were seen on the wall to the right; the same marble-topped table; the same sweep of the staircase to the left. Familiar Hartnell objects were displayed on the hall table, offering 'the sensory experience of continued contact' with the designer for the Mitchisons (Auslander, 2005, p. 1020).

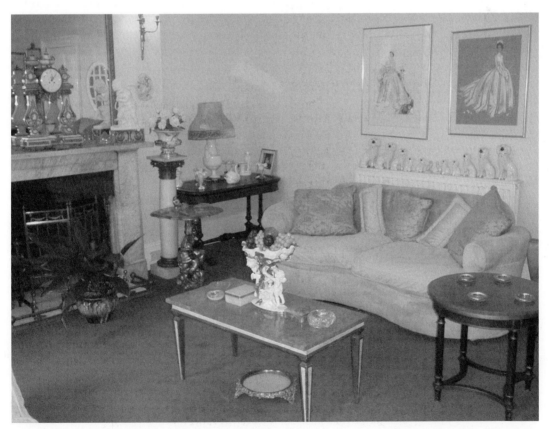

FIGURE 7.2 *Norman Hartnell's furniture and decorative objects on display in the drawing room at the archive house, the former home of Hartnell's business manager George Mitchison, courtesy of the Hartnell-Mitchison Archive.*

Leora Auslander writes that 'while intimate things are crucial objectifications of intimate relations, the space in which they are housed is equally fundamental. Memories are often literally housed, with dwellings and the objects they contain proving the key to remembrance'. The Mitchisons recreated the space in which to house Hartnell's objects, displaying his things as what Auslander has described as 'memory cues' (2005, p. 1020). She writes, 'people never really outgrow their need to incarnate in objects those they love' (2005, p. 1019). In this case, the material culture in the archive house very literally embodies the absent Hartnell, and since the death of the Mitchisons, the objects are the embodiment of three people for their surviving daughter (also Hartnell's goddaughter). It is this intimate context for my encounter with Hartnell's archive and possessions that also shaped my research methodology and brought me closer to the identity of the man I studied.

Unpacking Hartnell's archive

An 'archive' is usually the term used by archivists to refer to paper documents, not three-dimensional objects. New forms of digital record-keeping arguably challenge this traditional form of categorization, although Hartnell's archive still only exists in material form and has not been digitized. The sensory experience of handling the wartime flimsy paper with traces of his handwriting and the smell of his worn garments, has not yet been replaced with the more abstract encounter with this 'stuff' on a computer screen. It also challenges Susan Grigg's now dated explanation of what archives are: 'Archives in the narrowest definition are records of organisations preserved by those organisations, and historical manuscripts are the surviving papers of individuals and families' (1991, p. 234). The Hartnell archive conflates these two definitions, as personal correspondence, photographs and clothing (for example), are layered together with paperwork generated as part of the everyday working life of the business. Also, the personal cannot be separated from the business, as Hartnell's ideas, decisions and signature on Hartnell letterhead paper reveal his character and identity and the rare love-letter helps to contextualize the business correspondence.

At the outset, the focus of my research was the paper archive, which on its own comprises layers of what Steedman has described as 'entrancing stories' (2001, p. x). The surroundings in which the paper archive was found seemed unimportant. Quickly, however, this focus widened to include the house that contains the archive, and the rest of its contents, after photographs found amongst the paper archive revealed that much of the furniture, decorative objects and the pictures on the walls of the house had furnished Hartnell's homes and business premises from as early as 1924.

Steedman's 2001 critical essay on Derrida's *Archive Fever*, the publication based on his lecture of 1994 with its focus on the Freud House Museum in which Freud's objects and his archive are housed, was a useful theoretical way in. She discusses Derrida's definition of the term 'archive' as taken from the Greek *arkheion*, 'initially a house, a domicile, an address – the residence of the archon . . . where the official documents were housed' (Derrida, 1998, pp. 1–2). Derrida writes that Freud's archives are 'under house arrest'. He continues, 'the dwelling, this place where they dwell permanently, marks this institutional passage from the private to the public' (1998, pp. 2–3). Unlike the Freud house, now a public museum, the house where Hartnell's archive and collection is held under 'house arrest' is still in the private domain and therefore has not made this journey. I had the responsibility of sifting through the layers of material, the traces of the past, the memories. Because the house and much of its contents embodies those that Hartnell's goddaughter has loved and lost, the gathering of evidence was a slow and respectful process.

Archive research, autobiography and personal criticism

A single archive can be a source of material for a variety of projects and each researcher will come to the same archive with a particular story to tell. Depending on the agenda of the researcher, different material will be singled out as relevant and useful to that end. Thus, a documentary film-maker recounting a version of the Queen's coronation in 1953 studied material in the Hartnell archive that included the original pencil and watercolour designs, the paper patterns and the embroidery samples that formed part of the design and making up of that gown.[2] In positioning myself as a researcher in Hartnell's archive, it was imperative that I questioned my methodological approach to the material and the reasons why Hartnell's personal identity, in particular his homosexuality, was important to my account of his life and work. In their discussion of women's autobiographical experiences, Sidonie Smith and Julia Watson write that:

> personal criticism is widely practiced by women, in homage to the textual practices they work on but also as integral to their efforts to reframe the critical act through feminist pedagogy and praxis. It is in part a response to the sterile evacuation of the personal voice in what has by now become institutionalized as theoretical discourse.
>
> 1998, p. 32

It also offers the opportunity for a theorist to critique her relationship to her object of study, and for some it offers the means to interpret and theorize personal experience (Smith and Watson, 1998, p. 32).

Personal archives are often a mixture of both transactional material and 'the flotsam of the individual life' (Hobbs, 2001, p. 128). Catherine Hobbs writes that personal records can be studied as documentation of individual character: 'there are glimpses of the inner soul as well as its outer manifestation in public activities' (2001, p. 126). These glimpses both presented themselves to me in the manner that Steedman suggests, 'giving permission', and subsequently became what I looked for in Hartnell's archive, allowing a particular narrative to be told. My research ultimately searched for what has hitherto been sidestepped in the writing of Hartnell's life and work: the issue of his queer identity and how this might relate to his creative output. The intention is to foster a new understanding of his couture design work and the Hartnell trademark and fashion brand through this particular lens. Hobbs writes that research in a personal archive 'uncovers much about the evolving personality and character traits of the author' and that 'personal archives reflect not only what a person does or thinks, but who they are, how they envision and experience their lives' (2001, p. 128). Although I did not originally set out with this intention in mind, my experience in Hartnell's archive reflects Hobbs' theory.

As Laura Doan has explained, the word 'queer' is a highly contested term, lacking in scholarly consensus. Used as an umbrella term for lesbian, gay, bisexual and transgendered histories and pastimes by some historians, others consider it to mean the disruption of stable sexual identities. Difficult to define, it can be a verb, noun and adjective, and indeed 'revels in the open-endedness's' of its definitions (Doan, 2011). To approach an archive with the intention of deliberately looking for hidden or purposefully overlooked queer histories amongst the material is to go against convention. Biddy Martin argues that 'lesbianism should be understood as "a position from which to speak" that "works to unsettle rather than to consolidate the boundaries around identity" ' (Martin in Smith and Watson, 1998, p. 34).

If the sexuality of the designer has been suppressed in design literature, then knowledge about the sexuality of the author who writes the designer's sexuality back into design literature is totally absent, although might be assumed. As a female academic who identifies as queer, my approach to Hartnell's archive and possessions looked to reclaim Hartnell's sexual subjectivity. In her article 'What's in and Out, Out There?' (1994), Laura Doan accepts that lesbian writers disrupt the academe. I considered Hartnell's sexuality as a legitimate subject of study, partly as a way of identifying with a shared history with the couturier and also as a way of opening up the field to other queer histories of design.

Perhaps in this way, my experience of living and working with another person's possessions reveals as much about my identity as that of Hartnell. Hartnell revealed how difficult negotiating life as a gay male dress designer had been for him in unpublished sections of his 1955 memoir *Silver & Gold*, a memoir written very much in the white, male, Western tradition, and in personal letters reflecting the culture of criminality pre-Liberation in which his profile as the Queen's dressmaker was carefully crafted for public consumption at the height of criminal prosecutions of homosexual men.

Early on in my research process, it was suggested that I was allowing myself to become too personally involved with the story of Hartnell's sexuality and his relationship with his colleague and close friend Mitchison and his family, at the expense of researching the designing and working practices of this famous fashion designer. This poses the question, should we as researchers try to stay completely disengaged and rational when engaging with a person's artefacts, or can we use our emotional, visceral responses to help contextualize them? I would argue that it was precisely my particular perspective that prompted an emotional response to each object associated with Hartnell's personal and working life. I decoded the possible meanings held within this material and visual culture within a queer theoretical framework, treating everything, including textual documents, photographs, sketches, letters, decorative objects and personal effects, as equally important.

Through the physical process of unpacking (and repacking) Hartnell's archive and possessions, I unpacked his identity within a space that embodied the man and those he had been closest to in life. I became literally wrapped up in my surroundings, where every cupboard in every room in the house revealed some object, slip of paper or personal snapshot photograph relating intimately to the man. This methodology drove my thesis forward. Had I encountered Hartnell's paper archive one box at a time within the reading rooms of, for example, the Archive of Art and Design at the V&A, disassociated from the context of Hartnell's collections, personal effects and his personal relationships, my research would not have taken the turn it did. A level of abstraction would have existed between myself and the couturier's paperwork and things.

Between 2005 and 2008, the empty house stood still in time as a memorial to Hartnell and the Mitchisons. The beds were made up, wardrobes still contained the couple's clothing, Doris' last packet of cigarettes sat on the table beside her armchair. The paper archive was stored amongst the roomfuls of Hartnell's collections of tinkling, Bohemian coloured glass candle sticks and chandeliers, Regency furniture, decorative art objects and framed portraits by Cecil Beaton of all the main British royal women. The archive was not then catalogued, systematized or stored according to best practice in terms of its conservation.

During the first three years, more and more paperwork and artefacts were found squirreled away in drawers and cupboards in the house. From lists on scraps of paper found hidden between the pages of a book, to a dinner shirt embroidered with Hartnell's initials, still in its packaging, material was retrieved as it was put out for the skip. My role was what Derrida has called the 'archon' – or guardian of the archive – and only I had the power to interpret it. After two years of working with the archive and through the dissemination of my work through conference papers, I became associated with the archive amongst others in the field. My continued contact with the house and its contents over time led to a deep emotional attachment. Almost feeling like home to me, I was the only resident for nearly three years. I sat on the chairs once owned and sat in by Hartnell and closely studied the hundreds of handwritten letters and annotated, sketched designs by him – marks made on paper by his own hand. Like the artist Rachel Lichtenstein, and her obsession with the disappeared Jewish cleric Rodinsky's room and what was left of his possessions, I became the 'caretaker in absentia' – the keeper of the archive house. As Iain Sinclair writes of Lichtenstein's research into Rodinsky's life (and by association her own Jewish family past) 'her task was to tell the story in which she now had the central part. To uncover the mystery of David Rodinsky by laying bare her own obsession with his life and work' (Lichtenstein and Sinclair, 2000, p. 79). Similarly, between 2005 and 2009, I played a central role in the reinterpretation of Hartnell's life and work and did what I could to influence decisions about what happened to his things. At every visit, I photographed the rooms in the house and the objects within, and as, after three years, the objects and furniture began to be sold, I photographed the spaces in the rooms left behind in the absence of these things. Parts of the collection slipped away, and these losses were out of my control. The Regency dining table and x-back chairs that had been a feature of many photographs taken of his interiors were sold, and the swan vase in which Constance Spry arranged flowers, that had been a feature of his drawing room schema from 1934, was given away because it was broken (see Figure 7.3).

Susan Grigg states that: 'Archival practice rests on the principles of provenance and original order: that materials should be acquired in whatever groupings reflect their initial use and maintained in their present structure and sequence within those groupings' (1991, p. 232). As much care as possible was taken to keep the Hartnell paper archive in its original order, as it was found, in particular the files of business documentation that had been clearly lifted directly from filing cabinets at 26 Bruton Street, despite their often muddled content in terms of date. This business correspondence is perhaps the only material of 'official character', historically considered archive material proper, and the ontological order of the paperwork is therefore important. Grigg writes, however, that provenance is now more important than functional order (1991, p. 232). The Hartnell archive today is very far removed from its original home, function and order, as its location reflects the intersection of his public and private life. The ontology and taxonomy of the rest of the collection (embroidery samples, sketches, personal effects, ephemera) has been part of a more invasive process on my part, in order to preserve the objects and to make them easier to find (sketches from same period boxed together, for example). Much of this material was found in old suitcases, but is now wrapped in layers of acid-free tissue and boxed.

Identifying and photographing objects took place at the kitchen table, and items were labelled with jam-pot stickers in a very domesticated setting (see Figure 7.4). Papers and artefacts were basically systemized by me and boxed in terms of theme, such as business franchises and licensing agreements; autobiographical writing; special events such as the coronation, 1953, the royal wedding, 1947, the royal tours overseas; and type of material, such as photographs, pencil and watercolour sketched designs, objects such as briefcases, embroidery samples, Hartnell designed/made garments and the remnants of Hartnell's personal library. A broad-brush chronological approach was taken within these themes led by the examples of the different

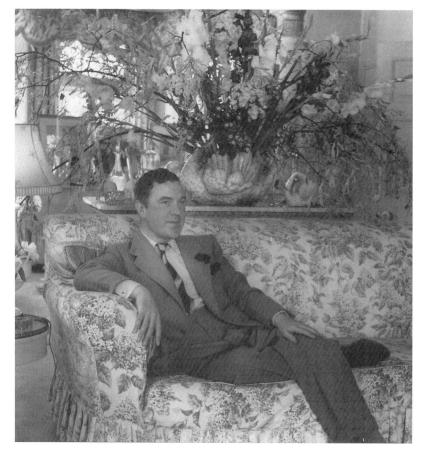

FIGURE 7.3 *Norman Hartnell seated in his drawing room at his country house Lovel Dene, Windsor, his swan vase on the table behind, 1953. De Groot, Amsterdam, courtesy of the Hartnell-Mitchison Archive.*

types of material found in the archive, which includes 40 boxes of paperwork, sketches and business paperwork and 22 boxes of garments.

During the seven years spent with this material, there has been keen interest in the public reputation of Hartnell and his work, from institutions such as Buckingham Palace – which has undertaken several major exhibitions of his royal couture designs – to the V&A in London.[3] In my capacity as archivist I have liaised between the archive and exhibition curators, researching and arranging appropriate loans and have given many papers and lectures on Hartnell's life and work. These exhibitions and conferences have differed greatly, however, in terms of content from the primary focus of my research, the private identity of the designer and how this impacted his life and work. The latter has been explored and disseminated strictly within the academy rather than publicly at royal palaces and national museums. These public and private faces of Hartnell are therefore reflected in the different arenas in which the research is disseminated. My emotional attachment to the archive and collection of this one man now takes a back seat. The material still resides in the house in which I lived and worked with it, and is boxed up and back

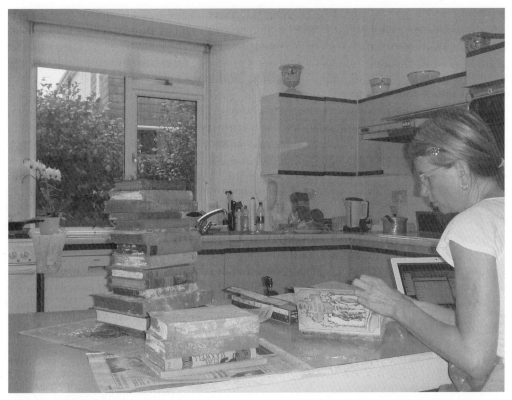

FIGURE 7.4 *The author cataloguing Norman Hartnell's books found in the cellar of the archive house in August 2008, courtesy of the Hartnell-Mitchison Archive.*

in the attic, and I am still the only researcher who knows exactly what the archive and collection comprises.

The year 2012 witnessed the British monarch's Diamond Jubilee celebrations. This was a busy year for a researcher whose subject of study is the royal designer who dressed the Queen from her childhood (1935) until his death (1979). I was involved in documentaries on the Queen's style and about her coronation,[4] conferences that focused on the subject of Modern Monarchy,[5] and have given lectures at the V&A about Hartnell's life and work to coincide with the national institution's exhibitions 'British Design 1948–2012' and 'Ballgowns: British Glamour Since 1950'.[6] Norman Hartnell's legacy, still favouring the subject of his royal styles rather than his couture fashion designs, was under scrutiny. The following year saw the Queen's coronation gown designed by Hartnell on display at Buckingham Palace and material from the Hartnell archive was once again on display to provide context. The years spent sorting and researching Hartnell's archive have provided me with insight into the man's life and work that goes far beyond the story of him dressing the Queen for her coronation. Yet this is the narrative that has been told and retold from the publishing of his 1955 memoir, *Silver & Gold* (Hartnell, 1955), to the exhibition devoted to the Queen's Coronation in 1953, which took place at Buckingham Palace in 2013. The coronation gown is a metaphor for his career in dress design and his legacy.

Conclusion

In conclusion, this essay has been an exploration into the biography of the lost Hartnell archive and collection and the impact that this collection of objects has had on me both professionally and personally. This has resulted in a many-layered, interdisciplinary project, underlining the archive house as what Auslander would describe as the 'imbrication of objects, space and place' (2005, p. 1027). The objects collected and loved by Hartnell became active agents in the construction of his identity and history as a celebrity couturier, as the clothes and accessories worn by him, the letters written by him, now embody the man. The memories of him still incarnated in these objects by those who loved him, add another layer of meaning to my research, adding to the seductive power of the archive and collection. It is the close contact I have had with the very broad range of objects designed, drawn, painted, annotated, read, contemplated, worn and kept close by him that has affected me emotionally, brought me closer to the man, and enabled a closer understanding of his identity and his design practice, moving beyond the constraints of the documents mentioned in the introduction.

Through self-disclosure and autobiographical, personal criticism, I have examined my rationale for queering Hartnell's archive. I also hope to have demonstrated that the personal identity of the researcher has an impact on how they approach their subject of study and their methodology in the archive, that my personal sexual identity directly led to my thesis that the sexual identity of the practitioner has an impact upon his/her creative output.

Notes

1   My AHRC-funded doctoral thesis *A Life in the Archive: The Dress, Design and Identity of the London Couturier Norman Hartnell, 1921–1979*, University of Brighton, 2012, analysed Hartnell's house style and signature looks in terms of fabric, colour and embellishment, mapping his personal taste in women's clothes designed by him and made up in his dressmaking and embroidery workrooms onto his fashion and royal dress design.

2   *The Coronation of Elizabeth II*. Dir. Jamie Muir, Blakeway Productions. Monday 4 June 2012, BBC 4.

3   Since 2005, examples of Norman Hartnell's royal couture designed for Her Majesty, Queen Elizabeth, the late Queen Mother, and our current monarch Her Majesty Elizabeth II have been included in dress exhibitions at Buckingham Palace including: 'Queen Elizabeth's White Wardrobe, Paris 1938', 2005; 'Dress for the Occasion, An Exhibition of Her Majesty The Queen's Evening Dresses and Jewellery at the Summer Opening of Buckingham Palace', 2006; 'Buckingham Palace: A Royal Wedding', 2007; 'Queen and Commonwealth: The Royal Tour', 2009; and 'The Queen's Year: Exhibition for the Summer Opening of Buckingham Palace', 2010. The V&A 2007 exhibition, 'The Golden Age of Couture: Paris London 1947–1957' chose to display three examples of Hartnell's royal couture for Her Majesty Queen Elizabeth II and Her Majesty Princess Margaret. The year 2012 also saw examples of Hartnell couture displayed at both the exhibitions 'Ballgowns: British Glamour Since 1950', 19 May 2012–6 January 2013, and 'British Design 1948–2012: Innovation in the Modern Age', 31 March–12 August 2012.

4   *The Coronation of Elizabeth II*. Dir. Jamie Muir, Blakeway Productions. Monday 4 June 2012, BBC 4.

5   'The Making of a Monarchy for the Modern World', Kensington Palace, 6 June 2012.

6   V&A Summer School Seminar, 'Introducing Norman Hartnell', 11 July 2012.

8

Kitsch, Enchantment and Power

The Bleeding Statues of Templemore in 1920

Ann Wilson

Introduction

In August 1920 in Templemore, a town in County Tipperary in Ireland, a group of Catholic devotional images – small, mass-produced statues of the sort common in Irish Catholic homes at the time – allegedly began to bleed. This unusual phenomenon attracted large numbers of people to the area, many interpreting it as a manifestation of some sort of divine power and hoping to experience emotional comfort or healing from interaction with the images. The bleeding was first observed by a 16-year-old farm labourer named James Walsh, who also saw a vision of the Virgin Mary in his home in Curraheen, about 10 km from Templemore. Shortly afterwards, religious statues were seen to move and bleed 'from the mouth and heart' in the house in Curraheen, and in another house in Templemore where his uncle lived, a newsagent called Thomas Dwan (Anonymous, 1920a, p. 5). Accounts of these incidents were published in local and national Irish newspapers, and in *The New York Times* on 22 August 1920. Within a few days, crowds converged on Templemore and Curraheen, and by early September thousands of pilgrims were arriving daily (Anonymous, 1920g, p. 4). Hugh Martin, an English journalist visiting Templemore, recalled encountering 'a throng so enormous as to make eating and sleeping a matter of the utmost difficulty'. He noted that by 'early afternoon there were thousands in the square. They came on farm carts, ass carts, outside cars, Fords, and bicycles, as well as by train' (Martin, 1921, pp. 95–96).

The bleeding statues were displayed at Dwan's premises in the town. According to Joice and Sydney Loch in their book *Ireland in Travail*, 'There was an amazing scene in the yard at the back of the house, where the statues were placed upon a table covered with a white cloth. Townspeople and countrypeople, grandmothers, and their grandchildren, husbands, wives, knelt in a crowd about the table, murmuring their prayers, and touching the statues with beads and prayer-books' (1922, p. 73).

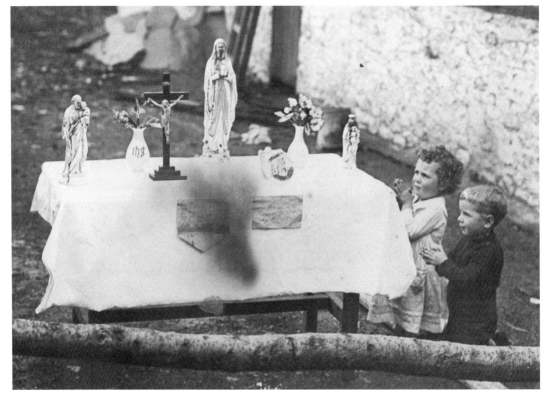

FIGURE 8.1 *Bleeding statues at Templemore, 1920, photo by W. D. Hogan. HOG183, courtesy of the National Library of Ireland.*

The phenomenon was also photographed (see Figure 8.1). An image from the W. D. Hogan collection in the National Library of Ireland, shows the table described by the Lochs, with two young children kneeling beside it, hands joined in prayer. The small, mass-produced objects placed on it, clearly displaying the stains from their bleeding, consist of a crucifix, a plaque showing the head of Christ with its crown of thorns, and three statues depicting Saint Joseph with the Christ Child, Our Lady of Lourdes, and Mary with the Christ Child.

Saint Sulpice and kitsch

The photograph shows these objects to have been very unremarkable examples of what became known as Saint Sulpice art, named after the area in Paris which during the nineteenth century became the worldwide centre for the sale of Catholic objects such as statues, holy cards and crucifixes (McDannell, 1995, pp. 168–170). Industrialized production led to the increased availability of vast quantities of religious images at very low prices, which also allowed for greater standardization and more Church control of their style and content. Catholic devotional images traditionally tended towards an idealized naturalism, in order to elicit a sense of spiritual connection and emotional elevation in the viewer who would be convinced by the lifelike 'truth' of what they were seeing, while being gently transported to a transcendent, heavenly state by its idealization. However, the imagery was mass-produced to such an enormous degree in media such as plaster and print, and with such varying levels of care and skill, that 'Saint Sulpice' progressively became a nickname for 'church art considered in bad taste'(Gamboni, 2007, p. 236). The French writer Émile Zola described it in his controversial novel *Lourdes* as characterized by 'a prettiness fit to make you cry, a silly sentimentality fit to make your heart turn with disgust!' (Zola, 1896, p. 419).

By the late nineteenth century, the majority of Catholic devotional images were of the Saint Sulpice type, and could be categorized as 'kitsch'; a term widely used in the twentieth century for cultural products that are cheap, derivative, formulaic and popular. A modern phenomenon, kitsch has been analysed by a succession of scholars who have concluded variously that it is a harmful and deceitful cultural weapon used by the powerful to charm and control the masses (Greenberg, 1939); that it is the product (and producer) of a class-based social system to which people adapt out of necessity (Bourdieu, 1979); or that it is a tool which can be manipulated by ordinary people to creatively construct and express their identities, functioning to reproduce but also resist the existing social order (De Certeau, 1984; Miller, 1987). More recently, Sam Binkley has introduced another way of approaching the relationship between humans and kitsch, arguing for a positive kitsch aesthetic that is deliberately not creative or critical, but which cultivates 'continuity, conformity and routine, which celebrate[s] sentiment and banality' and works in society 'to replenish stocks of ontological security, and to shore up a sense of cosmic coherence in an unstable world of challenge, innovation and creativity' (2000, pp. 134–135).

All these approaches have in common the fact that they grant considerable social power to kitsch, based on the way it works, or is made to work, within society, despite its low status within the traditional cultural hierarchy. This interest in the social functioning of everyday objects and images of all kinds, the power they can exercise, and their relationship with humans, has also been a recent focus of other disciplines such as social anthropology. Alfred Gell, for instance, has claimed that some images can have a particular agency in specific social and historical contexts, because the impact they have on a viewer evokes certain ideas and emotional states, and these ideas and emotional states in turn lead the viewer to take social action (1998, p. 12). Gell used the term 'enchantment' to describe the effect of such objects on a person, and claimed that many of the most powerful are 'crude and uninteresting artefacts, whose importance rests solely on their mediatory function in a particular social context' (1998, p. 68).

The Irish Roman Catholic context

Objects such as those that 'bled' in Templemore, despite their lowly aesthetic and economic status, had become associated with significant power and authority within the discourse of Roman Catholicism, a discourse that became increasingly influential in Ireland during the nineteenth century. Irish Catholicism in the early nineteenth century had been characterized by a heterogeneity of belief and practice, featuring a co-existence of orthodox, church-centred Roman Catholic beliefs and practices, popular devotions centred on pilgrimages and holy wells, and fairy beliefs. Irish devotions differed from related Catholic practices in other countries in some important respects. They tended, for instance, to focus on places in the landscape that had over time become associated with the sacred, such as mountain summits, islands, lakes, streams and springs; the latter generally referred to as holy wells. In a survey of pilgrimage shrines throughout Europe, Mary Lee Nolan has pointed out the importance in Ireland, compared to the rest of Europe, of natural objects and features like stones, trees and wells, as vehicles of holiness, and the relative unimportance of images (1983, p. 431). Michael Carroll has also noted what he terms the 'shapelessness' of Irish Catholicism, the 'clear predilection for objects that were relatively shapeless and nonfigurative ... piles of stones, pools of water, irregularly shaped boulders' and contrasts this with the focus on images of madonnas and saints in Mediterranean countries (1999, p. 49). This may have been a result of the iconoclasm associated with the Reformation of the sixteenth century, and the Penal Laws that were in force from 1691 to 1829, which meant that Ireland was precluded from having the level of religious material culture associated with other Catholic countries at this time.

From around the mid-nineteenth century, however, the Irish Church under the leadership of Cardinal Paul Cullen (1803–1878) increased its efforts to Romanize and standardize the behaviour of both its clergy and laity. Internationally, during this period, Catholicism was becoming characterized by a focus on, and a requirement to submit to, the Roman centre and an emphasis on the obedience and piety of the faithful, all of which marked the emergence of the Catholic Church as a highly unified international (or supra-national) entity. In Ireland, it built more and bigger churches so that Catholic practice could be contained and controlled within them as much as possible, and introduced numerous papally-sanctioned devotions so that Irish Catholics were regularly occupied with approved religious practices. By the late nineteenth century, a transformation, which Emmett Larkin has famously termed a 'devotional revolution', had taken place (1972). By the early twentieth century, popular Catholic piety had been significantly redirected towards the fixed, emphatically figurative and relatively semantically unambiguous imagery of international Roman Catholicism. This consisted of a small range of formulaic representations, principally statues and pictures of Christ shown crucified or as the Sacred Heart, of the Virgin with the Christ Child, and as Our Lady of Lourdes, the Immaculate Conception, Our Lady of Perpetual Succour, and Our Lady of Good Counsel, and of Saint Joseph (see Figures 8.2, 8.3, 8.4). These images were closely tied into, and promoted, the Rome-centred, authoritarian and anti-intellectual Catholicism, which became dominant throughout the Catholic world from the nineteenth century. They were given a special significance through prayers and devotions sanctioned and promoted by the Vatican, and in church buildings their physical placement on elaborate shrines and altars distinguished them as important and authoritative, but also as accessible and appealing to the faithful, who were invited to interact with them through prayer, touch, lighting candles and leaving gifts such as flowers.

Thus, even during peaceful, unremarkable times and in the absence of extraordinary manifestations such as bleeding, devotional images were given significant agency in Irish Catholicism. In his autobiography, for instance, Sean Ó Faoláin recalled childhood visits to the church of St Peter and Paul in early-twentieth-century Cork:

My mother often led me to pray at the tall crucifixion in the dim southwestern corner . . . As we knelt there under the pendent body of Christ, with the Magdalen, St John the Divine and the Virgin grouped sadly beneath, she never failed to whisper to me that the Virgin's foot had performed many miracles of healing. And sure enough (what further proof did I want?) I would, now and again, see a poor black-shawled woman pause there, rub the Virgin's foot with her spittle and then rub the spittle to her eyes, nose, lips, throat and heart, genuflect, sigh upward at the bleeding face of the Redeemer and shuffle away. The painted foot was worn to the white bone of its plaster by these pious rubbings.

Ó Faoláin, 1965, p. 19

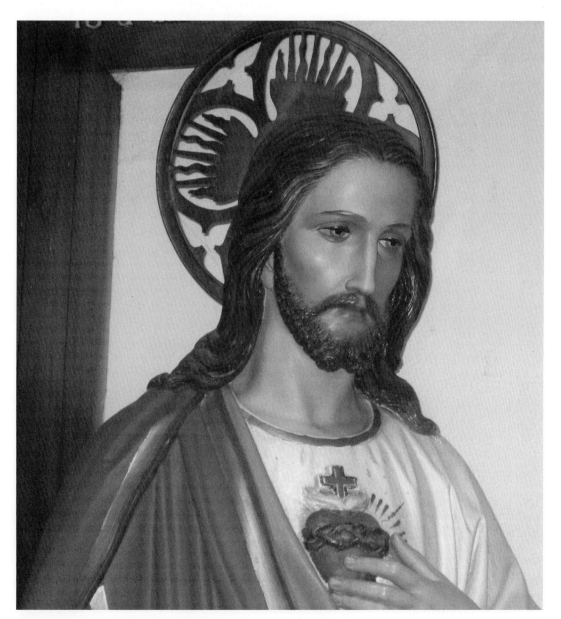

FIGURE 8.2 *Mayer & Co., Sacred Heart, statue detail, before 1925, Vincentian Church, Sunday's Well, Cork, 2009. Photograph by Ann Wilson.*

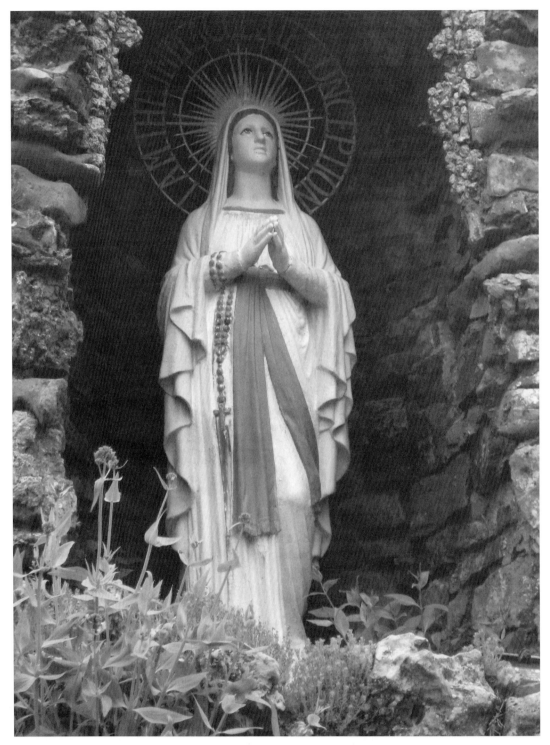

FIGURE 8.3 *Unknown maker, Lourdes grotto, detail, 1918, Church of St John the Baptist, Cashel, Co. Tipperary, 2009. Photograph by Ann Wilson.*

FIGURE 8.4 *Unknown maker,* Our Lady of Perpetual Succour, *painting, possibly 1867, St Alphonsus church, Limerick, 2009. Photograph by Jim Wilson.*

War and national identity

People in Templemore in August 1920, were experiencing anything but peaceful, unremarkable times. Between January 1919 and July 1921, a volunteer Irish Republican Army (IRA) fought a war of independence against British forces in Ireland, and local newspapers reported numerous violent incidents in the Templemore area, partly because of the Royal Irish Constabulary (RIC) barracks located there. In this atmosphere of heightened fear and tension, the bleeding of statues, which were already regarded as powerful Catholic mediators, became very meaningful, and could be readily interpreted by the town's citizens as a divine communication, a physical sign of empathy from the figures represented by the images, weeping blood in response to their sorrows. Many saw it as signalling a longed-for positive intervention, and the presence of the statues in Dwan's premises was regarded as having protected Templemore from complete destruction during an attack by the RIC on 20 August. It was claimed that 'our Lady had saved Templemore', and Walsh gathered people to kneel around the statues and recite the Rosary in Irish (Anonymous, 1920a, p. 5; Anonymous, 1920g, p. 4).

The bleeding statues were also seen as asserting the Catholic Irish identity of the population in the face of the non-Catholic British opponent, a superior spiritual power which would win out against the much more substantial, but merely worldly, advantages of the enemy. This was not the only time when international Catholic images were appropriated onto the side of the Irish. Our Lady of Lourdes, in particular, was considered by many Irish Catholics to have a special interest in, and identification with, Ireland. A Lourdes grotto in Cashel, a town about 30 km from Templemore, was erected in 1918 by the townspeople in gratitude for her role in the 'national struggle against conscription' (Anonymous, 1921, p. 6) (see Figure 8.3). It was consecrated in 1921 by John Harty, Archbishop of Cashel, whose speech on the occasion expressed both his gratitude at Ireland's avoidance of conscription, and his belief that Our Lady of Lourdes would shortly obtain Irish freedom from foreign rule. Our Lady of Perpetual Succour – a thirteenth- or fourteenth-century Byzantine painting which was (and still is) housed in the Redemptorist church of Saint Alphonsus at Via Merulana in Rome, copies of which were introduced to Ireland in the nineteenth century – was also seen as having a special interest in Ireland (see Figure 8.4). The Irish priest John Coyle even suggested that it might have been responsible for the downfall of the 'infamous Cromwell', the English leader whose army invaded Ireland in the seventeenth century:

> we may take it as at least a noteworthy coincidence that in the same year, 1658, in which the hunted exiles [Irish friars who fled from Cromwell's persecutions to Rome] knelt round the Picture of Our Lady of Perpetual Succour in Rome, praying for Ireland, Cromwell was called to his account, and Ireland and England rid of that bloodthirsty tyrant.
>
> Coyle, 1913, pp. 47–48

In August 1920, the bleeding of the holy statues changed the course of events, in that it resulted in an unofficial truce and temporary peace in Templemore, as the RIC withdrew because of the crowds of civilians now filling the town, and local IRA volunteers moved in and kept order, organizing traffic and helping the pilgrims, thus reinforcing the connection between the Catholic images and the fight for Irish freedom (Anonymous, 1920d, p. 1; Anonymous, 1920j, p. 6). These opportunist volunteers charged money for their services, which went into a fund for buying arms, and many of the more helpful also received tips from grateful pilgrims (Reynolds, 2006, pp. 24–25).

The IRA leadership allowed this situation to continue for about three weeks, after which they decided that it was no longer to their advantage, and that the war should be resumed. Some of the money given to the volunteers was being spent on alcohol, and discipline was loosening. They therefore brought the truce to an abrupt end by ambushing an RIC barracks on 29 September, killing two men and causing a series of reprisals which resulted in the mass exodus of pilgrims, stall-holders and other visitors. The town was emptied, and the statues stopped bleeding (Reynolds, 2006, p. 27). The extraordinary powers which they had suddenly manifested disappeared just as quickly, once the context changed.

The physical cause of the bleeding statues has never been definitively ascertained, nor whether it was intended as a prank or something more serious. While the majority of IRA men were practising Catholics, and many believed simply and unquestioningly in the supernatural power of the statues, the leadership of the organization was more sceptical and suspicious. A local delegation interviewed Walsh and concluded that he was either 'mentally abnormal or a hypocrite', and he was summoned to Dublin to be interrogated by Dan Breen, a senior IRA member, who decided he was a fake (Reynolds, 2006, pp. 25–26). A 'bleeding' statue, which may or may not have been one of those that performed in Templemore, was later broken, revealing inside an alarm-clock mechanism connected to a fountain-pen insert containing a mixture of sheep's blood and water, all of which was concealed inside the statue. Whether Walsh was an agent or a victim of deception was never established, but not long after the bleeding statues phenomenon he suddenly departed for Australia, voluntarily or otherwise, and never returned (Reynolds, 2006, p. 27).

Enchantment and agency

As well as fostering a sense of group identity and power in response to uncertainty and danger, the bleeding statues also attracted to the Templemore area large numbers of individuals with particular personal agendas, many of whom were willing to make long, uncomfortable and expensive journeys to see the images, or possibly even to make physical contact with them. The Lochs noted that the phenomenon particularly attracted 'the sick in body and the sick in soul', people with a need in their lives for the physical and emotional healing that they felt the objects could in some way facilitate (1922, p. 73). And, indeed, many miraculous effects were attributed to them (Anonymous, 1920d, p. 1; Anonymous, 1920h, p. 4; Anonymous, 1920i, p. 4). Cures were achieved through praying in front of or touching the statues, or by rubbing them against the afflicted area: 11-year-old Cornelius Galvin, for instance, was partially cured of 'acute hip disease' by having one of Dwan's bleeding statues rubbed against his hip, and after Walsh rubbed a bleeding crucifix on the badly injured knee of a young soldier called Martin Monaghan, the latter was reported to have regained almost full use of his leg (Anonymous, 1920b, p. 2; Anonymous, 1920k, p. 6). Such was the intensity of the communal emotional atmosphere that a Catholic RIC constable was alleged to have resigned his job and entered a religious order after a statue he owned began to bleed, and a soldier was reported to have converted to Catholicism (Anonymous, 1920c, p. 5). Other strange phenomena in the area were also noted around this time, including a number of apparitions of the Virgin and the emergence of a spring – which briefly became known as a 'holy well' and was associated with healing powers – from the floor of Walsh's bedroom (Anonymous, 1920d, p. 1; Anonymous, 1920e, p. 4). The Templemore incident highlights the fact that Irish Catholics were perfectly happy to combine the use of mass-produced Roman Catholic imagery with older strategies for harnessing the supernatural, instead of replacing one with the other. Therefore, as was the case before the 'devotional revolution', a range of apparently incompatible belief systems seems to have comfortably co-existed.

The enthusiasm with which Irish Catholics embraced devotional images, and the extent of the powers granted them, caused debate in the late nineteenth and early twentieth centuries. Some Catholic commentators saw their social power as a force for good in Irish society, enabling people to deal with the very harsh conditions of their lives. W. J. Lockington, for instance, a Jesuit priest visiting Ireland from New Zealand, was very impressed with the interaction between Irish Catholics and religious images, and in a passage which itself gives a very active role to the images discussed, describes the way this interaction helped people come to terms with their difficult lives:

> It tore one's very heartstrings to enter those poor rooms [of Irish cabins], and, by the flickering light of the shrine lamp, see our Lady of Perpetual Succour looking across the room at a worn and gasping saint lying paralysed and pain-twisted; or to see our Lady of Lourdes trying to comfort a poor widow as she kneels at the desolate hearth . . . And impossible as it may seem, our Blessed Lady does accomplish her task.
>
> Lockington, 1920, p. 15

The writer Michael McCarthy, on the other hand, responded with 'a feeling of disgust' to a scene he witnessed in front of a Calvary in the Augustinian church in Thomas Street in Dublin:

> I saw them tremblingly put forth their dirty right hands and rub the palms and backs of them against the coloured clay of the statue of the Virgin, moving their hands over its breast and arms and hands. And then I saw them rub their hands, after contact with the statue, against their own dirty foreheads.
>
> McCarthy, 1902, pp. 332–333

McCarthy concluded that 'those are the Irish who cannot get on in life. This is the teaching they get; this is the religion to which they sacrifice their lives' (1902, p. 333). Both Lockington and McCarthy perceive that Irish Catholics are susceptible to enchantment, in Gell's sense, by devotional images, as well as socially constructed and differentiated by that susceptibility, as in Bourdieu's model. Lockington sees the resulting social agency as a force for good, helping people to cope with difficult circumstances, whereas for McCarthy it is pernicious, one of the factors keeping Irish people at a primitive level of social and economic development. As David Morgan has observed, the problem that iconoclasts – opponents of religious images–have with them is not that they are empty and powerless, but, as with Greenberg's conception of kitsch, their danger lies in the fact that they are *too* powerful: 'not that they are vacant signifiers propped up by human vanity but that they possess an autonomy, a life of their own, a power over the human imagination' (2005, p. 142).

However, many Catholic clergy also reportedly responded with reserve and caution to the bleeding statues in Templemore. The prescribed (as opposed to actual) role, if any, of religious images in the lives of the faithful has in fact always been a problematic issue for the Christian Church. From its inception, great powers were granted to them – in the seventh century, for instance, paintings of the Virgin were recorded as having saved Constantinople from its enemies (Belting, 1994, pp. 495–496). Nevertheless, in response to repeated iconoclastic challenges, the official Church institution has needed to continually make a clear distinction between acceptable

Christian veneration of an image, because of what it represents, and what could very easily be perceived as unacceptable pagan idolatry of the image itself, in its own right. The decrees of the Second Council of Nicaea (AD 787), therefore, endorsed the value of using Christian images, but limited that use to 'veneration', emphasizing that 'he who venerates the image, venerates the person represented in that image' (quoted in Belting, 1994, p. 506).

In the thirteenth century, Saints Thomas Aquinas (c. 1225–1274) and Bonaventure (1221–1274) formulated three main justifications for religious imagery, which have provided the basis for the institutional Church approach ever since: to educate people, especially the illiterate; to help people memorize religious truths; and to excite religious emotion. The Protestant Reformation, which began in 1517, challenged the Church structure of beliefs and practices, including the use of imagery, resulting in the fragmentation of Christianity and producing some iconoclastic Protestant groupings. However, the Catholic Counter Reformation reasserted its endorsement of religious imagery at the twenty-fifth session of the Council of Trent in December 1563. Again, to ward off accusations of idolatry, the decrees of Trent, which formed the basis for nineteenth-century Roman Catholicism, specifically deny any power to images themselves, insisting that there is no question that 'any divinity or virtue is believed to be in them on account of which they are to be worshipped; or that anything is to be asked of them' (Buckley, 1851, p. 215). The section on 'Veneration of Images', written in 1910 for the *Catholic Encyclopaedia*, emphasized that natural law 'forbids the obvious absurdity of addressing prayers or any sort of absolute worship to a manufactured image', but argues that this is not a problem so long as the prototype (the thing that is represented) is worshipped, and not the sign (the representation itself), and that the two remain clearly differentiated (Fortescue, 1910).

In relation to the Templemore statues, many of the clergy became uncomfortable with the extraordinary powers with which they became associated: one priest was reported to have declared that the people were 'stark mad', and another spoke out publicly against the statues and advised his parishioners to shun them. The parish priest of Cashel, Monsignor Innocent Ryan, urged people in a letter to the press not to put their faith in statues or crucifixes, but in the Blessed Sacrament, reaffirming the centrality of the Eucharist (rather than wonder-working images) in Catholic belief and practice (Ryan, 1920, p. 6). However, when Walsh visited Ryan to show him how the miracle worked, a large crowd gathered outside, and 'to relieve the situation, and to satisfy the devotion of the people, one of these statues was given to the public to kiss or touch in the spacious yard before the church' (Anonymous, 1920f, p. 3). Thus the priest's authority was forced to yield before the potency of the images, and presenting the statue to the public in front of the church can only be seen as a form of damage limitation, an effort to link its power to the Church institution, rather than vice versa. On another occasion, a group of prominent Templemore citizens gathered around the statues to offer prayers aloud in thanks for their protection of the town against RIC attacks, seemingly without the usual need for a clerical mediator (Anonymous, 1920a, p. 5).

Conclusion

Catholic images have always had the capacity, in certain contexts, to exercise great social power. Their mass-production in the nineteenth century increased this, since there were more of them distributed more widely, while also allowing greater control and standardization of their content and style by the Church. The accessible, sentimental and repetitive aesthetic of many of these mass-produced images put them into the category of kitsch, and, if anything, enhanced rather than diminished their power to convince, reassure and enchant on a mass scale.

The Templemore phenomenon highlights the potential agency of such objects in Ireland in 1920, and how it could be harnessed by different groups with often conflicting agendas. The Church establishment successfully deployed devotional images to charm and control the population, as in Greenberg's model, but Irish Catholics also put them to uses that suited their own needs, so that they functioned not only to console and reassure, as Binkley argues, but also to construct, bolster and assert group and national identity, suggesting, in line with Miller's thesis, an active creativity on the part of the Catholic masses, with its potential for resisting as well as reproducing the social order, rather than a merely passive obedience.

In the tense and violent context of Templemore in 1920, the bleeding statues for a brief period greatly exceeded the limitations imposed by official Church discourse on the social role of devotional images, and even those of the much wider norms of popular Catholicism, first by their bleeding and then by the wave of miraculous apparitions and cures with which they were associated, to the extent that they threatened the authority of the very institution from which they derived their power in the first place. Their history suggests that kitsch, in certain contexts, can be a very powerful social agent, neither good nor bad in itself but capable of being used by different groups in the service of either, or both, and also, once deployed, difficult to direct and restrain.

9

'Magic Toyshops'

Narrative and Meaning in the Women's Sex Shop

Fran Carter

Introduction

For the last 20 years, British women have been able to buy sexual objects in shops dedicated not only to the pursuit of female pleasure, but to a notion of female empowerment achieved through the consumption of highly designed sexualized goods. The concept of the shop selling sex products specifically, if not exclusively, to women arguably arrived with Sh!, a female-oriented sex shop situated in London's Hoxton. Opened in 1992 by owners Kathryn Hoyle and Sophie Walters, the shop made an explicit challenge to the traditional notion of the sex shop as an exclusively male domain.[1] Myla, selling sex toys alongside luxury lingerie, came to London's Notting Hill in 1999, and Sam Roddick's luxury erotic boutique Coco de Mer arrived in Covent Garden in 2001. Other shops have followed elsewhere: Nua, which has franchises in Brighton, Manchester and Sheffield; Tickled and She Said in Brighton amongst them.[2] Conceived 'as an antidote to sleazy sex shops' (Sh!, 2013), the women's sex shop has had to radically reposition itself within the market in order to distance itself from the image of murky anonymity inspired by the 'traditional' male-oriented sex shop, which inhabits both the urban back streets of our larger cities and the hinterlands of our imaginations.

Material culture's engagement with consumption prioritizes the 'transformative capacities people possess when they deal with objects' (Woodward, 2007, p. 26). The designed spaces of the sex shop, as well as the objects for sale in them, surely do cultural work on behalf of prevailing discourses around female sexuality, offering a plurality of sexualized identities to women realized through the consumption of 'love objects' in which notions of sexual agency are invested via design. Thus, the women's sex shop materializes, and indeed relies upon, a discourse of empowerment in order to sell its sexualized products to women. While shops may differ in terms of the ethos they propose and the particular narratives they employ, all engage with an understanding widely circulated in current popular culture that through the consumption of practices such as pole dancing, neo-burlesque or the purchase of luxury underwear and designer sex toys, women are empowering themselves, borrowing from forums and practices once associated with female subjectivity and subverting them in complex ways to facilitate explorations of female sexual agency: 'The sexualisation of contemporary British culture has in part been enabled by a neo-liberal rhetoric of agency, choice and self-determination, which within sexuality discourses have produced an "up for it" femininity, a sexually savvy and active woman who can participate appropriately in consumer practices in the production of her choice biography' (Evans *et al.*, 2010, p. 115). Sh!, She Said, Coco de Mer *et al.* utilize a range of visual strategies both inside and outside the shops in order to re-gender and re-code shops as specifically feminine environments. Sh!, for example, presents a violently sugar-pink façade to the street, while Coco de Mer has archly beautiful windows featuring a tasteful assemblage of curiously suggestive and expensive 'objets d'art' (see Figure 9.1). Variously, these shops seek to normalize female sexual consumption by positioning it within the apparently oppositional frameworks of both domesticity and style, thus, on the one hand, the design of shop interiors may reference a supermarket and, on the other, a turn of the century bordello.

It is this process of transformation constructed in spaces and things that frames the interests of this essay. It takes as a fundamental premise that women's motives, meanings and experiences in shopping for sexualized objects *matter* in terms of theorizing contemporary sexual cultures. Moreover, it is the adoption of a methodology that prioritizes the lived experience of consumers, which is central to the notion of incorporating what Woodward calls the 'multiple interpretations, practices and manipulations' of consumers as they negotiate the slippery meanings of sexualized objects and spaces (Woodward, 2007, p. 4). Drawing on a number of interviews carried out with women sex shoppers, this essay draws out the complexities

FIGURE 9.1 *The exterior of Coco de Mer in London's Covent Garden. Photograph by Fran Carter.*

and contradictions inherent in the embodied challenge made by the women's sex shop to the dominant sexual paradigm invested in the design of the 'traditional' male sex shop.[3] Overwhelmingly, it asks how women read and negotiate the various and sometimes contradictory constructions of feminine sexual fulfilment embedded in the objects on offer in the women-orientated sex shop.

The imagined sex shop

The heterosexual male sex shop is represented by some of my participants as 'threatening', 'male dominated', 'intimidating' and overwhelmingly, by almost all participants, as 'uncomfortable' for the female consumer. However, evidence suggests that for the women interviewed it is impossible to 'imagine' the women-focused sex shop without a corresponding 'imagining' of the male shop, and thus the masculine sex shop becomes the 'defining model' for all conceptions of the female-orientated shop. Visually, the image of the traditional sex shop looms large in the collective female imagination, its stereotypical location on a dingy side alley in an area characterized by its bookmakers, barber shops and tagareen stores, the sweetly cloying smell of years of furtive urination around a darkened doorway, the grimy blacked-out windows with their stuttering neon signs – the women I interviewed uniformly constructed the male sex shop using the terms 'seedy', 'sordid' or 'sleazy' (see Figure 9.2). While some women had been inside

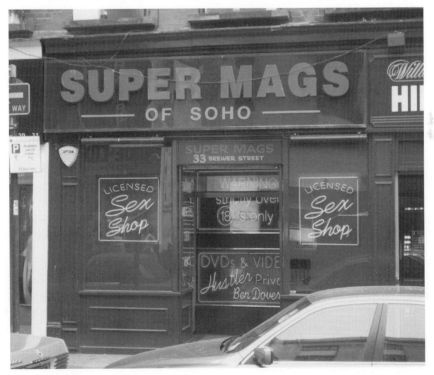

FIGURE 9.2 *The 'traditional' sex shop with its opaque frontage and neon signage, Soho, London. Photograph by Fran Carter.*

'traditional' male sex shops, others had not, but the traditional sex shop was still a fertile and persistent presence throughout interviews:

> I imagine it as being dark, my imagining is that they're not particularly clean, tidy and neat because the outsides often look so grubby . . . Erm, my imagining is lots and lots of magazines with covers with pornographic pictures of women that would make me very uncomfortable . . . I have this idea that they sell things that would make me uncomfortable; I can't think what they would be but . . .

> Louise

While the imagined sex shop is a familiar story in many of the accounts gathered for this research, there is an alternative narrative to be found lurking in the spaces left by the first; one of exploration, curiosity, the desire to make a purchase, even an attempt at feminine colonization of a wholly masculine sphere. Therefore, overwhelmingly, the women's sex shop must be conceptualized in opposition to this notion of the traditional sex shop, its existence and its materialization is dependent on it being '*different to*', on its '*not being*' 'the kind of place that dirty old men go to in the middle of Soho . . . the sort of place that sort of men in raincoats might go to and you get paper, erm you get things in paper bags' (Sexy Kitten). The women-focused shop must represent itself as a necessary corollary to the potential threat of the male-focused sex shop, the 'safe space' in which women may consume sexual goods framed as sexual freedoms, the consumption of pleasure without danger. If the sex shop is to be re-made, then new feminized narratives must eclipse those of the paradigmatic masculine shop and, here, design is utilized as key to this project of reappropriation.

'Posh means you can walk in anywhere'

Interview participants testified that it is the '*poshing up*' of products, product display and interior spaces that is the overwhelmingly significant strategy by which the sex shop is 'made over'. While an uneasy symbiosis between aesthetics and the notion of female sexual empowerment is at the centre of its appeal, women's sexual consumption emerges as semantically complex. The coding of objects and spaces as upmarket and aesthetically appealing must also work hard to provide an *alibi* for the consumption of sexualized objects, as Kate suggests, explaining the luxuriousness of Coco de Mer: 'It wants to make it look like there's nothing wrong with it'. This strategy, however, was not successful with all participants. Anna is 'disappointed' by the nature of Sh!'s products, which she feels embody a kind of 'soft', sensual construction of female sexuality:

> To be honest I was a little bit disappointed, I thought because it was predominantly female orientated it might be . . . I expected more, I don't know what exactly I expected more of but I expected it to be a bit more out there maybe, or . . . it almost seemed like a gift shop . . . in a way . . . you could buy sort of candles, like a boxed set with candles and massage oil and condoms and things like that.

> Anna

Anna resents the lack of challenge to a normative sexual narrative embodied in the shop and its products. Furthermore, for Veronica, the luxuriousness of the shop and the aestheticizing of the product do not serve to make female sexual consumption more acceptable, but neutralize the object:

> I think I felt a look but don't touch kind of thing, it did very much seem to be, even designer, which is a little bit crazy at the end of the day most of the things are just going one hole or another . . . I think it made the sexual experience very detached and I think there's a very detached feeling about it, that it's something that you wouldn't . . . That you would put on your table rather than actually use . . . I did feel it was much less sexual, that you wouldn't use these things.
>
> Veronica

Attwood (2005) recognizes the centrality of 'style and fashion' to the marketing of women's sexual products, but takes it as axiomatic that a proliferation of products purporting to provide a technologically assisted orgasm means that masturbation is a key discourse in sexual consumption:

> In the instance of marketing sex products to women, style and fashion have become particularly important resources in constructing a safe language for the repackaging of sex as a pleasure for women. The foregrounding of auto-eroticism is also key in this process, as evidenced by the speed with which the Rabbit vibrator has become one of the most visible contemporary signs of active female sexuality.
>
> Attwood, 2005, p. 395

In contrast, Veronica's emphatic assertion that the extreme aestheticizing of some sexualized products obscures, even nullifies, their function is echoed by Annabel in discussing the presentation of goods at Coco de Mer:

> It's almost like it's not really about sex – almost . . . some of the objects in Coco de Mer are designed to not look like they're anything to do with sex somehow. I mean there are some phallic shapes as far as I can remember there are some phallic shaped dildos, vibrators whatever but there's also these odd kind of ones, is there one called the Bone? . . . I don't know what it could be, but it doesn't look like a sex toy or a vibrator. So it's a sex shop that's trying very hard to almost be not a sex shop.
>
> Annabel

The Bone is a toy designed by product designer Tom Dixon. Made from a nine-inch wedge of hygienic resin, the sculptural shape is reminiscent of a hipbone or perhaps a Brancusi sculpture, and sells for approximately £120 (see Figure 9.3). While at the 2012 London Design Festival, Dixon proposed that most sex toys 'are . . . far removed from the pleasure and sensuality of the act' (Drumm, 2012, p. 26). Ironically, his statement inverts the observations of both Veronica and Annabel, whose testimonies concur that in the context of high design the sexualized object itself becomes desexualized.

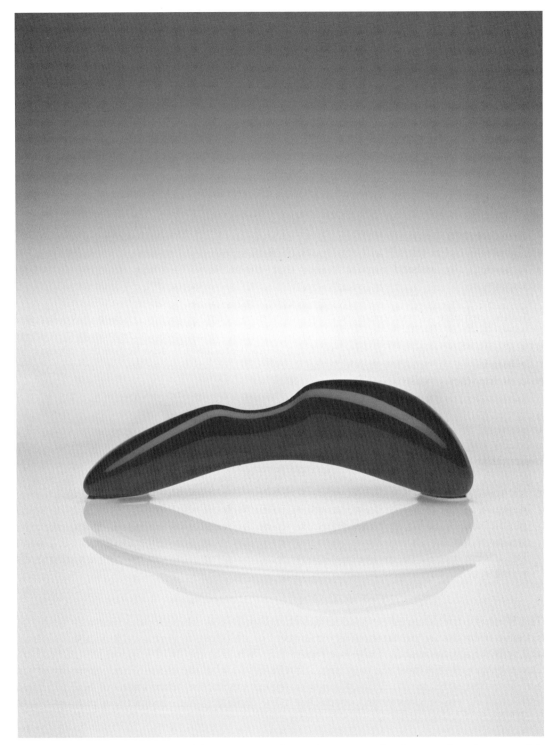

FIGURE 9.3 *The Bone, designed by Tom Dixon for Myla, an upmarket lingerie shop first opened in 1999 in London's Notting Hill. Courtesy of Tom Dixon Studio.*

Kate and Marley, however, are more sympathetic to the signifying properties of stylish goods and interior spaces, illustrating in what ways these draw on existing design genres to make an appeal to women via the use of an already familiar narrative of feminine sexuality:

K: Isn't Coco de Mer, haven't they got like a . . . Is it them that's got a sofa'y chaise
     longue thing? Is that them and a big table in the front, haven't they got a lot of like
     gilt, the gold . . .[inaud]
M: If I'm thinking of the right place, it's quite lavish and quite like lovely and luxurious
     and it's not . . . it doesn't make you [inaud]
K: It makes you think of burlesque and things like that, like not particularly like seedy
     and . . .
M: Not seedy and horrible and . . .
K: But it's not tacky or funny either.
M: It's stylish and it looks high end because it's decorated lavishly and for that reason it
     doesn't feel horrible.

Kate and Marley

For them, burlesque acts as a sort of design shorthand for a style of sexuality already well established as not only chic, but drawing on a post-feminist identity, which prioritizes style and irony. Thus, shops such as Coco de Mer, Sh! and She Said exploit visual motifs and styles, which code interiors and products via a particular style of mediated femininity that foregrounds sexual display. The rococo exuberance, which characterizes Coco de Mer's interior space, Sh!'s vivid pink paint, ostrich feather corset or *fin de siècle* style chaise longue, all come with their own set of associations or significations around female sexuality for those design-savvy consumers, such as Kate and Marley, who can read them (see Figure 9.4). The popularity of neo-Burlesque since the early 1990s has spawned an associated aesthetic style, which loosely references the late nineteenth century and relies more perhaps on a nostalgic notion of the boudoir or bordello than a bawdy stage variety show. It has, however, retained a sense of self-parody or irony, which has enabled it to be seen as reappropriation rather than female subjectification. Attwood, citing Rosalind Gill (2007), suggests that burlesque forms 'part of the development of a postfeminist sensibility "organized around notions of choice, empowerment, self-surveillance, and sexual difference, and articulated in an ironic and knowing register"' (Attwood, 2011, p. 204).

Essentially in Britain, neo-burlesque has been adopted by a middle class, stereotypically Brighton-living cognoscenti who espouse its claims to female empowerment on the part of both performers and its largely female audience and thus as a style of interior décor, 'burlesque' as materialized in furnishings, colour ways and wallpapers, is uniquely appropriate to the women's sex shop. Attwood draws on Debra Ferreday (2008) in suggesting that:

The construction of the vintage feminine 'look' associated with neo-burlesque (Ferreday, 2008) also challenges practices of femininity which are 'grounded in shame', focused on 'erasure' and 'disguise', and which conceal both the labour and the anxiety that they involve. In contrast, vintage femininity is shame-less, foregrounds an alternative D.I.Y. approach and resists 'the notion that feminism and femininity are mutually exclusive, and that the enthusiastic pleasure taken in feminine identity is inherently problematic.

Attwood, 2011, p. 206

FIGURE 9.4 *The interior of Sh! is clearly coded to denote femininity while the ostrich feathered, corseted costume also references burlesque style. Photograph by Fran Carter.*

This account of neo-burlesque chimes closely with the expressed rationale of the women's sex shop. Furthermore, thanks 'to the fashion for sleaze style and the love of irony on the part of "cool" tastemakers' (McRobbie, 2004, p. 1), the ubiquity of 'porn chic' has provided an additional context and a consumer sympathy for styles that are generally understood as signalling a 'knowing' or 'empowering' style of female sexuality. 'Porn chic' is a term used variously by both academic and popular writers to describe the appropriation of codes and conventions of masculinist pornography by other areas of culture such as advertising, fashion photography, dance, and so on, 'producing texts which constantly refer to, pastiche, parody and deconstruct the latter' (McNair, 2002, p. 61). In that Coco de Mer's rococo flock wallpaper may be constructed as 'pastiche', and all the shops (and the goods for sale in them) under discussion here are certainly aestheticized, the women's sex shop might be said to fit neatly into McNair and McRobbie's construction of the genre. Interestingly, Emily makes an emphatic link between 'ethics' and the upmarket nature of Coco de Mer's design aesthetic. She identifies the 'classiness' of the designed products for sale as a way of establishing the acceptability or validity of female sexual consumption: 'So it's easier to go to Coco de Mer and make it a bit posh because if it's got a diamond on it, it can't be utterly disgusting and depraved. Which is fine by me, actually – disgusting and depraved. But I think for a lot of people they find it very difficult' (Emily).

McNair's assertion that 'such texts *must* be sanitized, if they are to find a space in mainstream culture' sits well with Emily's account of the effect of moving female sexuality upmarket (2002, p. 72). But while the 'text' must be 'sanitized' to be acceptable as a part of mainstream consumer culture, the women's sex shop must still occupy the liminal space lying between 'acceptability' and challenge (to a hegemonic male sexual archetype) in order that it may be permitted to make its particular offer of sexual self-actualization or empowerment to women. It is this challenge, implicit in neo-burlesque style, that serves to increase the commodity value of the women's sex shop: 'And statements of rebellion and opposition are, in this economy, just as saleable as, if not more so than, those of submission to, or acceptance of, the state of things as they are' (McNair, 2002, p. 10).

Thus, if a sexual commodity must speak at once of both challenge and of acceptability, in what other ways is design utilized in order to comfort and reassure the occasionally tentative consumer of the women's sex shop? My participants suggest that one way in which it does this is through a discourse of 'fun'.

Fun in the sex shop

Several women prioritize the fun and humour encapsulated in the products for sale in the women's sex shop. Louise, for example, who is overwhelmingly positive about Sh!'s women-centric ethos, stresses this notion repeatedly: 'It's very fun, very open and a very fun atmosphere . . . [and later] . . . it looked very friendly and cheerful and bright and fun really . . . There wasn't anything that would make me feel uncomfortable, pictures on the walls or magazines on display that would make me feel uncomfortable' (Louise). Louise stresses that it is, at least in part, the fun and playfulness that have contributed to her feeling 'comfortable' not only with sexual consumption but ultimately with her own sexuality. The following exchange between Georgina and Melanie, who are discussing the display table of vibrators situated on the ground floor of Sh!, further draws on the normalizing and 'sanitizing' power of 'fun' (see Figure 9.5). Here, it is the 'fun' that enables Georgina and Melanie to engage actively with what might otherwise have been challenging objects:

G: It wasn't too kind of formal 'oh this is 1700 watts'. It was like 'do you need to close the door' or 'do you need to turn the music up' sort of thing which was quite amusing! And all the ones which looked interesting were all you 'had to turn the music up'.

M: They have all these little features, double features and the more features the louder obviously, because all the workings are very loud. I think it was really good that they had that table in the middle because you feel like you're almost gathering round, again it was just like women looking at tops, it was exactly the same thing. You know picking them up and reading and looking and then picking another one and there's no sense of discomfort or awkwardness which is what I would have expected if I went to a normal sex shop and maybe there were men loitering around.

Melanie and Georgina

Here, Sh!'s table of vibrators utilises three discourses – fun, everyday consumption and women's shopping as social activity. Melanie is clear that it is this sense of familiarity and light-heartedness, these normalizing discourses, that ease sexual consumption in terms of making it accessible to women. The narrative of fun is played out in the design of vibrators, dildos, anal stimulators and so on, many of which privilege humour and whimsy alongside high performance technology and saturated colours. Alongside infinite variations on the inevitable rabbit theme, anthropomorphized dildos and vibrators feature bright primary colours and happy, smiling faces. A range from German company Fun Factory is distinguished by names such as, 'Flexi Felix', 'Dolly Dolphin', 'Dinky Digger' and 'Paddy Penguin': 'Paddy Penguin . . . is a companion in demand for those late hours of the night. With his diverse structure, tantalizing curve and a tapered nose which stimulates spot-on, this little guy in tailcoats spreads pleasure wherever he goes' (Fun Factory online catalogue, 2013).

In the specific context of the women's sex shop, the product has been, in McNair's term 'sanitized' (2002, p. 72). The toy has been 'domesticated', its potency dulled via a performance in which the object has transformed its identity in order to communicate the soothing message that sexual consumption in the women's sex shop is 'ok absolutely, or *more ok*' (Hoyle). In the case of the sex toy, however, it is the challenging element that constitutes the object's power; it

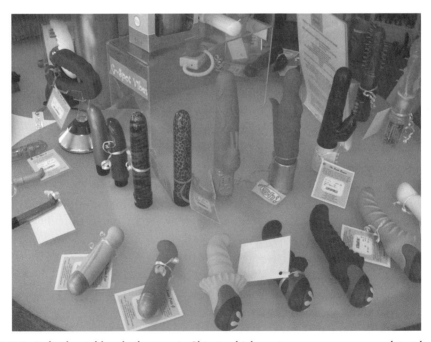

FIGURE 9.5 *A display table of vibrators in Sh! at which customers are encouraged to play with the goods. Photograph by Fran Carter.*

is vital that the sexual commodity treads a twisted path between the perverse and the domestic if it is to contribute to 'empowering' the female consumer through a project of appropriation.

However, just as the harnessing of high design as an alibi for female sexual consumption is problematic for some participants, the sanitizing power of 'fun' may have complex significations. Ann Summers is characterized by participants as: 'high streety' (Kate), a place for 'for having a laugh with people really ... it was just tacky and disgusting' (Emily), 'it's a bit commercial' (Anna), it is 'a different category of place' (Annabel). The style of 'fun' in evidence in the various novelty products available at Ann Summers (the Inflatable Willy Ball, Glow in the Dark Willy Straws, Clone a Pussy Moulding Kit and so on), is one element of a tranche of markers utilized by my participants in distinguishing the high street store from Sh!, Coco de Mer, She Said and others. Thus, having fun in the sex shop potentially involves a sophisticated reading of tone and nuance in order to distinguish between the fun that is not simply 'sanitizing' but confers a level of legitimacy on women's sexual consumption – and the tacky fun, which my participants associate with Ann Summers, as expressed here by Emily:

> I think Ann Summers is for men.
> 	Yes? That's interesting. What makes you say that?
> [laughing] Because everything's so disgusting and tacky and erm you know like they have plastic underwear. ... Ann Summers is marketed towards women who are driven by what they think men want. Like you know nurses outfits and I'm sure that's alright for people but it's the – it's tacky.
>
> Emily

For Emily, the version of fun on offer in Sh! is 'slightly different' to that on offer in Ann Summers. It is 'driven by what they [women] think men want'. Furthermore, for Louise, critique of Ann Summers also coalesces around class distinctions: 'It was like kind of going into the Primark equivalent of sex toys, you know ... It was just a very bargain basement, cheap type of experience, where Sh! made me feel really positive and excited' (Louise).

Conclusion

Thus, for the female consumer to access a form of sexual empowerment that may be seen as truly agentic in nature, it is necessary to have the *right type* of fun in the *right kind* of sex shop. Overwhelmingly, the transformative power of goods rests on design that accesses notions of 'fun' without 'tackiness'. To achieve this balance, goods must harness the various classed discourses of luxury and aesthetics and moreover, while the design of goods must retain some element of subversive power – a 'memory' of the 'perverse' – objects must be sufficiently removed from pornographic stylings to be understood as offering access to a discourse around agentic sexual expression. While Attwood suggests that 'sexual representations, products and services are becoming accessible to a wider group of consumers' (Attwood, 2006, p. 82), my participants represent their relationship with the women's sex shop and its goods as involving a negotiation between complex and often contradictory embedded meanings, which coexist in a state of tension. While all shops seek overwhelmingly to code themselves in opposition to the traditional male-focused shop, design here is understood by consumers as a project of distinction or differentiation as much as facilitation. For while these aestheticized goods and spaces may propose, to use Emily's term, a 'palatable' version of feminine sexuality, they may also serve to regulate access to participation in the discourse of sexual self-empowerment proffered, since that access may be dependent on certain class and taste understandings on the part of the consumer. While design elements borrowed from the traditional sex shop have been reappropriated and re-coded to denote feminine sexual empowerment, the objects for sale in the women's sex shop and the spaces in which they are displayed also retain for some women potent traces of other, and older, masculinist significations.

Notes

1   Ann Summers shops were bought in 1972 by Ralph and David Gold, developed from a 'traditional' sex shop into an established high-street brand. While Ann Summers does portray itself as 'woman friendly', most of my research participants did not identify the brand as a 'women's sex shop' for various reasons outlined in part in this essay.

2   Some changes have inevitably taken place during the life of this research. Tickled has now been taken over by She Said and Nua no longer exists in Brighton; its premises have been taken over by another branch of She Said.

3   Fifteen women were interviewed at different times over the life of this research but predominantly in 2007 and 2008. Research focused on in-depth, semi-structured interviews with consumers, but a sex shop owner, a shop manager and a designer of sex toys were also interviewed. Participants were accessed via a number of methods, most successfully from leaflets placed in Sh! and snowballing. Analysis of the data drew on the work of Mauthener and Doucet's 'Reflections on a Voice Centred Relational Method of Data Analysis' (1998).

SECTION 4

Mediating Relationships

10

Material Memories

The Making of a Collodion Memory-Text

Christina Edwards

Introduction

Rather than about concretely depicted and absent objects, photography is about the temporality of unconscious thought processes: the wish to see more, a wish that will never be fulfilled. But the essential dynamism of photographs lies in their implosive character . . . We can never quite understand them. It is not a question of nostalgia or of bygone days, but rather of filling out incomplete emanations of the past oneself. Photography has an essentially enigmatic nature which forces us to interrogate it. In front of a [family] photograph, we become archaeologists, the image reactivates affective, obtuse, uneasy time – the time of memory.

Sandbye, 1999, p. 184

It is said that it is impossible to cross the same river twice. This could also be said of viewing a photograph – the image may appear to be the same, but the interpretation and response to the photograph will be different, as the viewer in the present has altered with time. In the repeated viewing of a family photograph, other memories become interlinked with the original image. Indeed, it is a similar phenomenon to memory itself – the more often a memory is replayed, the deeper the groove, the easier it is to access – the more an image is viewed, the greater a part of our own mythology it becomes. According to Susan Engel:

We all tend to put ourselves at the centre of the past. Why else create one? Why else remember? Even when we recall events that had ramifications for others, events in which we played a small part, we tend to magnify our own role and shift things so that they more directly relate to us . . . If five people were involved in an event, each will tell of that event so that he or she, the teller, appears as the central character.

Engel, 1999, p. 4

Family, memory, photography

In 2008, I was awarded a PhD in Fine Art Practice, with the award equally weighted between a final exhibition and a written thesis. The exhibition 'Material Memories' consisted of a collection of ambrotypes and cyanotypes and took place at the School of Art, University of Wales, Aberystwyth, from February to March. The images were created by projecting transparencies from my family archive onto sensitized glass plates using the wet collodion process. Ambrotypes are collodion negative images on glass, which when viewed against a black background appear as positive images. The 125 glass plates were exhibited on a black box-like structure, with a ledge surrounding the structure on which the plates rested (see Figure 10.1). Along a shallow shelf around the gallery were cyanotype prints, which were printed from the glass plates, in nineteenth-century daylight printing frames. 'Material Memories' was a meditation on the function and place of family photographs – the images came in and out of view as the visitor walked round the central display – from negative to positive, the free-transformation of silver on glass lending these vernacular images a particular and distinct appearance elevated and recontextualized. Images usually viewed in a domestic setting were made public, transformed through the disparity of process and subject.

FIGURE 10.1 *Christina Edwards, 'Material Memories' exhibition, School of Art, University of Wales, Aberystwyth, February 2008, courtesy of Christina Edwards.*

My mother died on 11 March 2006; my father on 26 June 2001. This re-visioning I had been exploring through my family archive became more urgent, my grief contributed a longing, a need to comprehend and to cope with loss. Re-reading Roland Barthes' *Camera Lucida* (1982), I found common ground with the author; intense loss and desire that previously I could only theoretically relate to, now was all too adjacent.

This impulse, to inhabit the image, has been a partially naive motivation behind my work, and the approach – of reproducing and reframing my own family photographs, enlarging, refocusing, repeating – echoes the very desire that Barthes described. In the darkroom, the process of making ambrotypes through revisiting my childhood images functions as ritual and meditation, and through this process I re-establish a sense of my identity, of who I am in the world. I reflect upon my child-self and assimilate that sense of self into the present-day adult. I create a sort of monumental history from these domestic documents, a commemoration and celebration of my family. Just as a commemorative daguerreotype or ambrotype might be encased with a fragment of the person's hair, this reframing of my family archive is my mediation, as 'death emphasises the impermanence of social experience and elicits attempts to preserve some aspects of it in permanent form. This impulse to preserve in the face of death is enacted through the use of material forms that provide tangible substance as mnemonic resource' (Bronfen in Hallam and Hockey, 2001, p. 25).

I recall the thrill I felt as a child, when I would come home to find the screen set up in the living room, the projector being assembled, the slide carousels ordered in accordance with my father's choosing. I would feign interest in the images of other people or buildings, becoming animated and endlessly enchanted in the many images of myself, alone and in the family group. The 'studium' of these images has become my 'punctum' (Barthes, 1982). That carefree child, always smiling, still resides within me, but, naturally, I am transformed through the passage of time; connected, yet distanced. The further from the photographic event, the more precious the opportunity is of seeing our past selves and those whom we have loved. Those outside the family cannot access this sense of familiarity; this recognition. In time, our individual visual, tactile relics of beloved family members drift from their original moorings. Familial records of kinship and documented rites of passage lose their meaning. The individual inhabitants of the photograph become unidentifiable; once cherished images turn into ephemeral detritus. Over time, the focus shifts from a personal cataloguing of people and events. The incidental details, the backdrop of our lives, unremarkable in the present moment, begin to enthral in retrospect – the furnishings, home décor, fashions, hairstyles, all pinpoint and render that moment intransient. Identification of family, friends and places is dependent on narrative memory. In many ways, the family photograph becomes a social and cultural document, as 'Family is structured by desire and disappointment, love and loss. Photographs, as the only material traces of an irrecoverable past, derive their power and their important cultural role from their embeddedness in the fundamental rites of family life' (Hirsch, 1997, p. 5).

My love of photography can be traced directly back to childhood. On family excursions, daytrips, holidays, outings and other 'significant' events, I was aware of my father taking pictures with his Canon 35 mm SLR camera – particularly when I was the subject. It is apparent that, from an early age, I wanted to be the viewer as well as the viewed. Scattered through the family archive are many instances where I have managed to persuade dad to let me 'point and click'. These slides, and some existing negatives, bear witness to my own early attempts at photography, my reciprocal subject being my father, then my mother, and later my siblings. They all function as a reflection of self, an early allo-portrait, a situating of self in the world, defined by those closest to me – my family.

As I grew from a child to a teenager, I predictably turned my back on childish things, even grew disinterested in my own pictorial history, which rooted me far too strongly into my family at a time when I strived for difference. Later, in my twenties, as a mother, I found joy in my children's experience of the world, making new memories, happy to allow my own to recede, taking the opportunity to let go of real or imagined hurts and wrongs. The 'reality' or otherwise of these fragmented recollections became irrelevant as the boundaries between reality and imagination had always been subjective in nature. Now, these images appear to me as a legacy; pieces of the puzzle, speaking of my origin. Instead of being a 'cul de sac' of memories of people long gone, creating the resulting imagery becomes a vital expression of myself, in this moment. The combination of process and subject, past and present, actively moves me towards a potential future.

On materiality and memory, the photograph as object

In my practice as an artist, I focus on the transposition of the indexical character of the photograph with the materiality of the object, the photograph, itself. Both elements are apparent, the visible 'markers' of process are part of the manifestation of photograph as photo-object. 'Material Memories' reproduced and restaged my own family photographs from the 1970s using the wet collodion process, which was invented in 1851. The familiar childhood images are transformed into ambrotypes, images on glass, which are viewed against a black background. The nature of the original slides is ephemeral, the format is that of an obsolete technology. The transparencies began as a familial record, employed in the emphasizing and delineating of group and individual identity, in a language that is familiar, even universal, and as such, invisible in the everyday context. Figure 10.2 is taken from a 35 mm colour slide. I sat between my mum, one of my sisters and my brother, yet the faces are indistinct, the details blurred. I can't reach that little girl, sitting on the back of the bench, nor see my mum and siblings clearly. I imagine I can recall the feeling of sitting there, the youngest of the family, yet bigger and higher than the others, wanting my dad's attention as always. The tones of the silver on glass lend the image a dream-like atmosphere. Despite the overexposed faces, our smiles are visible.

Figure 10.3 is from another image taken on the same day. In the centre of the frame sits my dad, caught in my viewfinder, flanked by mum, sister and brother. I took this snapshot of my family. They are all smiling for me. The sky is bright above their heads. Figure 10.4 is a cropped close-up of my smiling face, my dad's silhouette is reflected in my eyes. This is me. This was me and my dad. Figure 10.5 shows mum and dad. This image is even more blurred and there are more markers of process on the plate, part of my darkroom meditation on love and loss. The making and viewing of this fragmented image comforts me and conveys some of my sense of loss now both my parents are dead. Through these images I mourn them and the child in me.

The isolation of subjectivity is assuaged by a reconnection with a broader human experience, a more generalized universal point of view, through the translation of memory into materialized form – glass, silver and chemistry. This process helps to solidify my sense of identity, it creates an existence not 'just' in my head.

Making images using the wet collodion process transports me to a time long before my lifetime, indeed, before my grandparents' lifetimes. There is a sense of going to the roots, the fundamental origins of photographic process, in the form of the most basic chemistry and equipment. The embodied nature of the process is in every detail – in the preparation of the

FIGURE 10.2 *Christina Edwards, 'Material Memories', 1970s family photograph (35 mm colour transparency) printed as an ambrotype (wet collodion on glass), 10 × 8 in, 2008, courtesy of Christina Edwards.*

plate, pouring the collodion, submerging the plate in silver solution, exposing and developing, using chemistry which has to be mixed from the raw chemicals, including ether, collodion, alcohol, silver nitrate, distilled water, ferrous sulphate and sodium thiosulphate as well as the manipulation of the camera lens and darkslide, with the use of light. The process of making ambrotypes is exactly the same as that documented by Frederick Scott Archer in 1851. This 'authenticity' can be seductive, with many contemporary wet plate practitioners finding themselves diverted from the actual making of images by the quest for genuine nineteenth-century equipment – for example Dallmeyer or Voigtlander lenses, cameras, darkslides, darkroom equipment and other ephemera – the paraphernalia becoming unlikely objects of desire. Clearly, there is a nostalgia inherent in working with a process such as this, but this is transmuted through the use of images from another era of photographic history. Since the advent of photography, it has entered into our consciousness, as a proof of resemblance, an evidential marker of existence, pervading every sphere of human endeavour, colouring and shaping our memories: 'the photograph stands as a central medium, infusing nineteenth- and twentieth-century memory. While carrying a visual image, a photograph's materiality is also important in sustaining its privileged position as a conduit of memory: here, image and material image are fused' (Edwards in Kwint *et al.*, 1999, p. 221).

FIGURE 10.3 *Christina Edwards, 'Material Memories', 1970s family photograph (35 mm colour transparency) printed as an ambrotype (wet collodion on glass), 10 × 8 in, 2008, courtesy of Christina Edwards.*

The images in 'Material Memories' demonstrate a fusing of disparate process and subject. The indexical, the content of the image, and the material, the physical being of the photo-object are co-present in a way that makes the focus of this analysis constantly shift from content, to image plane, to process. The materials deployed in this endeavour are as visible in the finished pieces as the subject (that which exists here, and that which is depicted here). An analogy could be drawn between this shifting of emphasis and the apparent trajectory of photographs existing in the public sphere – many of which may have begun their existence as part of a commercial transaction such as a portrait by an end-of-pier photographer, for example, travelling to the private domain of a frame or album in the family home, then back to the public as an exhibit, or stored as an example of genre in a museum, perhaps. The viewing, the reception, is bound by the context.

The conflation of exterior, objective 'photo-reality' and interior, subjective, human experience, is echoed or mimicked in the collapse of photographic history, as evidenced in this incorporation of nineteenth- and twentieth-century means to convey a contemporary notion. As virtual imaging, in the form of digital photography, subtly subsumes the conventional photographic 'codes' – a new technology growing familiar through this appropriation, absorbing and making redundant (in a popular sense) analogue photography – meanings in photographs become ever more layered and complex. Indeed, it is arguable that it is only since the advent of the 'digital

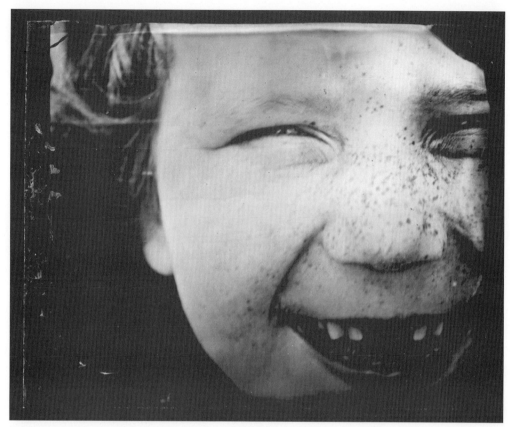

FIGURE 10.4 *Christina Edwards, 'Material Memories', 1970s family photograph (35 mm colour transparency) printed as an ambrotype (wet collodion on glass), 5 × 4 in, 2008, courtesy of Christina Edwards.*

age' and our first steps in the progression of digital lens-based media that the very physicality, the materiality of the photograph has been brought to the fore in cultural studies:

> Like relics, photographs are validated by their social biography: ordinary remains such as family snapshots become treasured, linking objects to traces of the past, the dead, a fetishized focus of devotion. Finally they return to the ordinary, indeed disposable object, the detritus of material culture, as they cease to have meaning for the living beyond a generalized pastness.
>
> Edwards in Kwint *et al.*, 1999, p. 4

Working with family snapshots in this way transcends the ordinary. I implement a certain awareness of genre in order to take a step outside my own subjective viewing of familial experience, and look back inwards, attempting objectivity. Whilst I can acknowledge the stereotypical poses or conventional events that the images depict, it is impossible to be truly objective in relation to one's own personal photographs. Roland Barthes, looking through his mother's photographs after her death, and subsequently describing what for him became the definitive image of his mother – known as 'The Winter Garden', an unpublished image of his mother and her brother as children – described this sense of knowing, and shock of recognition

FIGURE 10.5 *Christina Edwards, 'Material Memories', 1970s family photograph (35 mm colour transparency) printed as an ambrotype (wet collodion on glass), 5 × 4 in, 2008, courtesy of Christina Edwards.*

in this way: 'the picture of his mother provokes a moment of self-recognition which, in the reading process, becomes a process of self-discovery, a discovery of a self-in-relation' (Barthes in Hirsch, 1997, pp. 226–227). This 'self-in-relation' is central in all our lives. Identity is strongly bound in who we are to others – mother, daughter, sister, lover, friend – and conversely, these relations define our sense of self. When one or other of these connections fails, for whatever reason, there is a sense of grief, of loss. Not least of a part of our self, those shared memories, all that past time, now less remembered.

Our personal photographs become an external manifestation of our identity, our proof of connections with others, proof that we live an observed life. For many, their personal photographs are of such value that if asked 'what would you save if your house was on fire', the apocryphal answer, after family members and pets, will be their family photo album.

Through this work, of re-viewing, reviving what would otherwise languish unseen, only viewed within the family, I am creating a space in which the invisible (the conventions, the commonalities of all families) is made evident, yet the indexical, originating image becomes open to new interpretations, freed from its restrictions of when, where and who. This indexical thread of my family isn't tantamount to the viewer. I am transforming my own personal history and the poignancy is heightened in the anonymity. It is as if they take on a dual role – for myself as the artist, I am aware of the who, the when, generally (sometimes more vague) the what and where (as time passes there are fewer people to recall when, or where, the image of swans on a lake was taken, or which castle I am standing on top of, waving at my parents), and in the restaging these elements become disassociated, we are left with residual traces, elegiac and elusive.

My dad's original transparencies date mainly from the early 1970s through to the early 1980s. A certain amount of discrimination on the photographer's part would have been incumbent at that time, as photographic materials were relatively costly. A selective eye would be necessary, although, the term 'snap-happy' is symbolic of this connection between holiday, happy occasion and photography. Currently, with digital imaging, this discriminatory factor is less relevant, or apparent, only becoming a consideration at the point when the virtual image is selected for printing. However, the language of family photographs stays the same whether taken with an analogue or digital camera, as the conventions remain unchanged.

In family photographs, one of the valued signifiers is that of recognition – everyone presenting their face to camera, representing themselves, how they want to be seen, how they expect to be remembered by others, or indeed viewed by their own future selves. In this context, the expectations perpetuate the way in which the camera is used. Despite the fact that family photographs traditionally remain within the family, we stand and pose for the camera as if for a public stage. The conventions surrounding the snapshot decree when and where photography is appropriate. Aspects of Kodak's early marketing of the instamatic camera, specifically aimed at encouraging women and children to take photographs, for example, reinforcing the link between memories and photography, has indelibly shaped our expectations of the photograph within the family (Munir and Phillips, 2005, p. 1665). This marketing has even been appropriated by the newer technology of digital imaging – emphasizing the 'same difference' aspect of digital photography in order to create a sense of familiarity – to ease the adoption of a new technology.

The re-visioning of the archive is a meditation on family, love, memory, loss, grief and recollection, situated within a historical framework – that is, in a combination of differing photographic processes and methods, spanning the centuries. Inextricably interwoven within the broader, photographic history is my own story, creating a fictional intervention in life's chronological narrative with the incorporation of aspects from a dimly remembered childhood.

Photographs as memory-text

The increasing study of memory-objects opens up the study of the combination of photography with/as object. The ambrotypes I created owe as much to the field of autoethnography as to visual and material culture. In the focus on the interplay between image content and surface, the carrier is brought to the fore in the re-siting of family images through an 'antiquarian' historical photographic process in a combination of there-then and here-now. For me, this practice of rep-resenting satiates the numinous desire for something irrecoverable, the past – exemplified in the viewing of one's own childhood self, and of others, now dead – the proleptic sight of those now lost to touch. In restaging these images in glass and silver, there is a tactility inherent in the process, which in some way lends comfort. This photographic intervention aids an acceptance of mortality, a coming to terms with grief and loss, and through this, an awareness and comprehension of my own transient state of being. There is a flow that happens, in all creative processes, time becomes irrelevant – there is a stillness, an eternal moment, residing within, and alongside, current everyday experience. In carrying out a physical and chemical process to make an image, there is a transcendence of the everyday. In the reviewing, the restaging of photographic memories, the past is rupturing the linear passage of time; the past invades the present.

The nexus of dream/reality/memory is made manifest within the apparency of a photograph. In the mind, memory subtly alters every remembered moment at each occasion of recollection (dependent on the you-now). Dreams are intensely vivid at the instant of awakening, fleeting and fading the more they are pursued. In photography, there is the possibility of communicating, in some way, the essence of a dream, the texture of memory. The photograph can carry the weight of a person's subjective experience in a strange, heady mix of interior and external, banal, mundane, yet ethereal and transformative. Life is composed of these bridges and stars, momentary access to the spiritual, the cosmic, embedded within the cemented experience of the daily routine. To transcend the predicated 'reality' is a joy, a gift, a momentary release. Through the alteration, the context of the 'memories' (or memory substitute in the case of the photograph, or even, as Barthes described, 'counter-memory') there is also the potential for healing, a commemorative process that transcends the personal through the recognition of the human commonalities, there is an intervention, a refocusing and extension of the image meaning.

Conclusion: photography/memory traces

Bringing my own, personal history into my practice is a way of celebrating the ordinary, in the creation of a memory text – visualized fragments. I reference the original photographer – my father – and transform these images, from their private world, into a public commemoration, a monumental documenting of a minor history:

> For all [Benjamin, Sontag, Barthes] photography is a melancholic object. Not an aide-memoire, a form for preserving memory, it is a memento mori. Photography is not only a reminder of our loved ones' death, it tells our impending own. It is evidence of the fact of death itself . . . Photography makes real the loss. But then it makes possible the apprehension of this loss. This is my recovery. As offering insight into the inexorable loss that is life, photography captures a reality that we would otherwise not see, that we would choose not to see. It holds out the promise of a kind of enlightenment. It is this that makes me enter the dark room of photography.
>
> Prosser, 2005, pp. 1–2

Those memory traces, Benjamin's 'involuntary memory', rise with ease to the surface through the viewing of the family album – hence the avoidance of this potential emotional minefield in times of convalescence – mental or physical. Moments of contemplation and reflection are best enjoyed in calmer times. An unexpected viewing of someone held dear in reminiscence can be either comforting, or cathartic, dependent on the current state of self. Unanticipated memories arising with viewing of family photos cause rifts in the everyday; fragments of the past intersect the present moment. For this reason, at times of trauma and loss, we are less likely to get out the family album. Rather, it is a measure of our recovery in these times, whether we can comfortably re-view past happiness. However, in general we tend to keep our photographs (even if they are removed from an album, or shoved in a drawer), for to cut out the errant family member, or friend with whom we no longer get on, to rip, tear or destroy the image in any way is an ultimately violent act. Just as early subjects of photographs might symbolically ward off evil, our photographs can hold some sort of talismanic aura, so that to damage an image of someone can feel as though we are causing harm to that person.

In our current digital age, where we are surrounded with sophisticated visual messages, it is easy to overlook the impact of photography on modern society. Our lives are overtly public, in part thanks to the internet: we can all share each others' thoughts and memories, in direct contrast to the private cherishing of early daguerreotypes and ambrotypes in hinged cases and lockets – made specifically for precious, personal contemplation.

In the immediacy of our contemporary experience, do we even remember events when we haven't photographed them? Do we now store our memories in our cameras, in our computers and mobile phones? Can we hold a mental image of anyone without periodic recourse to a visual prompt? Does photography overwrite previous mnemonic impressions, traces?

Photography is still. It creates moments. Today, the majority of digital cameras have a film mode and people are growing more accustomed to viewing themselves in motion, their 'plastic' appearance. The exterior evidence runs counter to our inner perception of how we think we come across, how we seem to others. That same dissonance on hearing oneself on tape, or on an answering machine message, presents itself when viewing oneself in motion on someone's phone or camera. These prevailing 'home modes' of communication have generated an unprecedented prioritizing of appearance.

Now, I find I rarely commemorate photographically, so careful have I become to be living now, in this moment, experiencing rather than documenting – exporting into the future – already cognizant of a future self who will have a desire to view and re-view this moment, this place, these people. The more that photographic images become my way of working, of being creative, the less I am able to forget the power and conventions of photography. I have become too self-conscious, even though this 'now' will shortly be past also. Instead, I find solace in a defined activity, incorporating pre-existing time-capsules into new works in a symbolic elegy of love and loss.

Through the combination of a nineteenth-century process and twentieth-century snapshot imagery, this past, these moments, are collapsed in on themselves via the photographic medium – remaking in an antiquated process, incorporating personal history – of the I-was-there kind. This conscious conflating of times, of processes, makes evident the vehicles for our memories, and our preconceptions of photography. In the twenty-first century, how can a nineteenth-century process be relevant? Yet, it is precisely the digital era that fuels a desire to return to a previous, more physical mode of photography. Looking through lenses that haven't been used in decades, making images in this way, physically binds me in temporal ties. The past, covert in presence, mingles with the present moment before the camera, becomes an object, in the future. The physicality of the wet plate collodion process enables a manifestation of memory; a tactile object of glass and silver, grounding ethereal moments in solid form.

Manipulation, of materials and moments, has always existed within photography. Making this connection overt through the layering of processes and time becomes a meditation on the nature of photography itself. Throughout photography's history, people have created their own personal narratives. We intervene, making space for contemplation, attempting to make sense of the human condition. This work is an articulation of this. Incorporating a process dating back over 150 years, combined with the far more recent history of my own childhood, I create objects representing memory, love and loss. Many of the images originated through my late father's camera. They are of me, and now, are by me. They become allo-portraits, signifiers of truth, identity and memory. 'Memento mori' become 'memento vivere'.

11

The Problematic Decision to Live

Irish-Romanian Home-Making and the Anthropology of Uncertainty

Adam Drazin

Freewill has to be experienced, not debated, like colour or the taste of potatoes.
WILLIAM GOLDING, 1959, P. 5

Introduction

Much of the work on home-making sees people as engaged inevitably in a quest for social certainty. My work among Irish-Romanians reveals something of the multiple dimensions of the notions of certainty and uncertainty in social life. Among people who have moved from Romania to Ireland – a diverse group, whose politico-economic situation in Europe has changed immensely over the last 10 years or so – the material home is not so much an expression of emotion as a negotiation of it. In the engagement with domestic material culture, emotionality seems displaced in time, either evidenced retrospectively or anticipated. A longer-term participatory engagement with people's unfolding lives in this situation comes to be crucial.

While some ethnographic research proceeds in holistically exploring a site such as a community which has a coherence, with different people being connected by social ties or place, in this work I was surprised by the lack of interconnection between very comparable households, which was very different from my previous experience in Romania. In Ireland, my ethnographic journey moved through many different homes, and small groups, making decisions as households or families. It seemed to me as though there was an absolute divide between research among different households. While among some people, the attempt to talk about specific objects in the home absolutely failed, and was incomprehensible, in other households, there was clearly a lot of attention given to decor, building and other aspects of the home. Some people come to Ireland on a particular scheme to work in their vocation, such as software or engineering. This means buying a house, stocking it with furniture, and so on. The decision to live in Ireland involves making friends, socializing, pubs, developing hobbies and learning about Ireland. My argument is that, first, domestic material objects, here, are ways in which to deal with futures and possibilities in a situation where people are placed under the impossible expectation of knowing their own mind about the future. Second, the movement of objects from being simple indices of possibilities (as a bunch of flowers indicates romance, although not necessarily that you yourself are actively romantic), to intentional manifestations of responsibilities and purposes, is significant for *feelings*. Love and ways of being purposive are not necessarily wholly separate, nor wholly integrated, and different materialities can show us a range of ways in which they are being articulated, by people and families such as Irish-Romanians.

Katrina's 'Letter of Intent'

The moment when Katrina and Ion decided to invite me to their home was an important one. On the desk upstairs in Katrina's house next to the computer was a big stack of papers with the striking title on the front 'Letter of Intent' (see Figure 11.1). This 300-page document set out for

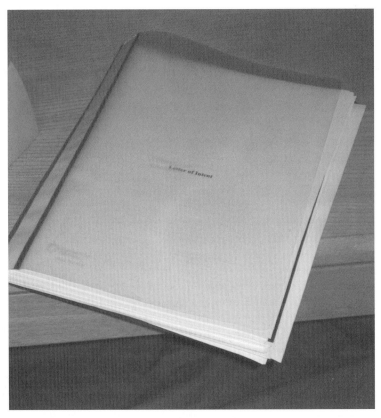

FIGURE 11.1 *Katrina's Letter of Intent. Photograph by Adam Drazin.*

the Irish Government Katrina's intentions in life, for the purposes of applying for a work and residency visa. While Romania joined the EU in 2007, the right to work only occurred in 2011. She had already been in Ireland for nearly four years. She moved when her boyfriend, Ion, was recruited from Romania for a job as a software engineer by one of Dublin's hi-tech companies. So Katrina switched from a degree course in Romania to one in Ireland. Upon graduating, after three years of study and part-time journalism work, her student visa finished and she had to apply for another. In her 'Letter of Intent', in fact, only a small portion expressed her own intentions on her own behalf. For the purposes of the document, her intentions amounted to the testimony of others: references from the people and companies who had employed her, the taxes she had paid, her salary, her first-class degree, information about her residence and landlord showing she had been resident in Ireland during this time, evidence of her boyfriend's secure job, the money they held in the bank, indicating she could support herself, and so on. In short, a mass of information – especially about home and money – was officially taken as things through which the State could indexically read her 'intent'.

Katrina and Ion lived in a two-bedroom terraced house in a relatively well-off area of Dublin near to the beach – a poorly-insulated 1980s house where, in the winter, ice formed on the inside of the kitchen window. At the back near the sliding French windows, a scattering of pebbles, shells and sticks adorned the fireplace, from their many walks beside the sea and from different locations exploring Ireland (see Figure 11.2). A bunch of dried and withered roses stood near to them, not gathered from nature, but a gift between the two of them that they never threw away. Beside the sofa were photo albums, with three years of pictures of Katrina, Ion, Ion's sister and his brother-in-law, on various holidays around Ireland, taken in the soft light characteristic of the Irish landscape. Upstairs in the main bedroom, were other mementoes and objects, mirrors, Katrina's grandmother's purse alongside 1920s-style artefacts. A cabinet held a range of cuddly toys from Romania – where these were, she commented, that was her home. Above the bed, on the ceiling, a series of luminous plastic stars spelled out their mutual pet name for one another.

At the time of my visit, Katrina's application had just been turned down. Quantitatively, she had a mass of supporting information, but qualitatively there was no individual instance among it all to set her apart from anyone else from Romania: for example, Irish family or one of the government's indispensible priority 'skills' areas.

What was clear was that if Katrina and Ion were to get married, she would automatically gain residence rights in Ireland. This was a double-bind. Obviously, they were not going to get

FIGURE 11.2 *Decoration in Katrina and Ion's home. Photograph by Adam Drazin.*

married because of this kind of issue. However, if they did marry, at that time or in the indeterminate future, they would risk the appearance of getting married for residence. Their marriage would risk appearing as something from which they clearly benefited, appearing as if it might have been done in a spirit of self-seeking or calculation.

Katrina does not think of herself as a 'migrant', but the State in some sense does. When people are migrants, they are often under intense pressure for self-knowledge, and to hold their intentions clearly in their minds. The poet Nick Laird lampoons this pressure in his poem 'The Immigration Form', in which the State asks a prospective 'immigrant', 'How intimate are you with breathing?' (Laird, 2007). It is not only the State, however, that is the source of this pressure – a person must justify their intentions to parents, family and children. To be a migrant without a clear plan is not socially acceptable, nor is sentiment an acceptable justification. Because of the complicated Foucauldian bind, which both extorts and creates un-affective individual intentions in these types of instance, it is not clear who is necessarily making the decisions. Self-knowledge as a migrant can emerge from an engagement with authority, rather than from simple choice.

Anthropology has also long been aware of the ways that agency, including the locus of intentionality, is distributed. Decisions are made and negotiated in groups or relationships, rather than by isolated Robinson Crusoe figures. What is important is that the group, family or relationship is the legitimate and appropriate one for the intention.

In situations of distributed agency, the material world assumes increased importance. Objects have the capacity to manifest in some sense a relationship or group (Douglas and Isherwood, 1978, pp. 71–90; Mauss, 1990), to express a quality of mind (Gell, 1997), and to do so in ways that appear as legitimate, unquestionable and accepted (Miller and Woodward, 1987, pp. 85–109). In this instance, many of the objects appear to express future trajectories, not to be confused with the conscious intentions of Ion and Katrina. In the eyes of the ethnographer, there is a story of love going on here, which is expressed in the particular objects I have singled out and described; objects that seem to embed nature into the home and express the naturalness of the wellsprings of emotion involved. Yet it is a story that would be demeaned if it were made too explicit.

Problematically, however, these objects' materiality is challenged. Thinking of the previous three years of Ion and Katrina building a life together, there is a process of social construction at work, which appears as an inevitable movement towards social certainty about who they are and where they stand. I read their domestic interior in terms of emotion and time, as a love story. Yet of what value is the materialization process in the event, the moment when I spoke with them? The records of their walks together, the photo albums, the arrangement of the bedroom, the dried roses – these appear at one moment permanent emotional fixtures, and in the next as ephemeral junk. The quality of materiality possessed by an object can seem permanent or transient (Buchli and Lucas, 2001; Miller, 2005). Houses can seem like natural features of the landscape and then suddenly like paper before the bulldozer, and often we choose them to be so and decide what is permanent and what is not.

By contrast with the spoken or written word (for example Katrina's Letter of Intent), the material futures we read into objects offer more subtle possibilities for expression and interpretation – much more grey, subjective and open to infinite degrees of negotiation. At the same time, Katrina's letter makes the future more abstract and evidently uncertain, in the sense of being unmaterialized, because the letter exists in the here-and-now; while the objects manifest certainty. As an ethnographer, I must admit that I privilege the subjective materiality of intentions above words.

Home-making as relating to future

Irish-Romanian homes commonly unmask the notion of a simple relationship between a warm home and a warm emotional feeling inside a person. The pressure to self-construct through self-knowledge is intense and artificial, revealing instead the disjunctures between knowledge and feeling; interior and exterior landscapes.

Studies of post-socialist Europe have commonly tackled these issues, of how home-making becomes a type of project in which identities are both *ascribed* from outside 'readers', and also apparently *intended* by home-makers. Caroline Humphrey (2002) offers one of the most subtle propositions of how this project has proceeded, has been challenged, and has (arguably) failed under the burden of its own presumption. Trying to become 'new Russians' through house-building, people draw from two wholly different resources of identity – European bourgeois modernity, as well as feudal Russian aristocracy. Monstrous concrete Frankensteins appear whose material form is testimony of experimentation more than 'transcendent' identities that will last:

> This reveals the unintended aspects of identity creation, the heaps and bits and pieces that have somehow ended up on the site, which of course are at the same time visible and 'readable' by everyone else. The slippage may be unintended but is no accident, since it reflects the general post-Soviet condition, which is characterized by uncertainty or irony toward any grand mythic projects.
>
> Humphrey, 2002, p. 176

Herein lie some of the difficulties of a material culture of emotion, in its dependence upon how one knows oneself, because it is dependent upon an anthropology of *un*certainty. Social life is prefigured as a quest for certainty. The person who has culture is presumed to be in a drive to create meanings that are somehow transcendent mythologies. There is a certain seductiveness here in the notion of the narrative. It is pleasant to think of our informants romantically, caught up in a story that is theirs.

However, when it comes to the material culture of the home, reading future stories into objects can be deceptive. Some objects manifest what Miller calls the 'blindingly obvious' (Miller and Woodward, 2007, p. 335), the oracular quality of the object, which in the words of Evans-Pritchard 'does not err':

> Azande often say 'the poison oracle does not err, it is our paper. What your paper is to you, the poison oracle is to us,' for they see in the art of writing the European's source of knowledge, accuracy, memory of events, and predictions of the future. The oracle tells Azande what to do at every crisis of life.
>
> Evans-Pritchard, 1976, p. 261

On the other hand, in a situation where someone has an identity as a 'migrant', they may be made to feel obliged to demonstrate that their future is a space of open possibility for them to make use of, in which certainty must be evidentially a quality of mind. The compulsion from this perspective is for the object world to be 'merely' an extension of self. Domestic objects would be expected to reflect intentions, but not to independently realize any meaningful qualities of their own.

Carmen on stereotypical Romanians and their homes

The State is not always a significant audience for Irish-Romanians in thinking about what one knows, intends or feels. For many people, it is a Romanian diasporic context that is more important, and domestic forms come to signify what sort of Romanian one is. Take Petru and Betty. They sold their small farmstead in Romania in order to finance moving to Ireland. What was their initial aim? Earning enough to build a house in Romania, to replace the one they had sold. After two years of living in a barely-furnished flat in Dublin, during which time they went out socially once (to the pub), they had managed to build a house in Romania and were purchasing things to furnish it. Were they intending to ever go back to Romania? No. Were they ever intending to buy a house in Ireland or start socializing? No. '*Asta e prostia*', Petru told me: 'That's the idiocy. The Romanian works like a fool. He builds a house and then he dies.' What was the house for? For their two children back in Romania. The physical home, present or absent, assumes great importance in these instances.

'We are not typical as Romanians', I was told by Carmen and by a friend of hers, as we sat in her flat. They told me how the typical Romanian spends nothing in Ireland at all, but saves up all their money. Their entire existence in Ireland is about saving and an ethic of saving, in order to build a life back in Romania. They also buy good-quality goods and send them to Romania, to the home they intend to live in. They buy a towel from Aldi to use here, and a good one from Marks & Spencer they send back unopened to Romania. They buy good jeans, and Nikes, and send them unworn to Romania; while in Ireland they wear second-hand clothes and 'adidas' (i.e. trainers) from Lidl.

This means that for this brand of 'typical' Romanian, the home is very minimalist. Life in Ireland comprises of attempting to spend as little money as possible – even if they are in fact spending money, the value of that money goes to Romania. They therefore do not invest their financial resources in Ireland. They go out rarely, if at all, to the pub, as a night out in Dublin can soak up a lot of money. Working hours are maximized, getting as many jobs or as much overtime as possible, so people can work a 60-hour week or more. People supposedly live in bare, spartan, rented accommodation and eat and socialize at home as much as possible in front of the TV (see Figure 11.3). An avoidance of actually making social contacts is implied, along with the risk of spending money on them.

The second 'Romanian stereotype' whom I was told during research I might well be interested in meeting, was a family who have bought a place, and are engaged in setting up home. The reason why I might want to meet them would be to witness their pride in feathering their nest. The ways in which this second form of 'typical Romanian' is reported as different from oneself varies. Maybe they are Irish citizens, or at least have very certain forms of documentation in their own names. Maybe they are married or have children. Maybe they are from a town or city rather than a rural area; went to university; have friends of all nationalities, not just Romanian; go out in the evenings; spend money in restaurants; shop at Marks & Spencer rather than Aldi or Lidl; shop in Dublin's Grafton Street on the south side of the river, not in Henry Street on the north side.

For people born in Romania, meanwhile, the two stereotypical home forms above offer ways of negotiating something of the wide variety of people from Romania. There is an immense variety, and it is debateable whether anyone has much in common with anyone else at all. Certainly, many people are very explicit that they do not want to socialize with other Romanians. Through stereotypical 'other' Romanians, different elements of identity can be negotiated – rural and urban people, less educated or more, different ethnicities, different religions (Orthodox

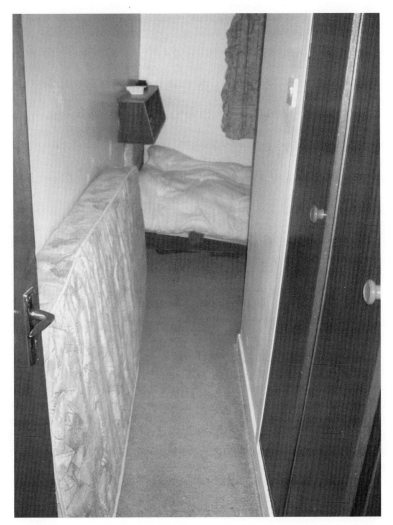

FIGURE 11.3 *Lack of home-making and intentions in Dublin flat. Photograph by Adam Drazin.*

or Protestant), different senses of class, people from Moldova in the East or Transylvania in the West, clever (*destept*) people and idiots (*fraiere*), farmers, factory workers and office workers, English speakers and monoglots, Irish citizens and non-Irish, Romanian speakers from inside the EU and those from outside it, Romanians who grew up in Romania and Romanians who grew up in Ireland. Most importantly, this broad canvas enables differentiation between good and bad Romanians – the bad Romanians being those other Romanians who are materialistic in one way or another, unlike oneself, who is not. In the particular instance of Irish-Romanians, materialistic stereotypes seem to be laid on thick and fast, while every person's experience and life is profoundly different.

Carmen, as many people, did not herself conform to either of the stereotypes, but wished to introduce me to others who fitted the bill. In her own case, she shifted in her conversation between talking about stereotypical friends who corresponded to one type or another, and talking about two alternative strategies in her own life. When I asked her why she was not a 'typical' Romanian, she said '*eu am hotarit cu sotul meu sa traim aici*' – 'I decided with my husband to live here'. In order to understand, we have to understand the specific meaning that she is ascribing to the word 'live' in this comment, in the context of the conversation. Living in Ireland implies not rigorously saving money with the intention of living in Romania, but rather engaging in social life in Ireland with the aim of settling. To live implies spending money on oneself now, having a *place* to live, and so on. To live implies a particular strategy, or rationalization, of living now and here.

Carmen moved to Ireland fully legally in the late 1990s, recruited in Romania to work for a cleaning company in Dublin. She already had a long CV of assorted professional jobs in Romania and elsewhere, and had travelled extensively. She was an au pair in France and in Sweden. She had for several years run a small manufacturing company in Romania, exporting to France; and she had worked for nearly two years as a translator for a clothes company that exported from Romania to Italy. When a company turned up recruiting in Bucharest for work in Ireland, she went along speculatively, at a time when she was sick of the pitfalls and wheeler-dealer nature of working in Romania. The people who interviewed her gave her very little impression of what on earth it was that she would be doing, beyond promising a surprisingly generous salary of IR£250 a fortnight, minus rent. She knew nothing about Ireland, so she got out an atlas with her father to check where Ireland was on the map, and she got out some guide books from the library.

Upon arrival, it transpired that the employer was a cleaning company. She lived at first in a huge house with nine other women, mostly Russians, in a nice, peaceful area of Dublin called Beaumont. She worked fully legally as a Romanian with her visa, PPS number, and so on. There was a small amount, IR£70, which disappeared from their pay packets each month, which the Irish managers never explained – she's not quite certain why she never asked about that. After a sequence of assorted dramas, job shifts, shifts in accommodation, and so on, she was promoted within the company. She also found a job for her husband, one that paid better than hers, and he came over to join her.

For several years she and her husband lived together in Dublin. As she said, they made the decision to *live* in Ireland. She moved job from being a supervisor in the cleaning company to being a supervisor in a hotel. They rented a nice flat near to the seafront in north-east Dublin – a peaceful townhouse converted into five apartments, mostly occupied by professional couples. They made friends and went out with work colleagues socially.

During their time in Dublin, however, they came to 'live different lives'. Much of this was concerned with work, as their social lives came to be organized with work colleagues, who did not overlap. The decision to 'live' in Ireland proved fatal for their 13-year marriage, and they decided to divorce. Taking stock of their situation, they had not managed to save much, nor to buy a house. They decided to move back to Romania to divorce and, having closed all their accounts in Ireland, said goodbye to everyone.

The process of separation and divorce, however, was very traumatic for Carmen, as ever more details about their past lives emerged. Carmen decided that, actually, she wanted a new start. She moved to Italy, then found out from friends in Ireland that her old job was still available. At this point, therefore, she made a decision to come back to Ireland, and do things differently this time around.

When I talked to Carmen, she was intending to implement the other type of strategy of living. She did not intend to socialize, spend money, live in a nice area, and so on. She intended to work hard, save money and build up capital in order to be able to buy a house, have a family (probably back in Romania), and so on. It was not 100 per cent certain that she would manage to do this. As we talked, her friend commented that Carmen would not manage to do this. Carmen countered that she would do, and she had to. Saving up capital takes a lot of self-discipline and is very difficult. It is exceptionally tricky, the suggestion was, when you are used to living in a 'normal' fashion.

In her second life in Dublin, Carmen was living in a rented bedsit in a converted Georgian house inherited from another Romanian tenant. The main part of the room was occupied by a bed, table and single chair. In a corner was a sink and small kitchen area, where she cooked on a set of rings. In the other corner, partition walls enclosed a cramped shower and toilet. Above the fireplace was a map of Romania and the Romanian national anthem, which begins 'Wake up Romanian' (*Desteapta te Romanule*) (see Figure 11.4). These belonged to the previous tenant, and she purposely left them there to remind her to 'wake up'. Likewise, she also hung an

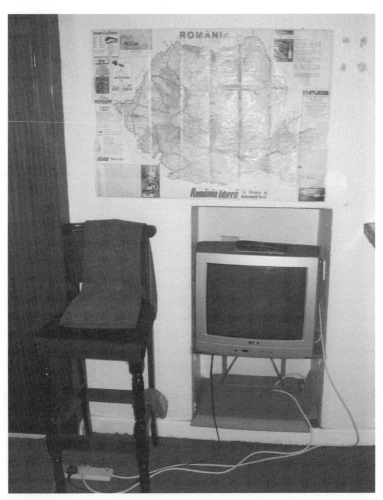

FIGURE 11.4 *In Carmen's flat: her map of Romania. Photograph by Adam Drazin.*

expensive watch by her door as a reminder. Carmen does not wear a watch. On her last visit to Romania, she bought an expensive one to wear to show people she had made something of herself. She keeps the watch on view to remind herself of the façade she used to give herself. Her intention was not to 'live' in Dublin, as before. Rather, she was going to suspend living in that sense, have a spartan existence and save money to return to Romania to live on.

The use of the term 'to live in Ireland' (in Romanian '*a trai in Irlanda*') has a number of characteristics here. Clearly, the term has a number of connotations that are different from simply existing and breathing, or being on Irish soil. The connotations of the term 'to live' are rendered clearer by contrast with the alternative mode of being in Ireland. To 'live in Ireland' implies a measure of intent. One is living now with the intention of living and being in Ireland in the future. In fact, of course, both the person who has decided not to live in Ireland, and the person who has, may still be in Ireland next year. Many people who have decided not to live in Ireland can exist in Ireland for years. The main difference is intention. Secondly, however, this is manifested in objects in the present, with implications for social relationships. Thus, intention, material home and household are being expressed and elided in this simple phrase 'to live'.

Conclusion: walls of the mind, walls of the home

Emotion, such as the phenomenon of love, exists not so much in direct relationships – for example with objects – but in the achievements and the slippages, and hence it exists in time and in social networks. The enduring, unquestionable drive behind a lot of Irish-Romanian life is an aspiration to build a trilogy: a material home, a (heterosexual) marriage, and to have children. This triple ideology, rooted in growing up in Romania, seems unquestionable and hegemonic. Different people may relate to it in different ways: while some may declare their commitment to these kinds of projects directly and consciously, others (for example, university-educated people) may talk about it from a distance through the stereotypes described above, or by outlining the ideas they have 'inherited' from parents. Yet the package of these three projects is always present somehow.

In describing the lives of certain of my informants, I have situated the emotions engendered in relationships and marriage within wider networks that support or defy this triple ideological aspiration. The exact material constitution of a home, and simple things such as how one shops or consumes, have profound implications for senses of love and mutual engagement between people. If 'to live' in Carmen's sense is to feel in the here-and-now, then objects in the home come to be ways of negotiating certainties of feelings – in the past, now, and in the future.

Simmell comments that the purest material expression of purposiveness is to be found in money, revealing the cultural and material situatedness of purpose (2004, p. 232). Futures here do not comprise only in knowing, but feeling. Objects are a medium through which futures unfold, much as relationships with pasts emerge through archaeological contexts.

The temporal dislocation or assertion of love, its evacuation from the present into future or past, or the absolute assertion of the here-and-now, is facilitated through objects. Through objects, we negotiate our relationships with the future, and these relationships are not uniform and singular, but varied and plural. Certain objects – money, or the written word – manifest purpose, certainty of mind and contemporaneity. Red roses or undecorated walls both can be creative in the emotional rhythms of Irish-Romanian life. Paints, televisions, carpets, mattresses, washing machines, even the physical home or house itself, indicate the ways in which it is not as simple as *whether* and *where* emotion is present or absent, but *when* it is present. The unpainted wall or the painted wall are both ways to locate ontologies of emotion in time. This is because feeling love, and knowing love, can be two different things. In conclusion, the material culture of emotion needs to explore better the ways in which uncertainty is materialized, because of the varied dimensions of materiality, certainty, intention and emotion in the lives of people such as Irish-Romanians.

12

Designing Meaningful and Lasting User Experiences

Jonathan Chapman

Introduction

If you were to mine a landfill site, you would see thick, choked geological strata of style descend before you, punctuated by zeitgeist objects whose archaeological discovery would serve to punctuate a design era more poignantly than any carbon dating methodology ever could.

As the biosphere chokes, we snigger at the fake 1970s walnut-veneered TV set lying face down in a ditch, or the recently ejected avocado bathroom suite from the 1980s, still standing earnestly to attention. Is it triumph perhaps? Affirmation of our transcendence beyond those aesthetic faux pas that we as consumers, sitting frigidly poised on the style-islands, have fought so hard to assemble, but which now sink beneath the smoggy swath of ecological decay we brewed in the making.

If we are to move toward a more sustainable future, we must first expose alternative understandings of the immaterial culture underpinning our stuff, and the manifold dialogues we are continually engaged in with the plethora of designed objects that touch our lives; arguing for an emotionally durable design approach that reduces the consumption and waste of natural resources by increasing the resilience of relationships established between people and things.

Meaning and the made

Although we may assign particular meaning to a given object, or material, meaning cannot exist outside the body. It is within us that meaning can be found. Of course, meaning may be represented, or prompted externally through the use of systems like language, images and form, for example. However, an object, material or space cannot hold meaning in and of itself – only our interpretation of these things will produce meaning.

In this way, meaning draws from lived experience – that which has happened to you up until this point – and is typically associated with sets of abstract relations and conditions, which create a lasting impression on us. Furthermore, meaning is a highly relative term that refers to the interpretation of both material and immaterial encounters. If we are, therefore, to have a discussion about the meaning of a poppy, we must first establish the various positions of the participants in that debate. To the English country gardener, for example, the poppy is a beautiful but short-lived speck of colour; to the veteran soldier, the poppy means remembrance of soldiers who died during wartime; to a Chinese mother, the meanings of the poppy are solely negative, and are to be avoided, as it is synonymous with the production of the drugs opium, morphine and heroin.

Meaning influences what we *see* in a given thing. As a preconscious state of mind, meaning gives a sense of direction for thought and potential action; a cognitive response to abstract features within a given encounter, such as experiencing a rat in a pet shop. Certain norms are at play here, of course, and a large degree of consensus delivers the meaning of this rat in a preformed state. However, meaning is also highly context-specific. If you take the same rat and put it in the kitchen of a hotel, then its meaning changes quite dramatically – same rat, very different meanings. So as we can see, it is not helpful to think of the object as being meaningful, but instead, the way we encounter and experience the object generates meaning, bespoke to each of us. It is the nature of these encounters that shapes and colours the meaning we preconsciously assign to such material experiences . . . not the material itself.

Whether deemed meaningful or not, the made world is a consequence – an emergent space in which the human species has progressively found ways to modify and enhance the world around us. The urban spaces we roam, buildings we inhabit, products we use and garments we wear, collectively represent our intellectual capacity to imagine a better world that is beyond our current level of experience. This innate capability to imagine a world just beyond, and then formulate (design) plans to realize those imaginings, is an essential determinant of what it is to be human – to reach beyond innate human limitations (Heskett, 2003). There is nothing new about this. Throughout human history, evidence of this enduring human characteristic can be found. Whether the selective rearing of high-yield livestock by our early ancestors, or the genetic modification of a given strain of fungus-resistant barley, through millennia of striving to enhance the conditions for life, we have evolved our processes and practices beyond recognition.

Belief

No designer ever knowingly set out to make the world a worse place. No designer ever jumped out of bed one Monday morning saying, 'Hey, I'm going to design a really unsustainable, meaningless product today!' The desire to produce lasting value and meaning in the world, through the things we create, is in the very DNA of all creative minds. In this way, it is clear that the shift toward designing longer-lasting products is something that most designers are already behind. On a corporate level, the desire is also evident, as customer satisfaction and consequent loyalty are tied in to such issues.

As we fumble our way through life, attempting to make sense of it along the way, our need to find explanation leads our minds beyond reason, and into the supernatural. On describing memorabilia and the power of inanimate objects, Bruce Hood, author of *Super Sense*

(Hood, 2009), undertook an experiment in which he first hands out a black 1930s fountain pen, which he falsely claims belonged to Albert Einstein. Everyone in the audience is desperate to hold it, and shows great reverence and awe toward the object, as though part of Einstein's soul somehow resides within it. Hood then holds aloft a tattered old cardigan, and asks who would be willing to volunteer by wearing it. Many offer to do so, until it is revealed that the cardigan belonged to Cromwell Street's notorious serial killer, Fred West. Promptly, almost all volunteers lower their hands. Hood claims that this change of heart reveals something odd: audience members sitting next to one of those who keep their hand raised, and are willing to wear the killer's cardigan, visibly recoil in repulsion of their neighbour's openness to this (Hood, 2009). The cardigan is no longer the prime source of repulsion, but more interestingly, the person who feels fine wearing it, or even handling it, must be avoided also (Chapman, 2013a).

So, what does design and meaning have to do with sustainability? Indeed, it may appear that generating meaningful synthesis between such apparently disconnected ideas is like trying to nail ice cubes together.

Meaning full

According to the director of London's Design Museum, Deyan Sudjic, we live in a world drowning in objects (Sudjic, 2008); households with a TV set in each room; kitchen cupboards stuffed with waffle makers, bread ovens, blenders and cappuccino whisks, and drawers swollen with a plethora of pocket-sized devices powered by batteries, which themselves are products that take several thousand times more energy to make than they will ever produce. One's material empire – with its aquariums, TV sets, plants, phones, lamps, clocks, scarves, lawnmowers, picture frames, door knobs, computers, shoes, cameras, bicycles, screwdrivers, jackets, carpets, sinks, cars or anything else for that matter – is made up of *stuff* (Chapman, 2013a). Like a shadow that follows you around, this stuff defines you, whether you like it or not – whether you planned it or not. Perhaps due to the normalcy of innovation, material culture is adopting an increasingly expendable, sacrificial persona. Today, an edgy sense of instability surrounds the made world, nurtured by continual change to render its offspring fleeting, transient and replaceable orphans of circumstance.

In this oversaturated world of people and things, durable attachments with objects are seldom witnessed. Most products deliver a predictable diatribe of information, which quickly transforms wonder into drudgery; serial disappointments are delivered through nothing more than a product's failure to maintain currency with the evolving values and needs of their user. The volume of waste produced by this cyclic pattern of short-term desire and disappointment is a major problem, not just in terms of space and where to put things, but, perhaps more notably, for its toxic corruption of the biosphere (Chapman, 2005).

Landfill sites are overloaded with fully functioning products; Hoovers that still suck and freezers that still chill; all of which still perform their tasks perfectly, in a utilitarian sense. In an more emotive sense, however, waste of this nature could be seen as nothing more than a symptom of a failed relationship between the subject and the object; a failure that led to the dumping of the static one by the newly evolved other.

Ecological destruction

One doesn't need to be an ardent environmentalist to see that there is little or no logic to the way we relate to our environment. We clear carbon absorptive forests to grow methane-producing meat, and smother vast areas of bio-diverse wilderness with ecologically inert urban sprawl, riddled with mazes of oil-dependent highways. Examples such as these are commonplace, and one could easily fill an entire essay just with horror stories such as these. Yet, however many examples you come across, one thing connects them all: they are each the result of an outmoded economic paradigm in which ecological systems are assigned zero monetary value.

In our evolutionary drive toward a faster, lighter, brighter and more technologically advanced material world, humans have wreaked havoc throughout all natural systems that support life on earth. Through our collective pursuit of modernity, we have wreaked unprecedented levels of destruction throughout all natural systems that support life on this planet. Since the mid-eighteenth century, more of nature has been destroyed than in all prior human history (Hawken *et al.*, 1999). Our species reached full behavioural modernity about 50,000 years ago, yet during the past 60 years alone we have stripped the world of a quarter of its topsoil and a third of its forest cover. In total, a third of all the planet's resources have been consumed within the past four decades (Burnie, 1999), all in the name of development and progress. As an inventive species, we can consider ourselves fortunate to have inherited a 3.8 billion-year-old reserve of natural capital (Hawken *et al.*, 1999). Within the past 150 years, we have mined, logged, trawled, drilled, scorched, levelled and poisoned the earth, toward the point of total collapse.

As ecological beings, we are embedded and mutually dependent on the rest of the natural world, but our understanding of reality does not reflect this basic geophysical reality (Boehnert, 2012). Humankind has conceived of itself as the sole proprietor of sentience, and the rest of the world as mindless and therefore not entitled to moral or ethical consideration (Bateson, 1979) – thus available for exploitation. As David Orr describes, the disordering of ecological systems and of the great biogeochemical cycles of the earth reflects a prior disorder in the thought, perception, imagination, intellectual priorities and loyalties inherent in the industrial mind. Ultimately, then, the ecological crisis concerns how we think and the institutions that purport to shape and refine the capacity to think (Orr, 2004).

Sociologist Robert Bocock tells us that consumption is founded on a lack – a desire always for something not there. Postmodern consumers, therefore, will never be satisfied. The more they consume, the more they will desire to consume (Bocock, 1993). Bocock – whose work examines the contribution of leading writers in the field, including Veblen, Simmel, Marx, Gramsci, Weber, Bourdieu, Lacan and Baudrillard – claims that consumer motivation, or the awakening of human need, is catalysed by a sense of imbalance or lack that steadily cultivates a restless state of being; material consumption is therefore motivated when discrepancies are experienced between actual and desired conditions. The types of consumptive behaviours that these conditions provoke range in scale from major lifestyle shifts, such as buying a larger property in a more affluent part of town, to something less dramatic, such as treating yourself to a new toothbrush (Chapman, 2005). The notion that many products possess symbolic features and that consumption of goods may depend more on their social meaning than their functional utility is a significant one for consumer research (Solomon, 1983). The myriad forms of consumption that derive from this phenomenon are varied, yet the root motivation is surprisingly consistent.

Disposable luxuries

The notion of a 'throwaway society' is nothing new, and has been in the public lexicon since 1955. In fact, it was as early as 1932 when American economist Bernard London first introduced the term 'planned obsolescence' – often referred to as 'death-dating' – as a means to stimulate spending among the very few that had money at that time (London, 1932). This proposed shift toward an increasingly disposable material world was initially intended as a solution to the dark economic crisis experienced during the Great Depression in the United States. The ecological impacts of this drive toward planned product failure could not have been anticipated or understood in the 1930s. Today, however, we are all too aware of the catastrophe-making character of these practices, and they simply cannot continue.

Of course, when new things are acquired, older things must be ejected from one's material empire, to make room, so to speak – out with the old, in with the new. This has led to the development of an increasingly 'disposable' character in material culture and design. Just over a century ago, disposability referred to small, low-cost products such as the Gillette disposable razor or paper napkins, whereas today – largely through the efforts of industrial strategy and advertising – it is culturally permissible to throw anything away anything from TV sets and vacuum cleaners to automobiles and an entire fitted bathroom (Chapman, 2013b). It should come as no surprise, then, that landfill sites and waste recycling facilities, are packed with stratum upon stratum of durable goods that slowly compact and surrender working order beneath a substantial volume of similar scrap (see Figure 12.1). Even waste that does find its way to recycling and sorting centres frequently ends up in stockpiles as the economic systems that support recycling and disassembly fail to support them. For example, in 2007 it was estimated that 250,000 tons of discarded but still usable cell phones sat in stockpiles in America, awaiting disposal (Slade, 2007).

Take the fashion industry, for example. In this fast-paced context, trends develop among large populations of consumers, and are followed with enthusiasm as a result of the trend's recognizable features (colour, cut, combination, etc.) being perceived as novel in some way. When enough people buy into this trend, however, the sense of novelty quickly peels away. Our affection for the things we spent so much money and time in acquiring is lost, and it isn't long before new novelty is noticed and pursued elsewhere. This ordinarily results in the purchasing of new things, and so the cycle continues.

One might instantly assume that trend is a negative thing. However, for a fashion designer to approach the creation of garments without considering trend would be like an architect approaching the creation of buildings without considering gravity. Trend is pervasive, it's out there whether you like it or not. Where a cultural trend is said to last 10 years or more, fashion trends are far more fleeting, often occupying a handful of weeks in any given year. Indeed, trend is a constantly evolving reality that is both followed and defined by fashion brands. This fact alone is at the heart of fashion's obsession with pace, newness and ephemera.

As Slade forcefully argues in his rousing book, *Made to Break: Technology and Obsolescence in America*, the concept of disposability was in fact a necessary condition for America's rejection of tradition and acceptance of change and impermanence (Slade, 2007). By choosing to support ever-shorter product lives, he argues that we may well be shortening the future of our way of life as well, with perilous implications for the very near future.

FIGURE 12.1 *Unwanted televisions and monitors await disposal. Photograph by Jonathan Chapman.*

A behavioural crisis

Peel back the slick, polished surface of the made world, and a dark, incoherent and altogether disturbing reality is revealed – one of misplaced agendas, obscure behavioural anomalies and harsh contradictions – showing how, at the root of it all, it is the underlying human condition that shapes our impending ecological crisis. As we inefficiently fumble our way through countless unsatisfactory embraces with material experiences – from skyscrapers to saltshakers – we temporarily connect with a longer-standing struggle to understand complex existential phenomena such as time, mortality, identity, value, selfhood and utopia, for example. So, like trout rising for hatching larvae, we roam the depths of ourselves, gazing constantly upward in endless anticipation of the existential nourishment we crave (Chapman, 2013b).

Indeed, the crisis of unsustainability is one of behaviour, and not of energy and materials alone. Prominent anthropologist, cyberneticist and systems thinker, Gregory Bateson, notably said that the world partly becomes – comes to be – how it is imagined (Bateson, 2000). Indeed, design plays a central role in imagining the products, systems and processes that constitute our material reality. This made world is an emergent property of our collective values, beliefs and aspirations. In this way, we can understand the world by looking at that which we have made, and then looking at our reflection cast by those objects.

Materials are powerful mediators, and are so much more than just skins to wrap technology; they are grossly undervalued in terms of their potential to contribute to the meaningfulness of human experience. Beyond their functional and utilitarian properties, materials connect us to a far deeper set of narratives surrounding complex and thorny issues of self, culture, society, economy and ecology. This meaningful *stuff*, therefore, shapes not only our made environment, but perhaps more importantly, our emotional experience of it.

Examining our personal relationships with the stuff we own brings us closer to the behavioural roots of our ecological crisis. In turn, this signposts new and critical directions for design to pursue; reframing materials as meaningful-matter that manipulates the way we encounter the made world, and the durability of the material relationships that form as a result. After all, design is surely about more than just the creation of more stuff; cooler, and slightly more on-trend versions of their discarded predecessors – isn't it?

In the discipline of design, we are familiar with seeing the world in this way. We understand that objects are so much more than the sum of their parts; they are signs, functions, meanings and styles. Seldom are they discussed purely as inert material entities devoid of character, as this is not their intention – both from the consumers' and the designers' points of view. As Julia Lohman describes: when communicating through objects, the meaning is created through the materiality of the object. The materials become the words; the design becomes the syntax. The piece speaks without the detour of language (Lohman cited in Williams, 2012).

Emotionally durable design

Emotionally durable design reduces the consumption and waste of natural resources by increasing the resilience of relationships established between consumers and products (Chapman, 2009). As Hazel Clark and David Brody of Parsons The New School for Design in New York state: emotionally durable design is a call for professionals and students alike to prioritize the relationships between design and its users, as a way of developing more sustainable attitudes to the design of things (Clark and Brody, 2009).

Emily Nicoll (2013) states: '*emotionally durable design* has a key role to play in helping address e-waste and obsolescence. It helps tackle the challenge of weaning people off their desire for the new, and helps shape new sustainable business models, so it is clearly an approach whose time is coming'. Significantly, 56 per cent of 18–25-year-olds state the importance of finding brands they can be loyal to and develop lasting relationships with (Euro RSCG Worldwide, 2011). In this way, emotionally durable design has the potential to present robust economic models for creating products, services and brand-loyal customers – driving future sales, upgrades, service and repair (Webb, 2013).

A number of academics call for a move away from the production of things, towards a less materialistic and ecologically burgeoning form of consumption in which experiences are the focus of our desire. In these scenarios, we consume experiences rather than objects, and sensations rather than stuff. The things we own become mere 'vehicles' or 'carriers' of meaning. Take denim jeans, for example: you have a close relationship with your jeans. Your jeans are like a second skin, worn and moulded and torn by your everyday experiences (see Figure 12.2). Purchased like blank canvases, jeans are worked on, sculpted and personified over time. Jeans are like familiar old friends providing animated narrative to life – a repository of memories – mapping events as and when they occur.

The social values affixed to the ageing of material surfaces are complex. Take leather, for example. A scuff or scratch on a pair of patent leather stilettos ruins them, whereas handmade leather brogues develop character and improve with such wear and tear. However, leather is an ecologically burgeoning material. For example, the average synthetic running shoe produces 8 kg CO_2. Primarily, this CO_2 is the result of materials processing, manufacturing, transportation and packaging. The average leather shoe produces 15 kg CO_2 – over twice as much (Berners-Lee, 2011). In addition to the high carbon intensity of cattle farming, the process of growing leather creates a great deal of methane, or CH_4 as it is scientifically known. As a greenhouse gas and main contributor to climate change, CH_4 is 25 times more potent per kilo than CO_2. And so there is a dichotomy here: synthetic materials are at times more sustainable than natural ones, as they can be kept within material flows on a cradle-to-cradle (C2C) or closed-loop methodology. On the one hand, leather can be used in a way that extends product life, and in so doing, reduces levels of consumption and waste. While on the other hand, leather has a heavy ecological burden.

Indeed, patina is an important design consideration to assist the extension of product lifespans in graceful and socially acceptable ways. Sometimes, it is acceptable for a given material to develop patina, and sometimes it is not. For example, cars should not be dinted and scratched, unless they're vintage cars, and then its considered charming (Chapman, 2013b). Japanese footwear brand Visvim design and make shoes that grow old gracefully, and construct them in such a way that they are actually repairable (see Figure 12.3). When the outsole wears off, it can be replaced. The shoe costs more to buy, but this is part of the story of the shoe, and the brand, and people buy into it.

Designers can reduce the need to consume by making stuff that lasts; things that withstand the test of time, with durable meanings and values that people want to keep and look after. The theory of emotionally durable design has potential here, as a strategic approach to reducing the consumption and waste of resources and energy. Design must challenge our social desire for a scratch-free, box-fresh world. The onset of ageing can concentrate, rather than weaken, the experience of an object. Emma Whiting's concept for Puma explores the idea of an 'evolving narrative experience'; a shoe that celebrates the process of ageing, and the accumulation of grime, wear and tear (see Figure 12.4). Certain areas of the textile are printed with a protective screen, and other areas are left exposed to the elements.

FIGURE 12.2 *Jeans are like a second skin, ageing and adapting with you. Photograph by Jonathan Chapman.*

FIGURE 12.3 *Visvim footwear is designed for repair, and ages well. Courtesy of Cubism Inc.*

According to Jasper Morrison, our perception of objects can be broken down as follows: the first encounter may well be based more on an evaluation of the object's cost, the quality of the object relating to the cost, the perceived usefulness of the object to us and the object's desirability. But later on, when it comes to living with an object, we forget all about the cost, and we have in mind the object's usefulness in relation to certain tasks, how much we enjoy using it and how much we appreciate it as a possession. It becomes a part of our lives, which we may not think about much, but that nevertheless exists, as witnessed when we move house (for example) and may be forced to confront the relationship we have with the object in deciding whether to keep it or not (Fukasawa and Morrison, 2007, pp. 53–54). In Fukasawa and Morrison's book, *Super Normal*, we are told how design, which used to be almost unknown as a profession, has become a major source of pollution. Encouraged by glossy lifestyle magazines and marketing departments, it has become a competition to make things as noticeable as possible by means of colour, shape and surprise. Its historic and idealistic purpose, to serve industry and the happy consuming masses at the same time, of conceiving things easier to make and better to live with, seems to have been side-tracked (Fukasawa and Morrison, 2007, pp. 8–10).

As *matter* that we must negotiate, products can literally shape our daily experience in ways that spark particular thoughts, and designers can therefore influence what these thoughts are. In addition, objects have the ability to be the locus of discussion about our potential futures; to explore through objects the logical conclusions to certain models of thought, be they politically partisan, positive (utopian) or negative (dystopian). Yet, beyond a small band of critical designers and activists, the design world is not a hotbed of political debate, and most designers neither wear their political agendas on their sleeves, nor make them explicit in their portfolios. Hence the link between design and politics that undeniably exists is downplayed and often overlooked entirely (Parsons, 2009).

FIGURE 12.4 *Evolving narrative experience by Emma Whiting, 2012. Courtesy of University of Brighton.*

Conclusion

In today's unsustainable world of goods, where products are desired, acquired, briefly used and then promptly discarded, the cycle of production, consumption and waste is spiralling out of control. For decades, designers have strived to put the ghost into the machine – to be meaning-makers. Yet, it is within *us* the spirit lurks. As a simultaneously creative and strategic activity, 'emotionally durable design' can be achieved through consideration of the following five elements:

- **Narrative:** users share, and develop, a unique personal history with the product.
- **Consciousness:** products are perceived as autonomous and in possession of their own free will.
- **Attachment:** users feel a strong emotional connection to a product.
- **Fiction:** the product inspires interactions and connections beyond just the physical relationship.
- **Surface:** the product ages gracefully and develops character through time and use.

Design's transition from a *world-making*, to a *world-breaking* enterprise has put it in a position of flux, in which urgent re-examination of the potential of design as an agent of positive change continues to gather in intensity. If design is the research, planning and visioning that lays the basis for the making of all objects, spaces or systems, then its influence over the sustainability of consumption is nothing short of critical. Like philosophers who do something about it, designers play a vital role in our transition toward more ecologically compatible systems and practices; an emerging synthesis of artist, inventor, economist and evolutionary strategist that roams the territory between value and action.

As the made world continues to develop in technological and scientific complexity, it can be said that the human condition itself has changed relatively little. And so today we find ourselves as primitive beings, transplanted into progressively abstract and technologically complex environments that are beyond our 'nature' as a species. In terms of biological evolution, it may be argued that we have come as far as we can usefully go, and if we intend to sustain progress, we must dramatically alter the parameters of life, through design. Whether faster processing speeds, taller structures, smarter textiles or smaller components, we must apply science, technology and design to realize our visions – whatever they may be – and make them livable.

Emotionally durable design provides a useful language to describe the contemporary relevance of designing responsible, well-made, tactile products, which the user can get to know and assign value to in the long term (Lacey, 2009). Objects that, through their materiality, grow old gracefully, and accumulate character and value through time. At which point, it becomes clear that durability is just as much about emotion, love, value and attachment as it is about fractured polymers, worn gaskets or blown circuitry.

BIBLIOGRAPHY

1 'I Love Giving Presents'

Adorno, T. (1997), *Minima Moralia* [1951], London: Verso.

Bhatti, M. (2006), ' "When I'm in the Garden I can Create my Own Paradise": Homes and Gardens in Later Life', *The Sociological Review*, 54(2), pp. 318–341.

Carrier, J. G. (1995), *Gifts and Commodities: Exchange and Western Capitalism Since 1700*, London: Routledge.

Geertz, C. (1993), *The Interpretation of Cultures* [1973], London: Fontana.

Godlier, M. (1999), *The Enigma of the Gift*, Cambridge: Polity Press.

Gregory, C. A. (1982), *Gifts and Commodities*, London: Academic Press.

Hurdley, R. (2006), 'Dismantling Mantelpieces: Narrating Identities and Materialising Culture in the Home', *Sociology*, 40(4), pp. 717–733.

Hurdley, R. (2013), *Home, Materiality, Memory and Belonging: Keeping Culture*, Basingstoke: Palgrave Macmillan.

Komter, A. (1996), 'Women, Gifts and Power', in A. Komter (ed.) *The Gift: An Interdisciplinary Perspective*, Amsterdam: Amsterdam University Press, pp. 119–131.

Marx, K. (1988), *Capital: A Critique of Political Economy* [1867], London: Penguin.

Mauss, M. (1990), *The Gift: The Form and Reason for Exchange in Archaic Societies* [1925], London: Routledge.

Mass Observation (2013), 'Mass Observation: Recording Everyday Life in Britain', www.massobs.org.uk/index.htm.

Mitchell, C. J. (1984), 'Case Studies', in R. Ellen (ed.) *Ethnographic Research: A Guide to General Conduct*, London: Academic Press, pp. 237–241.

Pollen, A. (2013), 'Research Methodology in Mass Observation Past and Present: "Scientifically, About as Valuable as a Chimpanzee's Tea Party at the Zoo"?', *History Workshop Journal*, 75, pp. 213–235.

Purbrick, L. (2007), *The Wedding Present: Domestic Life Beyond Consumption*, Farnham: Ashgate.

Sheridan, D. (1996), ' "Damned Anecdotes and Dangerous Confabulations": Mass-Observation as Life History', *Mass-Observation Archive Occasional Paper*, 7, Brighton: University of Sussex Library.

Sheridan, D., Street, B. and Bloome, D. (2000), *Writing Ourselves: Mass Observation and Literacy Practices*, Cresskill, NJ: Hampton Press.

Slater, D. (1997), *Consumer Culture and Modernity*, Cambridge: Polity.

Stanley, L. (2001), 'Mass Observation's Fieldwork Methods', in P. Atkinson, S. Delamont, A. Coffey, J. Lofland and L. Lofland (eds) *Handbook of Ethnography*, London: Sage, pp. 92–108.

Slater, D. (1997), *Consumer Culture and Modernity*, Cambridge, Polity.

2 (S)mother's Love, or, Baby Knitting

Alford, C. F. (2006), *Psychology and the Natural Law of Reparation*, Cambridge: Cambridge University Press.

Bakhtin, M. (1984), *Rabelais and His World* (trans. H. Iswolsky), Bloomington, IN: Indiana University Press.

Bamberger, J. (1974), 'The Myth of Matriarchy: Why Men Rule in Primitive Society', in M. Zimbalist Rosaldo and L. Lamphere (eds) *Woman, Culture and Society*, Redwood City, CA: Stanford University Press, pp. 263–280.

Banyard, K. (2010), *The Equality Illusion*, London: Faber & Faber.

Barthes, R. (1973), *Mythologies*, London: Paladin.

Bauer, D. M. and McKinstry, S. J. (1992) (eds), *Feminism, Bakhtin, and the Dialogic*, New York, NY: State University of New York Press.

Benjamin, J. (1988), *Bonds of Love: Psychoanalysis, Feminism and the Problems of Domination*, New York, NY: Pantheon Books.

Blaffer Hrdy, S. (1999), *Mother Nature: Natural Selection and the Female of the Species*, London: Chatto & Windus.

Boris, E. (1994), *Home to Work: Motherhood and the Politics of Industrial Homework in the United States*, Cambridge: Cambridge University Press.

Davidoff, L. (1973), *The Best Circles: Society, Etiquette and the Season*, London: Croom Helm Publishing.

Davidoff, L. and Hall, C. (2002), *Family Fortunes: Men and Women of the English Middle Class 1780–1850*, 2nd edition, London: Routledge.

Dufresne, T. (2000), *Tales from the Freudian Crypt: The Death Drive in Text and Context*, Palo Alto, CA: Stanford University Press.

Gauntlett, D. (2011), *Making is Connecting*, London: Polity Press.

Goodwin, S. and Huppatz, K. (2010), *The Good Mother: Contemporary Motherhoods in Australia*, Oxford: Blackwell.

Hirschon, R. (1993), 'Open Body/Closed Space; the Transformation of Female Sexuality' in S. Ardener (ed.) *Defining Females: The Nature of Women in Society*, Oxford: Berg, pp. 66–81.

Hollows, J. (2006), 'Can I Go Home Yet? Feminism, Post Feminism and Domesticity', in J. Hollows and R. Moseley (eds) *Feminism in Popular Culture*, Oxford: Berg, pp. 97–118.

Keltner, S. (2010), *Kristeva*, Malden: Polity Press.

Klein, M. (1988), *Love, Guilt and Reparation*, 2nd edition, New York, NY: Vintage.

Kristeva, J. (1982), *Powers of Horror: An Essay in Abjection*, New York, NY: Columbia University Press.

Miller, D. (1998), *Shopping, Place and Identity*, London: Routledge.

Mowery Kieffer, S. (2004), *Fiberarts Design Book 7*, New York, NY: Lark Books.

Nelson, M. K. and Smith, J. (1999), *Working Hard and Making Do*, Berkeley, CA: University of California Press.

Pagett, M. (2007), *Make Your Own Sex Toys: 50 Quick and Easy D.I.Y. Projects*, San Francisco, CA: Chronicle Books.

Reynolds, H. (1999), ' "Your Clothes are Materials of War": The British Government Promotion of Home Sewing During the Second World War', in B. Burman (ed.) *The Culture of Sewing*, Oxford: Berg, pp. 327–340.

Rigdon, R. and Stewart, Z. (2007), *AntiCraft: Knitting, Beading and Stitching for the Slightly Sinister*, Cincinnati, OH: North Light Books.

Ruddick, S. (2004), 'Maternal Thinking as a Feminist Standpoint', in S. Harding (ed.) *The Feminist Standpoint Theory Reader: Intellectual and Political Controversies*, London: Routledge, pp. 161–168.

Salecl, R. (2004), *On Anxiety*, London: Routledge.

Samuel, R. (1996), *Theatres of Memory*, 2nd edition, London: Verso.

Scott, J. (2003), *Textile Perspectives in Mixed Media Sculpture*, Hungerford: D & N Publishing.

Sparke, P. (1995), *As Long as it's Pink: The Sexual Politics of Taste*, London: Pandora.

Stafford, J. (2007), *DomikniTrix: Whip Your Knitting Into Shape*, Cincinnati, OH: North Light Books.

Strawn, S. M. (2007), *Knitting America: A Glorious Heritage from Warm Socks to High Art*, Minneapolis, MN: Voyager Press.

Turney, J. (2009), *The Culture of Knitting*, Oxford: Berg.
Warwick, A. and Cavallaro, D. (1998), *Fashioning the Frame: Boundaries, Dress and the Body*, Oxford: Berg.

3 Sex, Birth and Nurture Unto Death

Barnett, P. (1999), 'Folds, Fragments, Surfaces: Towards a Poetics of Cloth' in *Textures of Memory: The Poetics of Cloth*, Nottingham: Angel Row Gallery, pp. 25–34.
'Barts Dog Gets an F'. The Simpsons, Season 2, Episode 16, 1991.
Constantine, M. and Reuter, L. (1997), *The Whole Cloth*, New York, NY: Monacelli Press.
Chase, P. (1976), 'Quilting: Reclaiming our Art', *Country Life*, 21, September, p. 9.
Cherenack, K. and van Pieterson, L. (2012), 'Smart Textiles: Challenges and Opportunities', *Journal of Applied Physics*, 112, 091301, http://dx.doi.org/10.1063/1.4742728.
Chu, A., Fink, P. W., Dobbins, J. A., Lin, G. Y., Scully, R. S. and Trevino, R. (2008), *Circuit Patterns are Implemented in Tightly Woven Cloth Instead of Stitched Conductive Thread*, Houston TX: Lyndon B. Johnson Space Center (patent application filed by NASA), ntrs.nasa.gov/archive/nasa/casi.ntrs.nasa.gov/20090016265_2009015493.pdf.
Dong, L. (2012), 'Coaxial Electrospinning Produces a Self-Supporting Micro/Nanofiber Electronic Light Source', *SPIE Newsroom*, 30 April, http://spie.org/x86807.xml.
Fry, G. (2002), *Stitched from the Soul: Slave Quilts from the Antebellum South*, Chapel Hill, NC: University of North Carolina Press.
Gavin, R. (2002), 'History of the Clothing Industry in Derry', in V. Wilson (ed.) *Fabrics and Fabrications*, Derry: Context Gallery.
Harper, C. (2001), 'Narelle Jubelin at Goldsmiths College, London', *Textile: The Journal of Cloth and Culture*, 1(3), November, pp. 210–229.
Holstein, J. (1973), *The Pieced Quilt: An American Design Tradition*, Boston, MA: New York Graphic Society.
How to Make an American Quilt (1995), Dir. Jocelyn Moorhouse.
Johnson, P. (2000), *Thinking Process in Art Textiles*, Bury St Edmunds: Art Gallery of Bury St Edmunds, pp. 17–24.
Lippard, L. (1993), 'Up, Down and Across: A New Frame for New Quilts' in C. Robinson (ed.) *The Artist and the Quilt*, New York, NY (2008): Knopf Press, p. 18.
Lowther, C. and Schultz, S. (eds) (2008), *Bright: Architectural Illumination and Light Installations*, Berlin: Die Gestalten Verlag.
Lucie-Smith, E. (1981), *The Story of Craft*, Ithaca, NY: Cornell University Press.
Maharaj, S. (2001), 'Textile Art – Who are You?', in J. Jefferies (ed.) *Reinventing Textiles: Volume Two: Gender and Identity*, Winchester: Telos Art Publishing, pp. 7–10.
NASA (2012), *Phase Change Fabrics Control Temperature*, Originating technology/NASA Contribution, www.nasa.gov/offices/ipp/centers/jsc/spinoff/PhaseChange.html.
Parker, R. (1984), *The Subversive Stitch: Embroidery and the Making of the Feminine*, London: The Women's Press Ltd.
Qi, J. (2012), 'How-To: Work with Shape-Memory Alloy', http://blog.makezine.com/2012/01/31/skill-builder-working-with-shape-memory-alloy/.
Smith, E. (2004), 'Soft Wear', *Selvedge magazine*, 00, May/June, pp. 26–31.
Smith, P. J. (1986), *Craft Today: Poetry of the Physical*, London: Weidenfeld & Nicolson.
Suit, V. (2004), 'Creativity Constrained', *Selvedge magazine*, 00, May/June, pp. 16–20.
Watney, S. (1997), *Craft*, London: Richard Salmon.
Wilson, V. (2002), 'Introduction to Quilts and Clothing', in *Fabrics and Fabrications*, Derry: Context Gallery.

4 Bringing Out the Past

Barthes, R. (1975), *The Pleasure of the Text* (trans. R. Miller), New York, NY: Hill & Wang.

Barthes, R. (1978), *A Lover's Discourse: Fragments*, New York, NY: Hill & Wang.

Barthes, R. (1981), *Camera Lucida: Reflections on Photography* (trans. R. Howard), New York, NY: Hill & Wang.

Barthes, R. (1985), *The Grain of the Voice: Interviews 1962–1980* (trans. L. Coverdale), Berkeley, CA: University of California Press.

Barthes, R. (1992), *Incidents* (trans. R. Howard), Berkeley, CA: University of California Press.

Burns, E. (1985), 'The Man Behind the Lady in Troubadour Lyric', *Romance Notes*, 25, pp. 254–270.

Burns, E. (2001), 'Courtly Love: Who Needs It? Recent Feminist Work in the Medieval French Tradition', *Signs*, 27, pp. 23–57.

Bush, R. (1998), *Affectionate Men: A Photographic History of a Century of Male Couples (1850s to 1950s)*, New York, NY: St Martin's Press.

Cohen, K. (1996), 'Locating the Photograph's "Prick": A Queer Tropology of Roland Barthes's *Camera Lucida*', *Chicago Art Journal*, 6, pp. 5–14.

Crompton, L. (1976), 'Homosexuals and the Death Penalty in Colonial America', *Journal of Homosexuality*, 1(3), pp. 277–293.

Deitcher, D. (1998), 'Looking at a Photograph, Looking for a History', in D. Bright (ed.) *The Passionate Camera: Photography and Bodies of Desire*, New York, NY: Routledge, pp. 23–26.

Deitcher, D. (2001), *Dear Friends: American Photographs of Men Together, 1840–1918*, New York, NY: Harry N. Abrams.

Ellenzweig, A. (1992), *The Homoerotic Photograph: Male Images From Durieu/Delacroix to Mapplethorpe*, New York, NY: Columbia University Press.

Foucault, M. (1980), *The History of Sexuality 1: An Introduction* (trans. R. Hurley), New York, NY: Vintage Books.

Foucault, M. (1997), 'Sex, Power, and the Politics of Identity', in P. Rabinow (ed.) *Ethics, Subjectivity, and Truth: The Essential Works of Michel Foucault*, New York, NY: New Press, pp. 166–173.

Gardiner, J. (1998), *Who's a Pretty Boy, Then?: One Hundred & Fifty Years of Gay Life in Pictures*, London: Serpent's Tail.

Ibson, J. (2002), *Picturing Men: A Century of Male Relationships in Everyday American Photography*, Washington, D.C.: Smithsonian Institution Press.

Iverson, M. (1994), 'What is a Photograph?', *Art History*, 17, pp. 451–463.

Iverson, M. (2007), *Beyond Pleasure: Freud, Lacan, Barthes*, University Park, PA: Pennsylvania State University Press.

Katz, J. (2001), *Love Stories: Sex between Men Before Homosexuality*, Chicago, IL: University of Chicago Press.

Kay, S. (2001), *Courtly Contradictions: The Emergence of the Literary Object in the Twelfth Century*, Redwood City, CA: Stanford University Press.

Kritzman, L. (1989), 'The Discourse of Desire and the Question of Gender', in S. Ungar and B. McGraw (eds) *Signs in Culture: Roland Barthes Today*, Iowa City, IA: University of Iowa Press, pp. 99–116.

Lacan, J. (1991), *The Seminar of Jacques Lacan, Book VII: The Ethics of Psychoanalysis, 1959–60* (ed. J. A. Miller, trans. D. Porter), New York, NY: W. W. Norton.

Lacan, J. (1994), *Livre IV: La Relation d'objet, 1956–57*, Paris: Seuil.

Lacan, J. (1998), *The Seminar of Jacques Lacan, Book XI: The Four Fundamental Concepts of Psychoanalysis* (ed. J. A. Miller, trans. A. Sheridan), New York, NY: W. W. Norton.

Lacan, J. (n.d.), *Seminar VIII: Transference, 1960–1961*, (trans. C. Gallagher), http://www.lutecium.org/mirror/www.valas.fr/IMG/pdf/THE-SEMINAR-OF-JACQUES-LACAN-VIII_le_transfert.pdf.

Ragland, E. (1995), 'Psychoanalysis and Courtly Love', *Arthuriana*, 5, pp. 1–20.

Restuccia, F. (2006), *Amorous Acts: Lacanian Ethics in Modernism, Film, and Queer Theory*, Redwood City, CA: Stanford University Press.

Robb, G. (2003), *Strangers: Homosexual Love in the Nineteenth Century*, New York, NY: W. W. Norton.

Shepherdson, C. (1995), 'History and the Real: Foucault with Lacan', *Postmodern Culture*, 5(2), http://muse.jhu.edu/journals/postmodern_culture/v005/5.2 shepherdson.html.

Smith, C. and Greig, C. (2003), *Women in Pants*, New York, NY: Harry N. Abrams.

Smith-Rosenberg, C. (1975), 'The Female World of Love and Ritual: Relations Between Women in Nineteenth-Century America', *Signs*, 1, pp. 1–29.

Warner, M. (1994), *Fear of a Queer Planet: Queer Politics and Social Theory*, Minneapolis, MN: University of Minnesota Press.

Waugh, T. (1996), *Hard to Imagine: Gay Male Eroticism in Photography and Film from Their Beginnings to Stonewall*, New York, NY: Columbia University Press.

Žižek, S. (1992), *Looking Awry: An Introduction to Jacques Lacan through Popular Culture*, Cambridge, MA: MIT Press.

Žižek, S. (1993), 'From Courtly Love to the Crying Game,' *New Left Review*, I, pp. 95–108.

5 The Genteel Craft of Subversion

Ackermann, R. (1810), *The Repository of Arts, Literature, Commerce, Manufactures, Fashion and Politics*, July, Vol. III, No. 18.

Anonymous (1810a), 'The History of the Shoemaking Craft', in *The Princely History of the Gentle Craft or, The Shoemaker's Glory: shewing what renowned Princes, Heroes, and Worthies, have been of the Shoemaker's Trade, in this and other Kingdoms. Likewise, why it is called, The Gentle Craft: and that they say, A Shoemaker's son is a Prince born.* Printed by T. Johnston: Falkirk.

Anonymous (1810b), 'The History of the King and the Cobler', in *The Princely History of the Gentle Craft or, The Shoemaker's Glory: shewing what renowned Princes, Heroes, and Worthies, have been of the Shoemaker's Trade, in this and other Kingdoms. Likewise, why it is called, The Gentle Craft: and that they say, A Shoemaker's son is a Prince born.* Printed by T. Johnston: Falkirk.

Anonymous (1827), *Crispin anecdotes: comprising interesting notices of shoemakers who have been distinguished for genius, enterprise, or eccentricity: also curious particulars relative to the origin, importance, & manufacture of shoes: with other matters illustrative of the history of the gentle craft*, Sheffield: J. Blackwell.

Blake, Mrs A. E. K. (ed.) (1911), *An Irish Beauty of the Regency compiled from 'mes souvenirs', – the unpublished journals of the Hon. Mrs. Calvert 1789–1822*, London: John Lane Company.

Bourdieu, P. (1984), *Distinction: A Social Critique of the Judgement of Taste*, Cambridge, MA: Harvard University Press.

Byrde, P. (2008), *Jane Austen Fashion: Fashion and Needlework in the Works of Jane Austen*, Ludlow: Moonrise Press.

Edwards, C. (2006), ' "Home is Where the Art is": Women, Handicrafts and Home Improvements 1750–1900', *Journal of Design History*, 19(1), pp. 11–21.

Hobsbawm, E. J. and Wallach Scott, J. (1980), 'Political Shoemakers', *Past & Present*, 89, pp. 86–114.

Letter to Penelope Geast (1783), Record Office for Leicestershire, Leicester & Rutland (DE5047/79/1-2), Leicester.

McGuire, N. (2010), *Inconspicuous Production: The Genteel Craft of Amateur Shoemaking in the Late Eighteenth and Early Nineteenth Centuries*, MA thesis (Design History and Material Culture), National College of Art and Design, Dublin.

Parker, R. (1984), *The Subversive Stitch: Embroidery and the Making of the Feminine*, London: The Women's Press Ltd.

Pitt Lennox, Lord W. (1878), *Fashion Then and Now: Illustrated by Anecdotes, Social, Political, Military, Dramatic and Sporting*, Vol. I. London: Chapman & Hall.

Riello, G. (2006), *A Foot in The Past: Consumers, Producers and Footwear in the Long Eighteenth Century*, Oxford: Oxford University Press.

St Aubyn, F. (1987), *Ivory: A History and Collector's Guide*, London: Thames & Hudson.

Sharp, K. (2004), 'Women's Creativity and Display in the Eighteenth-Century British Domestic Interior' in S. McKellar and P. Sparke (eds) *Interior Design and Identity*, Manchester: Manchester University Press, pp. 10–26.

Stirling, A. M. W. (ed.) (1913), *The Letter-Bag of Lady Elizabeth Spencer-Stanhope (1806–73)*, London: John Lane.

Swann, J. (1982), *Shoes*, London: B.T. Batsford Ltd.

Veblen, T. (1899, 1915 edition), *The Theory of the Leisure Class: An Economic Study of Institutions*, New York, NY: Macmillan.

Vickery, A. (1998), *The Gentleman's Daughter: Women's Lives in Georgian England*, New Haven, CT: Yale University Press.

Vickery, A. (2009), *Behind Closed Doors: At Home in Georgian England*, New Haven, CT: Yale University Press.

Young, L. (2003), *Middle-Class Culture in the Nineteenth Century*, New York, NY: Palgrave Macmillan.

6 Performing Masculinity Through Objects in Postwar America

A Woman of Fashion (1898), *Etiquette for Americans*, Chicago, IL: Herbert S. Stone & Company.

Anonymous (1865), *The Habits of Good Society*, New York, NY: Carleton.

Anonymous (1956), 'Playboy's Penthouse Apartment: A Second Look at a High, Handsome Haven – Pre-planned and Furnished for the Bachelor in Town', *Playboy*, October, pp. 65–70.

Anonymous (1958), 'Meet the Playboy Reader', *Playboy*, April, pp. 63, 76–77.

Anonymous (1959a), 'Playing the Piper: A Paean to the Pipe: An Elegant, Masculine Way to Smoke', *Playboy*, September, pp. 75–80, 97–98.

Anonymous (1959b), 'Invitation to a Playboy Christmas', *Playboy*, December, pp. 83–87.

Anonymous (1962), 'What Sort of Man Reads Playboy', *Playboy*, March, p. 43.

Attwood, W. (1958), 'The American Male: Why Does the Work So Hard?', *Look*, March 4, pp. 70–75.

Auslander, L. (1996), 'The Gendering of Consumer Practices in Nineteenth-Century France', in V. de Grazia and E. Furlough (eds) *The Sex of Things*, Berkeley, CA: University of California Press, pp. 79–112.

Burns E. (2007), *The Smoke of the Gods: A Social History of Tobacco*, Philadelphia, PA: Temple University Press.

Cuordileone, K. (2000), ' "Politics in an Age of Anxiety": Cold War Political Culture and the Crisis in American Masculinity, 1949–1960', *Journal of American History*, 87(2), pp. 515–545.

Ehrenreich, B. (1983), *The Hearts of Men: American Dreams and the Flight from Commitment*, New York, NY: Anchor Books.

Gately, I. (2003), *Tobacco: A Cultural History of How an Exotic Plant Seduced Civilization*, New York, NY: Grove Press.

Gelber, S. (1999), *Hobbies*, New York, NY: Columbia University Press.

Gilbert, J. (2005), *Men in the Middle: Searching for Masculinity in the 1950s*, Chicago, IL: University of Chicago Press.

Green, W. (1904), *A Dictionary of Etiquette*, New York, NY: Brentano's.

Hefner, H. (1953), *Playboy*, Volume 1, Number 1, November, p. 7.

Hefner, H. (1998), 'Introduction', in G. Edgren, *Inside the Playboy Mansion*, Santa Monica, CA: General Publishing Group, pp. 7–12.

Humphry, C. (1897), *Manners for Men*, London: James Bowden.

Leonard, G. B. Jr. (1958), 'The American Male: Why is He Afraid to be Different?' *Look*, 14 February, pp. 95–103.

Louis, S. (1881), *Decorum*, New York, NY: Union Publishing House.

Lynes, R. (1949), 'High-brow, Low-brow, Middle-brow', *Time*, April, pp. 99–101.

Moskin, R. (1959), 'The American Male: Why Do Women Dominate Him?', *Look*, 5 February, pp. 76–80.

Riesman, D. (1950), *The Lonely Crowd*, New Haven, CT: Yale University Press.

Roberts, H. (1913), *Putnam's Handbook of Etiquette*, New York, NY: G. P. Putnam's Sons.

Schlesinger, A. Jr. (1958), 'The Crisis of American Masculinity', *Esquire*, November, pp. 63–65.

Weber, C. (1962), *Weber's Guide to Pipes and Pipe Smoking*, New York, NY: Cornerstone Publishing.

Whyte, W. (1956), *The Organization Man*, New York, NY: Simon & Schuster.

Wylie, P. (1958), 'The Womanization of America', *Playboy*, October, pp. 51–52, 77–79.

Young, J. (1881), *Our Deportment*, Springfield, MA: W. C. King & Co.

7 Seduced by the Archive

Attfield, J. (2000), *Wild Things*, Oxford: Berg.

Auslander, L. (2005), 'Beyond Words', *The American Historical Review*, 110(4), October, pp. 1015–1045.

Belk, R. (1995), *Collecting in a Consumer Society*, London: Routledge.

Derrida, J. (1998), *Archive Fever: A Freudian Impression* (trans. E. Prenowitz), Chicago, IL: The University of Chicago Press.

Doan, L. (1994), 'What's in and Out, Out There? Disciplining the Lesbian Author(s)', *American Literary History*, 6(3), Curriculum and Criticism (Autumn), pp. 572–582.

Doan, L. (2011), 'Welcome and Keynote Presentation', *Sexuality and the Archive: A Colloquium on Method*, 18 February, King's College London.

Elliott, B. (2006), 'Art Deco Hybridity, Interior Design, and Sexuality between the Wars: Two Double Acts: Phyllis Barron and Dorothy Larcher/Eyre de Lanux and Evelyn Wyld', in L. Doan (ed.) *Sapphic Modernities: Sexuality, Women and National Culture*, Basingstoke: Palgrave Macmillan, pp. 228–239.

Grigg, S. (1991), 'Archival Practice and the Foundations of Historical Method', *The Journal of American History*, 78(1), June, pp. 238–239.

Hartnell, N. (1955), *Silver and Gold*, London: Evans Brothers.

Hattrick, J. (2012), 'Collecting and Displaying Identity, Intimacy and Memory in the Staged Interiors of the Royal Couturier Norman Hartnell', in S. H. Dudley, A. J. Barnes, J. Vinnie, J. Petrov and J. Walklate (eds) *Narrating Objects, Collecting Stories*, London: Routledge, pp. 136–152.

Hobbs, C. (2001), 'The Character of Personal Archives: Reflections on the Value of Records of Individuals', *Archivaria*, 52, Fall, pp. 126–135.

Ideal Home (1947), Cover, November. Courtesy The Hartnell-Mitchison Archive.

Kopytoff, I. (1986), 'The Cultural Biography of Things: Commoditization as Process', in A. Appadurai (ed.) *The Social Life of Things: Commodities in Cultural Perspective*, Cambridge: Cambridge University Press, pp. 64–93.

Lichtenstein, R. and Sinclair, I. (2000), *Rodinsky's Room*, London: Granta.

Maple & Co. Ltd. Valuers London, W1 (1939), *Inventory & Valuation 'The Towers' 12, Park Village West, N.W.* Courtesy The Hartnell-Mitchison Archive.

Martin, B. (1998), 'Lesbian Identity and Autobiographical Difference(s)', in S. Smith and J. Watson (eds) *Women, Autobiography, Theory: A Reader*, Madison, WI: University of Wisconsin Press, pp. 380–393.

McNeil, P. (2010), 'Crafting Queer Spaces: Privacy and Posturing', in A. Myzelev and J. Potvin (eds) *Fashion, Interior Design and the Contours of Modern Identity*, Farnham: Ashgate, pp. 19–42.

Prescott, A. (2008), 'The Textuality of the Archive.' in L. Craven (ed) *What are Archives? Cultural and Theoretical Perspectives: A Reader*, Farnham: Ashgate, pp. 31–51.

Prown, J. D. (1993), 'The Truth of Material Culture: History of Fiction?' in S. Lubar and W. D. Kingery (eds) *History from Things: Essays on Material Culture*, London and Washington: Smithsonian Institution Press, pp. 1–19.

Smith, S. and Watson, J. (2002), *Interfaces/Women/Autobiography/Image/Performance*, Michigan: University of Michigan Press.

Smith, S. and Watson, J. (1998), 'Introduction: Situating Subjectivity in Women's Autobiographical Practices', in S. Smith and J. Watson (eds) *Women, Autobiography, Theory: A Reader*, Madison, WI: University of Wisconsin Press, pp. 3–52.

Steedman, C. (2001), *Dust*, Manchester: Manchester University Press.

The Coronation of Elizabeth II. Dir. Jamie Muir, Blakeway Productions, Monday 4 June 2012, BBC 4.

Tulloch, C. (1998), ' "Out of Many, One People": The Relativity of Dress, Race and Ethnicity to Jamaica, 1880–1907', *Fashion Theory*, 2(4), pp. 359–382.

Williams, C. (2008), 'Personal Papers: Perceptions and Practices', in L. Craven (ed.) *What are Archives? Cultural and Theoretical Perspectives: A Reader*, Farnham: Ashgate, pp. 53–67.

Williams, J. J. (2012), 'Queer 2.0', *The Chronicle of Higher Education*, 1 January, http://chronicle.com/article/Queer-20/130156/.

Yee, S. (2007), 'The Archive', in S. Turkle (ed.) *Evocative Objects: Things We Think With*, Cambridge, MA, and London: The MIT Press.

8 Kitsch, Enchantment and Power

Anonymous (1920a), 'Amazing Story of Supposed Miraculous Occurrences in Templemore', *Anglo-Celt*, 28 August, p. 5.

Anonymous (1920b), 'Limerick Youth Partially Cured after Visit to Templemore', *Limerick Leader*, 25 August, p. 2.

Anonymous (1920c), 'Police and Templemore Happenings', *Irish Independent*, 9 September, p. 5.

Anonymous (1920d), ' "Statues Bleed" Again. Marvellous Stories of Cures from Templemore', *Anglo-Celt*, 4 September, p. 1.

Anonymous (1920e), 'Templemore, a Visitor's Impressions', *Meath Chronicle*, 25 September, p. 4.

Anonymous (1920f), 'Templemore Cures', *Anglo-Celt*, 18 September, p. 3.

Anonymous (1920g), 'Templemore Miracles, Graphic Description of the Miraculous Statues', *Limerick Leader*, 10 September, p. 4.

Anonymous (1920h), 'Templemore Pilgrimage. Further Cures Reported', *Irish Independent*, 2 September, p. 4.

Anonymous (1920i), 'Templemore Wonder. Further Cures Claimed', *Irish Independent*, 30 August, p. 4.

Anonymous (1920j), 'The Templemore Wonders, Some Interesting Impressions', *Limerick Leader*, 20 September, p. 6.

Anonymous (1920k), Untitled article, *Irish Independent*, 23 August, p. 6.

Anonymous (1921), 'Cashel Commemorates Victory over Conscription. The Dean's Promise', *Freeman's Journal*, 10 October, p. 6.

Belting, H. (1994), *Likeness and Presence, a History of the Image before the Era of Art*, Chicago, IL: University of Chicago Press.

Binkley, S. (2000), 'Kitsch as a Repetitive System: A Problem for the Theory of Taste Hierarchy', *Journal of Material Culture*, 5(2), pp. 131–152.

Bourdieu, P. (1979, 1984), *Distinction: A Social Critique of the Judgement of Taste* (trans. R. Nice), Cambridge, MA: Harvard University Press.

Buckley, T. A. (trans.) (1851), *Canons and Decrees of the Council of Trent*, London: Routledge.

Carroll, M. P. (1999), *Irish Pilgrimage, Holy Wells and Popular Catholic Devotion*, Baltimore, MD: Johns Hopkins University Press.

Coyle, J. B. (1913), *Our Lady of Perpetual Succour and Ireland*, Dublin: M. H. Gill & Son.

De Certeau, M. (1984), *The Practice of Everyday Life* (trans. S. Rendall), Berkeley, CA: University of California Press.

Fortesque, A. (1910), 'Veneration of Images', in *The Catholic Encyclopaedia*, New York, NY: Robert Appleton Company, http://www.newadvent.org/cathen/07664a.htm.

Gamboni, D. (2007), *The Destruction of Art: Iconoclasm and Vandalism Since the French Revolution*, London: Reaktion Books.

Gell, A. (1998), *Art and Agency*, Oxford: Oxford University Press.

Greenberg, C. (1939), 'Avant Garde and Kitsch', in C. Harrison and P. Wood (eds) (1992) *Art in Theory, 1900–1990: An Anthology of Changing Ideas*, Oxford: Blackwell, pp. 539–548.

Larkin, E. (1972), 'The Devotional Revolution in Ireland, 1850–75', *American Historical Review*, LXXVII, pp. 625–652.

Loch, J. M. N. and Loch, S. (1922), *Ireland in Travail*, London: John Murray.

Lockington, W. J. (1920), *The Soul of Ireland*, New York, NY: Macmillan.

Martin, H. (1921), *Ireland in Insurrection; an Englishman's Record of Fact*, London: Daniel O'Connor.

McCarthy, M. J. F. (1902), *Priests and People in Ireland*, Dublin: Hodges Figgis.

McDannell, C. (1995), *Material Christianity: Religion and Popular Culture in America*, New Haven, CT: Yale University Press.

Miller, D. (1987), *Material Culture and Mass Consumption*, Oxford: Basil Blackwell.

Morgan, D. (2005), *The Sacred Gaze, Religious Visual Culture in Theory and Practice*, Berkeley, CA: University of California Press.

Nolan, M. L. (1983), 'Irish Pilgrimage: The Different Tradition', *Annals of the Association of American Geographers*, 73(3), September, pp. 421–438.

Ó'Faoláin, S. (1965), *Vive Moi!*, London: Rupert Hart-Davis.

Reynolds, J. J. (2006), *'Violence and Visionaries' – A Study of the Anglo-Irish War 1919–21 in Templemore with Specific Reference to the 'Templemore Miracles', 1920*, M.A. Thesis (History and Local Studies), University of Limerick.

Ryan, Monsignor I. (1920), 'The Reported Miracles at Cashel', *Irish Times*, 18 September, p. 6.

Zola, É. (1896), *Lourdes* (trans. E. A. Vizetelly), London: Chatto & Windus.

9 'Magic Toyshops'

Attwood, F. (2005), 'Fashion and Passion: Marketing Sex to Women', *Sexualities*, 8(4), pp. 392–406.

Attwood, F. (2006), 'Sexed up: Theorizing the Sexualisation of Culture', *Sexualities*, 9(1), pp. 77–94.

Attwood, F. (2011), 'Through the Looking Glass? Sexual Agency and Subjectification Online', in R. Gill and C. Scharff (eds) *New Femininities: Post Feminism, Neoliberalism, and Subjectivity*, Basingstoke: Palgrave Macmillan, pp. 203–214.

Drumm, P. (2012), 'London Design Festival 2012: Tom Dixon on How to Design a Vibrator', *Core*, 77, http://www.core77.com/blog/design_festivals/london_design_festival_2012_tom_dixon_on_how_to_design_a_vibrator_23504.asp.

Evans, A., Riley, S. and Shankar, A. (2010), 'Technologies of Sexiness: Theorizing Women's Engagement in the Sexualization of Culture', *Feminism & Psychology*, 20(1), pp. 114–131.

Ferreday, D. (2008), '"Showing the Girl": The New Burlesque', *Feminist Theory*, 9(1), pp. 47–65.

Fun Factory (2013), Online catalogue, http://www.funfactory.com.

Gill, R. (2007), *Gender and the Media*, Cambridge: Polity Press.

Hebdige, D. (1979), *Subculture: The Meaning of Style*, London: Methuen.

Mauthner, N. and Doucet, A. (1998), 'Reflections on a Voice-Centred Relational Method of Data Analysis', in J. Ribbens and R. Edwards (eds) *Feminist Dilemmas in Qualitative Research: Private Lives and Public Texts*, London: Sage, pp. 119–146.

McNair, B. (2002), *Striptease Culture: Sex, Media and the Democratization of Desire*, London: Routledge.
McRobbie, A. (2004), 'The Rise and Rise of Porn Chic', *Times Higher Education*, http://www.timeshighereducation.co.uk/182087.article.
Sh! (2013), Sh! Women's Erotic Emporium Online, http://www.sh-womenstore.com/.
Woodward, I. (2007), *Understanding Material Culture*, Los Angeles, CA: Sage.

10 Material Memories

Acland, C. R. (ed.) (2007), *Residual Media*, Minneapolis, MN: University of Minnesota Press.
Bal, M., Crewe, J. and Spitzer, L. (eds) (1999), *Acts of Memory: Cultural Recall in the Present*, Hanover, PA: University Press of New England.
Barthes, R. (1982), *Camera Lucida*, London: Jonathan Cape Ltd.
Batchen, G. (2001), *Each Wild Idea: Writing, Photography, History*, Cambridge, MA: MIT Press.
Edwards, E. (2001), *Raw Histories: Photographs, Anthropology and Museums*, Oxford: Berg.
Edwards, E. and Hart, J. (2004), *Photographs Objects Histories: On the Materiality of Images*, London: Routledge.
Engel, S. (1999), *Context is Everything: The Nature of Memory*, New York, NY: WH Freeman & Co.
Hallam, E. and Hockey, J. (2001), *Death, Memory, and Material Culture*, Oxford: Berg.
Hirsch, M. (1997), *Family Frames: Photography, Narrative, and Postmemory*, Cambridge, MA: Harvard University Press.
King, N. (2000), *Memory, Narrative, Identity: Remembering the Self*, Edinburgh: Edinburgh University Press.
Kwint, M., Breward, C. and Aynsley, J. (eds) (1999), *Material Memories: Design and Evocation*, Oxford: Berg.
Munir, K. A. and Phillips, N. (2005), 'The Birth of the "Kodak Moment": Institutional Entrepreneurship and the Adoption of New Technologies', *Organization Studies*, 26(11), pp. 1665–1687.
Prosser, J. (2005), *Light in the Dark Room: Photography and Loss*, Minneapolis, MN: University of Minnesota Press.
Radstone, S. (2000), *Memory and Methodology*, Oxford: Berg.
Radstone, S. and Hodgkin, K. (2006), *Memory Cultures: Memory, Subjectivity, and Recognition*, New Brunswick, NJ: Transaction Publishers.
Rugg, L. H. (1997), *Picturing Ourselves: Photography & Autobiography*, Chicago, IL: University of Chicago Press.
Sandbye, M. (1999), 'Photographic Anamnesia: The Past in the Present', in L. K. Bertelsen, R. Gade and M. Sandbye (eds) *Symbolic Imprints: Essays on Photography and Visual Culture*, Aarhus: Aarhus University Press, pp. 180–201.
Spence, J. and Holland, P. (1991), *Family Snaps: The Meaning of Domestic Photography*, London: Virago.

11 The Problematic Decision to Live

Buchli, V. and Lucas, G. (2001), *Archaeologies of the Contemporary Past*, London: Routledge.
Corcoran, M. and Peillon, M. (2006), *Uncertain Ireland*, Dublin: Institute of Public Administration.
Douglas, M. and Isherwood, B. (1978), *The World of Goods*, London: Allen Lane.
Drazin, A. (2005), 'Architecture Without Architects: Building Home and State in Romania', in *Home Cultures*, 2(2), pp. 195–220.
Evans-Pritchard, E. E. (1976), *Witchcraft, Magic and Oracles Among the Azande*, abridged edition, Oxford: Oxford University Press.

Gell, A. (1997), *Art and Agency*, Oxford: Clarendon Press.

Golding, W. (1959), *Free Fall*, London: Faber & Faber.

Humphrey, C. (2002), *The Unmaking of Soviet Life: Everyday Economies after Socialism*, London: Cornell University Press.

Laird, N. (2007), *On Purpose*, London: Faber & Faber.

Mauss, M. (1990), *The Gift: The Form and Reason for Exchange in Archaic Societies*, reprinted edition, London: Routledge.

Miller, D. (1987), *Material Culture and Mass Consumption*, London: Routledge.

Miller, D. (2005), *Materiality*, London: Routledge.

Miller, D. and Woodward, S. (2007), 'Manifesto for a Study of Denim', *Social Anthropology*, 15(3), pp. 335–351.

Simmel, G. (2004), *The Philosophy of Money*, London: Routledge.

12 Designing Meaningful and Lasting User Experiences

Bateson, G. (1979), *Mind and Nature: A Necessary Unity*, New York, NY: E. P. Dutton.

Bateson, G. (2000), *Steps to an Ecology of Mind: Collected Essays in Anthropology, Psychiatry, Evolution, and Epistemology*, Chicago, IL: University of Chicago Press.

Berners-Lee, M. (2011), *How Bad Are Bananas? The Carbon Footprint of Everything*, Vancouver: Greystone Books.

Bocock, R. (1993), *Consumption: Key Ideas*, Abingdon: Routledge.

Boehnert, J. (2012), *The Visual Communication of Ecological Literacy: Designing, Learning and Emergent Ecological Perception*, PhD thesis, University of Brighton, http://www.eco-labs.org/.

Burnie, D. (1999), *Get a Grip on Ecology*, Lewes: The Ivy Press.

Chapman, J. (2005), *Emotionally Durable Design: Objects, Experiences and Empathy*, London: Earthscan.

Chapman, J. (2009), 'Design for [Emotional] Durability', *Design Issues*, 25(4), Autumn, pp. 29–35.

Chapman, J. (2013a), 'Emotionally Sustaining Design', in J. Girard and S. Walker (eds) *The Handbook of Design for Sustainability*, London: Bloomsbury Academic, pp. 363–374.

Chapman, J. (2013b), 'Meaningful Stuff: Towards Longer Lasting Products', in E. Karana, O. Pedgley and V. Rognoli (eds) *Materials Experience: Fundamentals of Materials and Design*, Oxford: Elsevier, pp. 135–144.

Clark, H. and Brody, D. (2009), *Design Studies: A Reader*, Oxford: Berg.

Euro RSCG Worldwide (2011), *Prosumer Report*, Vol 11, Geneva: Euro RSCG Worldwide.

Fukasawa, N. and Morrison, J. (2007), *Super Normal: Sensations of the Ordinary*, London: Lars Muller Publishers.

Hawken, P., Lovins, A. and Hunter Lovins, L. (1999), *Natural Capitalism: Creating the Next Industrial Revolution*, Snowmass, CO: Little, Brown & Company.

Heskett, J. (2003), *Toothpicks & Logos*, Oxford: Oxford University Press.

Hood, B. (2009), *Super Sense: From Superstition to Religion – the Brain Science of Belief*, London: Constable & Robinson.

Lacey, E. (2009), 'Contemporary Ceramic Design for Meaningful Interaction and Emotional Durability: A Case Study', *International Journal of Design*, 3(2), pp. 87–92.

London, B. (1932), *Ending the Depression Through Planned Obsolescence*, New York, NY http://catalog.hathitrust.org/Record/006829435.

Nicoll, E. (2013), General Manager of Sustainability, Sony Europe, quoted in a testimonial for the University of Brighton, UK, 17 July.

Orr, D. (2004), *Earth in Mind: On Education, Environment, and the Human Prospect*, Washington, DC: Island Press.

Parsons, T. (2009), *Thinking Objects: Contemporary Approaches to Product Design*, Lausanne: AVA
Publishing.

Slade, G. (2007), *Made to Break: Technology and Obsolescence in America*, Cambridge, MA: Harvard
University Press.

Solomon, M. (1983), 'The Role of Products as Social Stimuli: A Symbolic Interactionism Perspective',
Journal of Consumer Research, 10(3), p. 319.

Sudjic, D. (2008), *The Language of Things*, London: Allen Lane.

Webb, F. (2013), 'Designing for a Sustainable Future', *Making It Magazine: Industry for Development*,
30 August, http://www.makingitmagazine.net/?p=6906.

Williams, G. (2012), *21 | Twenty One: 21 Designers for Twenty-first Century Britain*, London: V&A
Publishing.

INDEX